Scenic Driving

WASHINGTON

Steve Giordano

FALCON®

Helena, Montana

_A_ **FALCON** GUIDE

Falcon® Publishing is continually expanding its list of guidebooks. You can order extra copies of this book and get information and prices for other Falcon® books by writing Falcon®, P.O. Box 1718, Helena, MT 59624, or by calling 1-800-582-2665. Also, please ask for a free copy of our current catalog listing all Falcon® books. Visit our web site at http:\\www.falconguide.com.

Front cover photo by James Randklev.
Back cover photo and all black-and-white photos by Steve Giordano.

Library of Congress Cataloging-in-Publication Data
Giordano, Steve, 1941-
    Scenic driving Washington / Steve Giordano
        p.   cm.
    ISBN 1-56044-577-7 (pbk.)
    1. Washington (State)--Guidebooks. 2. Automobile travel--
Washington (State)--Guidebooks.   I. Title.
F889.3.G56   1997
917.9704'43--dc21   97-14787
                                                                                   CIP

CAUTION

All participants in recreational activities suggested by this book must assume the responsibility for their own actions and safety. The information contained in this guidebook cannot replace sound judgment and good decision–making skills, which help reduce risk exposure, nor does the scope of this book allow for disclosure of all the potential hazards and risks involved in such activities.

Learn as much as possible about the recreational activities you participate in, prepare for the unexpected, and be cautious. The reward will be a safer and more enjoyable experience.

 Text pages printed on recycled paper.

Contents

Acknowledgments

Many people contributed immeasurably to this book. John and Roberta Wolcott lent huge enthusiasm—and no small amount of research—to the project.

Eager Washington State Parks, USDA Forest Service and National Park Service personnel, and chambers of commerce staff and volunteers went overboard in sharing their resources and suggestions.

Major contributions were made by the Washington State Department of Transportation, in particular Patti Miller-Crowley, assistant manager of the Heritage Corridors Program, and Brent Olsen, public information officer.

Joan Tannen, program manager of the National Scenic Byways Clearinghouse (a partnership of the American Automobile Association, Transportation, Travel, and Tourism Institute, and the Federal Highway Administration) provided invaluable assistance, as did Elizabeth Fisher of the U.S. Department of Transportation.

My wife and fellow traveler, who in addition to her day job as a TV producer is a theater and opera critic and travel writer in her spare time, contributed invaluable impressions of places and sights on the scenic drives.

My Falcon Press editors, Megan Hiller and Randall Green, displayed guidance, courtesy, patience, and skill beyond any writer's hope.

Thank you all.

Map Legend

Scenic Drive - paved		Interstate	
Scenic Drive - gravel		U. S. Highway	
Scenic Sidetrip - paved		State and County Roads	
Scenic Sidetrip - gravel		Forest Service Roads	000
Interstate		Pass	
Other Roads (paved)		Peak and Elevation	9,782 ft.
Other Roads (gravel)			
Railroad		Glaciers	
City		Wilderness Area National/State Park Indian Reservations	
Boardwalk			
Ranger Station		National Forest Boundary	
Buildings			
Point of Interest		State Boundary	W A
Campground			
Ski Area		Map Orientation	N
Hiking Trail		Scale of Miles	0 0.5 1 Miles
River/Creek		Scenic Drive Location	★
Waterfall			
Lakes			

Locator Map

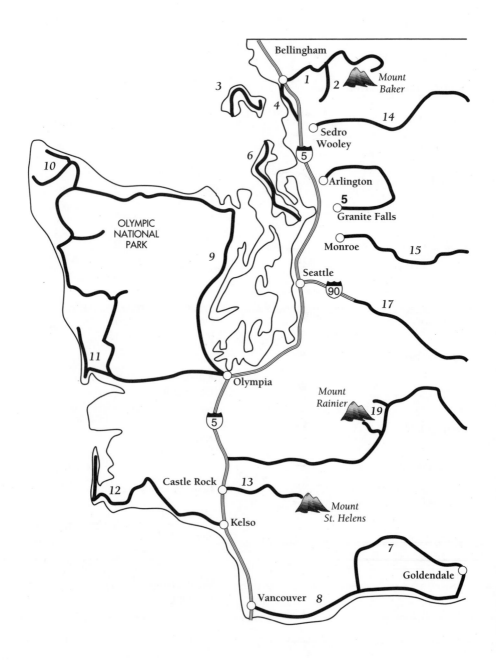

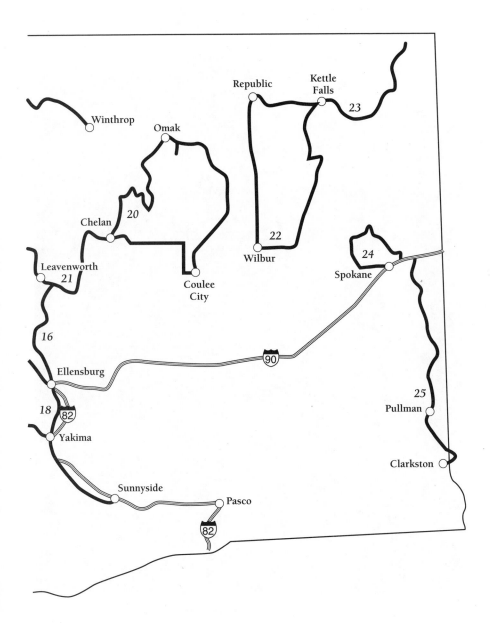

Middle Fork Bridge on Mosquito Lake Road (Drive 1).

Introduction

For the freedom of the open road, family road trips are the next best thing to the excitement of long-haul trucking. My father reminded me recently that as a kid, my life's ambition was to become a trucker. I had forgotten all about it, but it helps explain the fun our family has on road trips—which I figure are even more fun than trucking, actually, because you can make up your own schedule as you go along. Even my "granddogs" in back stand alert for the next park or woods or lake opportunity.

I first fell in love with Washington during a driving vacation in the winter of 1970. The infinite variety of gray tones in the sky, the incessant drizzle, the teddy-bear-tummy-look of the rolling forests, and the surprisingly chipper nature of the people, all combined to give me the impression that human life in Washington was the life of nature, the life of the wondrous outdoors. A quarter of a century of living here has proved true my first impressions, but with one exception: dust. As drizzly rain rules western Washington in the winter, dust reigns statewide on dirt roads much of the rest of the year.

Southeastern Washington, including the Palouse hills south of Spokane, is actually the northern end of the Great American Desert. No trees have grown in the region for several million years, where the annual rainfall is less than 12 inches. But that meager rainfall adds up quickly to form the mighty Columbia River, whose drainage basin blankets 260,000 square miles that range over ten degrees of latitude. The Columbia Plateau extends eastward across the southern two-thirds of the state from the volcanic Cascade Mountains beyond the border with Idaho. Indians of the plateau lived as hunters and gatherers for ten thousand years in this land of strong contrasts. Their encyclopedic knowledge of the different environments was their main survival tool. Through all this land, the Columbia River winds like a dropped bootlace, flowing in all directions of the compass. Because of all the dams, vast sections of the river are actually lakes. Several of this book's drives will take you along far reaches of the Columbia, and even across it on two ferries.

There were originally four transcontinental roads across the United States and one of them, the Yellowstone Trail, ran through Washington on its way from Plymouth, Massachusetts, to Seattle. The Yellowstone Trail was a collection of different roads that met and connected one coast with the other. Within Washington they consisted of the Evergreen Highway (Portland to Walla Walla), Washington Highway 410 (Aberdeen to Lewiston, Idaho) and the Inland Empire Highway, which zigged and zagged between Ellensburg, Yakima, Walla Walla, and Spokane to the Canadian border. An original 3-mile segment of this road, the Old Grandview Pavement Road in the Yakima Valley, is all that remains of the initial pavement.

Western Washington's rain, in spite of its distressing reputation, is not really all that much. Seattle gets about 38 inches per year, which is less than New York; Bellingham about 33. In the "rain shadow" of the Olympic Peninsula, the town of Sequim (pronounced "Squim") gets about 17 inches of rain per year, and some of the San Juan Islands get around 22. Of course, the mountains that cause this near dryness, the Olympics, absorb the southwesterly brunt of Pacific storms by getting more than 100 inches per year.

A favored activity for some hardy people is storm watching on Washington's Olympic Peninsula coast. The experience is an actual tourism draw, as travelers pull their rigs into coastal campgrounds and Seattle weekenders rent cottages and lodge rooms all for the sake of experiencing the brutal beauty of a winter storm.

The rain forest growth that results from this precipitation is a sight to behold. There are as many shades of green in the forest as there are shades of gray in the sky. Mosses and lichens grow thick and luxurious, both on the trees and on the ground, providing abundant food for the wildlife that live in Olympic National Park. The thick forest canopy blocks so much light, even on sunny days, that in places the forest floor seems to be in perpetual twilight.

The wilds of Washington's Cascade Mountains are made accessible to everyone via three east-west highways, each one a scenic drive in this book. Whether you prefer to get out the binoculars at a breathtaking overlook or pack in from a highway trailhead on the Pacific Crest National Scenic Trail, there seems to be no end to the great viewing opportunities. In the North Cascades, which include North Cascades National Park, there was nary a paved cross-mountain road until 1972. Even now the North Cascades Highway, Washington Highway 20, is closed by snow four to six months a year. Because much of WA 20 cuts through the park, the drive is one of the most pristine imaginable. The Cascades are young and their peaks jagged. Glaciers flow in all directions, supplying unbelievably beautiful mountain lakes and streams. The National Park Service wants to maintain the surroundings in as natural a state as possible; as a consequence, the only traveler services along one 80-mile stretch are a few campgrounds. The other two east-west Washington highways across the Cascades, U.S. Highway 2 and Interstate Highway 90, pass through the Mount Baker-Snoqualmie National Forest. Running north to south in the Cascades and its drainage areas, the national forest has 1.7 million acres. Even with 40 percent of it set aside as wilderness areas, there are still more than 1,400 miles of trails for public use. These include trails for hikers, mountain bikers, cross-country skiers, and snowmobilers. Many of these are easily accessed by the cross-mountain highways.

The Maryhill Museum (Drive 8).

The beauties of Washington's mountain drives are more than enough to satisfy the most experienced traveler. Swiftly moving streams fall away on all sides, rock walls jut straight up from the roadside, forest canopy hangs entirely over the road in some places, and in the fall, the changing of the leaves in the mountain passes gives off a near-neon glow. These mountain highways are open all year, but winter drivers are reminded that all this wild and rugged nature so close at hand comes at a price: avalanches can stop traffic for a few days once or twice each winter. The Cascades get a lot of snow—the Mount Baker Ski Area averages 595 inches per year, the most of any ski area in the country.

A man named Ohiyesa, a Santee Dakota physician and author, expressed this sentiment in 1911: "Whenever, in the course of the daily hunt the red hunter comes upon a scene that is strikingly beautiful or sublime—a black thundercloud with the rainbow's glowing arch above the mountain, a white waterfall in the heart of a green gorge; a vast prairie tinged with the blood-red of sunset—he pauses for an instant in the attitude of worship." He could have been writing about Mount Rainier National Park or the route to Mount St. Helens. Both are close to indescribable to people who have never seen them. Their scale is enormous; their contrasting terrains between forest and alpine are striking. Their gorges and river valleys seem sculpted by giants, and their perpetually snow-and-ice-covered peaks appear as beacons to everyone within a hundred miles.

The two scenic places, Mount Rainier National Park and Mount St. Helens National Volcanic Monument, each have terrain and activities suitable for everyone, no matter what your interest. It would be tough to exhaust the rangers' and volunteers' knowledge of the areas, but if you do, they know where you can find out more. Be sure to take extra film and keep the camera ready, because the photo opportunities are unlimited. Each bend in the road reveals a new and striking scene, whether it is an elk taking an afternoon nap in the mudflow valley below Mount St. Helens, or an immense wall of perpendicular columnar basalt across the gorge, with Mount Rainier in the background. You can drive through or around a national park in a day and gain a real sense of the spectacular scope and grandeur of this semi-untouched part of the world.

Only serious hikers, packers, and skiers venture far beyond the few available roads through the wilderness. They soon learn just how primitive the Washington wilds can be. For the rest of us, Washington has eighty-two state parks with campgrounds and fifty-one more that are designated for day-use only. The state's public lands are guardians of these wilds, their snow-capped peaks, glaciers, alpine lakes, cascading rivers, and conifer-blanketed hills and valleys that seem to go on forever.

Safety

Much of western Washington is mountain territory—remote, and not always with roadside services nearby. Be sure your car has plenty of gas and oil and is in good repair. Take along some spares beyond the spare tire— water, food, warm clothes, shoes, rain gear, and maybe a backpack shovel. That's all the stuff I used to carry in my car when I was a volunteer on the Mount Baker Ski Patrol. I was always ready for anything in the mountains, and in five years I didn't need any of it. But you never know.

How To Use This Guide

As the locator map shows, some drives can be linked together for a more extensive trip. This is especially true on the Olympic Peninsula, in central Washington near Chelan and Leavenworth, and in the northeastern part of the state. Most drives can easily be covered in a day, but a few, notably the Olympic Peninsula, could require two or more days. Of course, all the drives offer lots of discoveries and out-of-vehicle experiences to tempt you into pulling off the road for a closer inspection and perhaps a memorable adventure or two. The chapters give suggestions along the way, and campgrounds are clearly indicated on the maps and in the chapter introductions.

The drives here are all on well-paved roads, with the exception of Drive 5 (Mountain Loop Highway) and Drive 7 (Ice Caves Route). In those two cases, some unpaved Forest Service roads are used, but they are quite well-maintained. The worst hazard might be dust from vehicles in front. If you have any doubt about road conditions, always check with the local ranger station.

More information about attractions on these drives is available from parks, communities, and business and travel bureaus eager to tempt you with maps, brochures, and answers to your questions. Refer to each chapter's "For more information" section and Appendix A for names, phone numbers, and addresses.

In my own view, the best experiences on road trips come from the human exchanges—from talking with the local people. Those are the experiences to remember: the after-the-lecture chat with the park ranger, coffee with some old-timers at the downtown lunch counter, or idle conversation with shopkeepers on a slow day. When prompted, people love to tell their stories, and there is more to be learned from listening than from any amount of reading.

Background reading is important, however. Some advance awareness of what a drive has to offer can only enhance the experience. The books listed in the "Further Reading" appendix will help you enjoy your experiences on Washington's scenic highways. They give texture and fascinating background to the descriptions and impressions in this book. Besides, other viewpoints can lend more substance to your own. Twenty-seven years in Washington have only begun to teach me what's around the next bend in the road, and the books listed in Appendix B have been a great resource. Be sure to check them out.

Drive 1: Mount Baker Highway

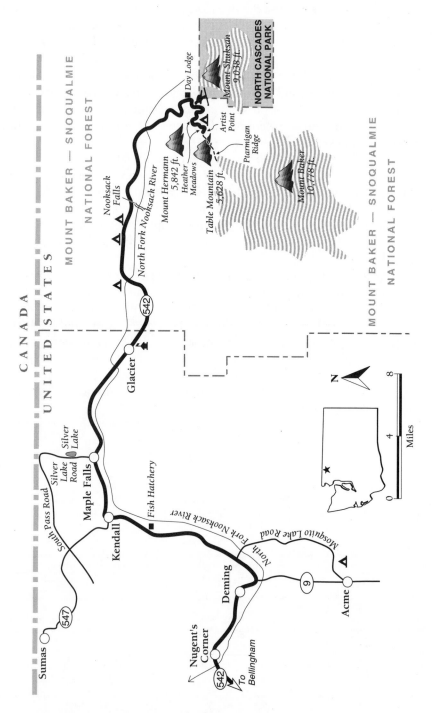

1

Mount Baker Highway

General description: A 60-mile drive through pastoral farmland and dense mountainside rain forest to an inspirational viewpoint showcasing Mount Baker.

Special attractions: Mount Baker-Snoqualmie National Forest, Mount Baker Wilderness Area, hiking, camping, fishing, river rafting.

Location: Northwest corner of Washington.

Highway number: Washington Highway 542.

Travel season: The Mount Baker Highway is open as far as the Mount Baker Ski Area year-round, but four-wheel-drive or traction devices may be required from November through March. The final few miles, past the ski area to Artist Point, while paved, are open only from late July through October, depending on snow conditions.

Camping: There are two Forest Service campgrounds on the highway and one group reservation site. Many other camping possibilities exist along the numerous wilderness access roads and trails. No overnight camping is allowed at Heather Meadows.

Services: The last gas station is in Maple Falls, about 32 miles before the eastern end of the highway at Artist Point. Both Maple Falls and Glacier have lodging, restaurants, and groceries.

Nearby attractions: Silver Lake Park (a 411-acre Whatcom County park open year-round), Nooksack Falls, Nooksack Salmon Hatchery.

For more information: Mount Baker Ski Area; Mount Baker-Snoqualmie National Forest; Outdoor Recreation Information Center; Mount Baker Ranger District; Glacier Public Service Center; Bellingham-Whatcom County Convention and Visitors Bureau; Whatcom County Parks (see Appendix A).

 ## The drive

The 60-mile Mount Baker Highway winds eastward from Interstate 5 in Bellingham, alongside the North Fork of the Nooksack River. It passes through pastoral farm land, small towns, and dense rain forests before climbing past the Mount Baker Ski Area to Artist Point, where you will find inspirational views of Mount Baker, the North Cascades, and the Canadian Coastal Range.

The scenic drive begins where Mount Baker Highway crosses the

Nooksack River at Nugent's Corner, Milepost 11 on Washington Highway 542. Glaciomarine drift formed the Nooksack Valley terrace between Nugent's Corner and Deming. The late Pleistocene fill has been eroded by the Nooksack River, leaving the deposits along the sides of the valley.

There is easy dirt road access to the river from the southeast side of the bridge at Nugent's Corner. You can drive down to camp, fish, or picnic on the river-rock beaches.

While Mount Baker itself may have been visible up to now, the approaching foothills beyond the town of Deming block the view until much later in the drive. Mount Baker was called *Koma Kulshan* by the coastal Lummi Indians, at least as interpreted by early white explorers and settlers. The name has stuck as part of the popular lore of Mount Baker. One Indian story describes a volcanic eruption. Kulshan, the mountain, once got so mad that a big piece fell off and slid down the mountain, resulting in a lot of fire and noise. The mountains blackened, the rivers heated. Fish cooked in the rivers and floated downstream, scaring the Indians and animals away. They returned after a year, and Kulshan has never again been mad.

The Mount Baker Vineyards, just west of Deming on both sides of the Mount Baker Highway, serve as the northernmost vineyard in the United States. The location along the Nooksack River provides a climate much like the wine regions of France. Nooksack Valley weather is a mini-climate characterized by what the Nooksack Indians call a "hole in the smoke." Coastal winds and nearby mountains work together to cause frequent blue skies over the Nooksack when everywhere else is cloudy and rainy. It doesn't happen all the time, of course, but often enough to allow the sun's rays through when the grapes need the heat.

You can visit the Mount Baker Vineyards at 4298 Mount Baker Highway, Deming, WA 98244, phone (360)592-2300. The tasting room is open year-round, Wednesday through Sunday, 11 A.M. to 5 P.M. Overnight RVs are welcome, no charge.

The Nooksack Indians have a small reservation in Deming, and their casino alongside the Mount Baker Highway is very popular with Canadian visitors. Canadians contribute up to forty percent of the retail economy of northern Washington. Deming is also home to the annual early June Deming Logging Show and Loggerodeo.

Just east of Deming, at the intersection of the Mount Baker Highway and Washington Highway 9 from Sedro-Woolley, look for a Chuckanut sandstone buttress on the left. Eagles have been spotted at the pond just east of the buttress. In the back wall of the quarry you can see an upright fossilized tree embedded in the sandstone. Glaciers pushed rock debris eastward up the Nooksack Valley at least this far. The glacial flow was opposite to today's westward river flows.

Nooksack Falls.

Just after Milepost 16, Mosquito Lake Road heads south from Welcome, between Welcome Valley Excavating and the Texaco station. During January and February, a 1-mile detour here will give you the best chance to see eagles on the lookout for salmon. Mosquito Lake Road crosses the North Fork of the Nooksack River here, and the bridge is a good vantage point. Up to one hundred bald eagles winter along the North Fork. The Mount Baker Highway, following the North Fork, crosses mudflow deposits from the mountain much of the way.

As you continue on the Mount Baker Highway, 4 miles past the Mosquito Lake Road turnoff, Fish Hatchery Road loops to the right of the highway and returns to it 0.5 mile later. The Nooksack Salmon Hatchery, operated by the Washington Department of Fisheries, is on Fish Hatchery Road. The site is open for viewing. To see the river up close, just scramble up the row of rocks on the left side. Those rocks are part of the dike of the North Fork and the roiling river is right there.

The Nooksack has Class III and IV rapids, ranging from "adventurous," with lots of waterslide-like waves and eddies and rapids with clean passages (good for family adventure), to "thrilling," with long rapids and powerful waves with big drops. Inexperienced rafters should ride the Nooksack with one of the local guide services.

The Nooksack Valley is still broad enough at this point to allow farming, but dairies and a horse ranch also dot the region. Just before Kendall, a right turn in the road is locally referred to as Zenderville. There are fourteen Zender families who live on this stretch of the Mount Baker Highway.

Dense forest and big trees begin near the town of Maple Falls. In the late fall, bigleaf maples turn colors, along with cottonwood, alder, and birch. The more staid greens are Douglas-fir, Western redcedar, and hemlock. The old-growth forest on both sides of the highway are remnants of a once-great forest that stretched from timberline in the mountains to the shores of Puget Sound just one hundred years ago. In Pulitzer prize-winner Annie Dillard's novel *The Living*, she writes that pioneer women in Bellingham and Nooksack River settlements had to compress their hoop skirts sideways to walk between the trees.

Indians have probably lived along the Nooksack River for the past eleven to twelve thousand years. Foothills Indians, like the Nooksack and Upper Skagit, fished the rivers for salmon and hunted deer, elk, and mountain goat. Goat hunting brought Indians closer to Mount Baker, at least to timberline, but there is no formal record of anyone climbing to the top of the mountain until 1868, when Edmund Coleman, an Englishman living in Victoria, British Columbia, made the journey.

The highway continues through the town of Maple Falls, site of an annual tongue-in-cheek Bigfoot Festival in September. From the center of

Maple Falls, there is a turnoff to the north for good year-round camping at Silver Lake Park. The park, 3 miles from the Mount Baker Highway, has cabins, campsites, RV sites, and horse stalls, plus swimming, boating, and fishing.

Continuing eastward from Maple Falls, the road descends through thick scrub and alder back to the valley floor and its abundance of Douglas-fir. It continues alongside the river to Glacier, on the western boundary of the Mount Baker-Snoqualmie National Forest. From here on, the Mount Baker Highway is entirely within the national forest, but a few bends in the road come close to the boundaries of the Mount Baker Wilderness and North Cascades National Park.

The three jurisdictions are served by the Glacier Public Service Center, just east of Glacier on the right. It is open until 4:30 P.M. There are good restrooms and a picnic area on the grounds. This is also where the officially designated Mount Baker Scenic Byway begins, the first such road designated by the Forest Service. In 1993, the state announced its version of the Mount Baker Scenic Highway, which begins at Interstate 5 in Bellingham and goes for 57 miles to Austin Pass, just past the Mount Baker Ski Area. Oddly, that is just 3 miles shy of Artist Point. The Forest Service route begins at the Glacier Public Service Center and continues for 24 miles up to the parking lot at Artist Point.

Glacier Public Service Center.

11

Before making any excursions on the mountain, stop by the service center, hosting information for both the Mount Baker-Snoqualimie National Forest and, on its eastern border, North Cascades National Park. The ranger on duty will inform you of the best areas to see for the season and any road closures and weather changes that may affect your plans. The rangers normally offer special hints about getting along in the wilderness and with its inhabitants. The Forest Service also offers free weekend interpretive programs on nature photography, geology, natural history, and wildlife in the Mount Baker region. Check at the Service Center for the schedule.

Busy summer weekends may see two thousand people at the service center. The building itself is on the National Register of Historic Places. It was built by the Civilian Conservation Corps (CCC) in 1938 and 1939, a fine example of Cascadian architecture. The style refers to rustic design that uses building materials native to the area.

Rustic campsites are available along the Nooksack River at Douglas Fir and Silver Fir campgrounds, and group campsites without drinking water are available at Excelsior Campground on a reservation basis. The Douglas Fir Campground sits alongside the river 2 miles east of the Glacier Public Service Center. It has thirty sites. Silver Fir Campground, 11 miles farther east, has twenty-one sites. Both charge a fee.

North Cascades National Park, which includes Mount Shuksan, requires permits for backcountry camping to insure that campsites don't become too crowded. If the service center is closed, you can get a permit from the front porch information board.

The drive to Glacier is a very gentle elevation climb through the heavily forested foothills. but now the valley begins to narrow and the climb alongside the river sharpens a bit. It is still relatively straight under an ever-thickening canopy of forest. In this stretch there are a few opportunities to turn off the highway to see some wonders of nature. Within 0.5 mile east of the service center, Glacier Creek Road cuts in from the right. One-third of a mile up Glacier Creek Road, Thompson Creek passes under a bridge which is an excellent spot to watch salmon heading upstream to spawn. The other off-highway sight is Nooksack Falls, accessible from Wells Creek Road on the right near Milepost 41. Wells Creek Road is gravel and not plowed in winter. The switchbacks continue down 0.33 mile to the parking area near the falls. Views are good from the bridge and behind the green chainlink fence. The river parts ever so briefly at the top of the falls, then pours in a double tumble 170 feet to the rocks below. If there is any moisture on the ground it will be slick, so don't be tempted by the narrow steep path that goes around the end of the fence.

Back on the Mount Baker Highway, keep an eye out for columnar Mount Baker andesite rock. Walls of it seem to thrust upward and teeter on the left side of the road. The rock was used extensively in the construction of the 1995 White Salmon Day Lodge at the ski area and in the 1994 remodel of the Heather Meadows Visitor Center.

By Milepost 47 the highway has crossed the river for the last time and begins its serious ascent to the ski area and beyond to Artist Point at 5,200 feet elevation. The last 14 miles are more of a steady climb, with some eye-popping views when the fog and clouds lift.

Mount Baker, with its surrounding peaks, valleys, rivers, and meadows, is a year-round attraction for alpine sports. Winter and spring skiing draw the most visitors because the snow season usually lasts about six months. The road beyond the ski area is snowed in all winter, but the highway up to the ski area is very well plowed and sanded daily. The ski season is much longer for backcountry telemarkers who are willing to climb above 5,000 feet.

The Mount Baker Ski Area is not actually located on the 10,778-foot volcano of the same name. It is on an arm of 9,127-foot Mount Shuksan. Since its opening in 1953, the ski area's proximity to British Columbia's Lower Mainland has had a lot to do with its popularity. The main ingredient, however, is the average 595-inches-per-year snowfall. There are usually 150 inches at the base by mid-season. Mount Baker's one thousand skiable acres cover two mountain faces, Pan Dome and Shuksan.

At about Milepost 51, a wide road to the left leads 0.25 mile to the White Salmon Day Lodge, a cooperative effort between the Mount Baker Ski Area and the Forest Service, designed by Bellingham architect Don Wilcox. Wilcox researched Cascadian architecture, looking at buildings in Oregon and thumbing through a book on old Forest Services lodges. The buildings Wilcox studied were the Multnomah Falls Lodge and Skamania Lodge on the Columbia River, which was made of recycled wood from old canneries. He particularly liked Sun Mountain Lodge after its $20 million remodel in 1990.

Some people feel the new lodge is more than just a building; it's a work of art. The construction called for local wood and stone, lots of mountain-type angles, and big glass viewing areas. It offers a fantastic view of Mount Shuksan, a mass of metamorphic rock on the Shuksan thrust fault. The mountain, thrust up ten million years ago, and its four glaciers lie within North Cascades National Park. The Hanging Glacier breaks off periodically and rumbles into the valley below. Skiers report sightings and soundings every winter.

Heather Meadows is in the divide between Mount Baker and Mount Shuksan, and part of the ski area sits on that divide. The area is a fragile subalpine environment with a short summer season. The meadows present pink and white heather, huckleberries, mountain ash, and mountain

Picture Lake with Mount Shuksan rising in the background.

hemlock. Picture Lake, normally thawing by June within Heather Meadows and near the ski area's older lodge, is the favorite stop for summer visitors. It features the photogenic Mount Shuksan in the background. A paved trail goes through the meadows and around the lake and is marked with interpretive signs.

There are no Cascadian CCC lodges at Mount Baker Ski Area, but the visitor center stands as a proud tribute to the men who formed the local CCC crews.

Up the road from the ski area, what was known for fifty-four years as the Austin Pass Warming Hut became the Heather Meadows Visitor Center in 1994. It was built by the CCC in 1940 and stands as a sentinel overlooking Bagley Lakes below Mount Hermann. It is open daily until 5 P.M. from July through September.

The CCC typically used local materials in construction, and that required the builders to lug stones from nearby andecite rock columns. Blacksmith hangers support the roof frames, and the floors and roof-support beams are old-growth Douglas-fir. The newer walls and doors are pine.

It served as a warming hut for skiers until the University of Washington rented it in 1960. Unfortunately, during their more than 20 years of tenancy, users tore down and burned the original pine walls to put up insulation and wall board to reduce drafts and keep the inside warm. After UW left, the Forest Service used the warming hut as a utility building for fifteen years, and trail crews lived in it during the summer. Now the Forest Service has restored it to its original CCC standards.

Its completion marks the last phase of the Heather Meadows Project, a revitalization program for this part of the Mount Baker-Snoqualmie National Forest. The project included paving the original road, built in 1934, to Artist Point. Barrier-free sections of the interpretive center's Fire and Ice Trail and the Artist Ridge Trail are also paved. Both interpretive trails feature information on the volcanic and glacial activity that shaped the region.

The sloped entrance ramp to the center was a controversial design aspect. It is one instance of modern accessibility needs clashing with historical accuracy. The main interpretive display is the building itself. In past years, visitors passed the hut on their way to Artist Point. Now the building sparks a lot of interest in passing hikers and drivers.

The walls were completely replaced to their original knotty pine. The use of pine in CCC buildings is unusual, but its purpose was to brighten the interior. A family of common flickers has been raising a family under high security in an outer wall.

The end of the Scenic Byway at Artist Point, with plenty of parking for cars, RVs, and tour busses, is a popular start for walks and day hikes in all directions. Be alert to the weather, though. There can be white-out fog at

Artist Point even in the summertime. The most popular walk is out on Ptarmigan Ridge, west toward the lower glaciers of Mount Baker itself. Take your binoculars for viewing the mountain goats, whistling marmots, and snowboard tracks that form graceful arcs on the glaciers across the valley. Take care on spring and early summer ice fields—either avoid the sloping ones or carry an ice axe.

Summer hikers are rewarded by an abundance of berries along the trails. Blueberries practically fall into your pockets, but you have to look a little harder for the huckleberries and salmonberries. The views of Mount Baker are truly breathtaking. The mountain is nearly one million years old, the result of a volcanic eruption. It is still an active volcano and venting steam can be seen 50 miles away in Bellingham. As one interpretation reads, "Magma seethes beneath the volcano's cool slopes. Future eruptions are almost certain to wipe away today's landscape, preparing a new surface for the next tide of life."

The glacier system on Mount Baker is one of the largest in the continental United States, draining into three major river systems. As for life on the glaciers, the only survivors are ice worms and red algae. At lower elevations, hikers can see mountain goats, elk, pika, and blue grouse, as well as huckleberries, blueberries, glacier lilies, and buttercups.

There are many trails into the 130,000-acre Mount Baker Wilderness. Bicycles, or any other mechanized vehicles except wheelchairs, are not allowed on wilderness trails. Hundreds of miles of Forest Service logging roads and trails are open to cycling and snowmobiling. From the upper reaches, the views of the Canadian Rockies and the San Juan Islands are spectacular.

Given the deliberately primitive conditions, and the quick-change weather conditions in the mountains, even day hikers should shoulder a pack with the usual survival essentials.

The south flank of Mount Baker is designated as a National Recreation Area. Access is via Baker Lake basin north of the town of Concrete on Washington Highway 20, the North Cascades Highway. Extensive hiker and stock trails crisscross the National Recreation Area. It also has traditionally been a popular snowmobiling area during winter months.

2

Mosquito Lake Road

General description: A side trip from the Mount Baker Highway that traverses 15 miles of bucolic countryside along the Middle Fork of the Nooksack River.

Special attractions: Bald eagle viewing at the Welcome Bridge. The one-lane Middle Fork Bridge is a National Historic Site.

Location: Northwest Washington, triangulating a corner between Washington Highway 542 and Washington Highway 9.

Highway number: None.

Travel season: The road is open year-round.

Camping: Hutchinson Creek Campground and River View Park.

Services: Gas and groceries in Welcome; groceries in Acme.

For more information: Department of Natural Resources (See Appendix A).

 ## The drive

The 35-mph road is rural, peaceful, and mostly quiet, a favorite for adventuresome bicyclists and drivers with the time and inclination to see what life is like away from the hubbub of towns and cities. The route is called a "selected local road" by official Washington highway maps.

Starting from the Mount Baker Highway, just after Milepost 16, Mosquito Lake Road heads south, descending until it crosses the North Fork of the Nooksack and then the North Fork Road. The Truck Road from Deming intersects Mosquito Lake Road from the right before the bridge.

The Welcome Fire Station is just south the bridge, a bit north of the old Kulshan townsite. The Welcome Senior Center, in the 1918 No. 41 Welcome schoolhouse building, is 1.5 miles farther.

It is a bit of a drive back in time because there has been no roadside development of the type that stretches farther and farther out the Mount Baker Highway from Bellingham. The 15 miles of Mosquito Lake Road were not even fully paved until recently. The road was once part of the Deming Trail, a shortcut from Deming to the flanks of Mount Baker that avoided the travails of the Glacier region. The trail followed the course of the North and Middle Forks of the Nooksack River and was one of the main routes for early mountain climbers. They hiked the Middle Fork to its source below the Coleman and Easton glaciers.

Drive 2: Mosquito Lake Road

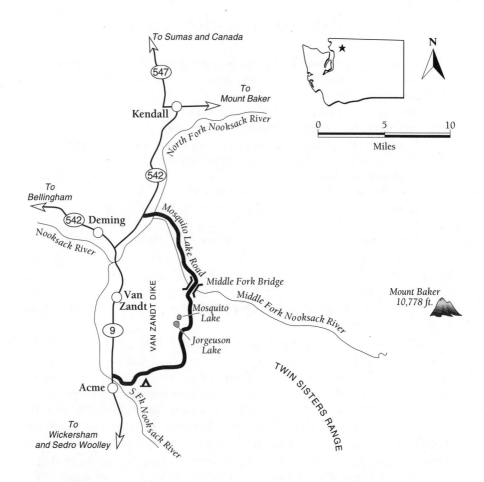

To Sumas and Canada

547

To Mount Baker

Kendall

North Fork Nooksack River

542

To Bellingham

542 Deming

Nooksack River

Mosquito Lake Road

Middle Fork Bridge

Van Zandt

VAN ZANDT DIKE

Mosquito Lake

Jorgeuson Lake

Middle Fork Nooksack River

Mount Baker 10,778 ft.

9

Acme

S Fk Nooksack River

To Wickersham and Sedro Woolley

TWIN SISTERS RANGE

N

0   5   10
Miles

By 1911 it had become enough of a road for Mount Baker Marathon racers to drive as far as the Heisler Ranch before they had to proceed on foot to the peak of the mountain. The ranch is near the Middle Fork Bridge, which allows present-day Mosquito Lake Road to continue south to Acme at Washington Highway 9.

Commerce and industry have come and gone from Mosquito Lake Road and left a hardy population that likes peace and quiet in its surroundings. The road is no longer a shortcut to anywhere, but rather a scenic byway with a life and appeal all its own. From its early trail days it became a supply road for pioneers who settled the river valley, and later a logging road that gave access to the surrounding old-growth forests. The drive is punctuated by several dirt logging roads that push ever farther toward the Mount Baker Wilderness.

The people of Mosquito Lake Road, between the Van Zandt Dike to the west and the Twin Sisters Mountains to the east, have always been resourceful. Before Would War II they mined peat moss from the big bog north of Mosquito and Jorgenson lakes and cut giant hemlocks with bent trunks to use as boat bows. Farms, mills, and a builder of hydroelectric equipment exist in harmony among the mossy woods, meadows, and fields of foxglove, berries, and overhanging ferns.

Most of the mills are gone, and the chicken farm doesn't cluck anymore, but the olivine mine still produces and cows and horses still dot the fields. There are plenty of elk in the woods uphill from Mosquito Lake road, but not in the numbers of yesteryear. They are rarely spotted near the road itself.

Much of the road follows the course of the Middle Fork of the Nooksack River, but cyclists should be advised that it is narrow and there is an elevation gain of 740 feet in the southern 5-mile section.

The one-lane Middle Fork Bridge is about midway on Mosquito Lake Road. It is one of six Whatcom County sites on the National Register of Historic Sites. The other one in the Mount Baker foothills is the Glacier Public Service Center, just east of Glacier on the Mount Baker Highway. Others include Boundary Marker 1 at Point Roberts, Fort Bellingham, Hovander Homestead, and the Sumas border station. There are twenty-two more national sites in the city of Bellingham.

After the bridge, Mosquito Lake Road passes within sight of its namesake, Mosquito Lake. The lake was so-named by surveyors "on account of insect pests they there encountered," according to the last postmaster of the town of Welcome, Frank B. Garrie, in 1923. Both Mosquito and adjacent Jorgenson lakes are surrounded by peat bogs in a glaciated valley.

A few miles south of the lake, the road crosses Hutchinson Creek in two places, 1 mile apart, before reaching the short gravel road on the left to Hutchinson Creek Campground. The campground is maintained by the

Mosquito Lake.

Washington State Department of Natural Resources. It is a wilderness campground, surrounded by wooded areas of evergreens, alder, and cottonwood. Hutchinson Creek runs alongside and is reputed to have good cutthroat fishing. The campground is about 0.33 mile off the main road. After taking the turn-off, keep on the road to the right.

The campground is divided into three day-use and eleven overnight areas. No water is supplied, but the creek is clear and cool and flows fast during the spring runoff. Boil, filter, or chemically treat your water before drinking, or buy bottled water at the nearby Acme General Store.

There is no fee for staying in Hutchinson, but there is a seven-day limit. It tends to fill quickly on holiday weekends. The campground is 2.4 miles from WA 9, just before the steep descent to the South Fork of the Nooksack and the town of Acme.

River View Park is just across the river from where Mosquito Lake Road dead-ends into WA 9 at Acme. For the RV crowd, the privately owned park has thirty spacious sites on flat grassland above the bank of the South Fork. The camp has wheelchair-accessible picnic tables, an ice machine, firewood, and big truck inner tubes for floating the river. It is a nice float downriver to Potter Road in Van Zandt, says owner Betty Lou Close. She also offers parking in a separate area for tubers who don't spend the night. Cost for parking is five dollars for the day, and Betty Lou will hang on to your wallet and keys, no charge.

Old farm machinery marks the entrance to River View Park.

3

Horseshoe Highway on Orcas Island

General description: This 20-mile Orcas Island drive visits a few exciting rural communities, winds around the shoreline of a deep fjord, and summits the highest point in the San Juan Islands—Mount Constitution.
Special attractions: Moran State Park, Mount Constitution, hiking, fishing.
Location: One of 172 San Juan Islands in Puget Sound.
Highway number: Orcas to Olga Road (also called the Horseshoe Highway) and Mount Constitution Road.
Travel season: Year-round except when the portion to Mount Constitution is closed during snowstorms or icy conditions.
Camping: Orcas island camping facilities include 151-site Moran State Park, open all year. Doe Bay Village Resort has 40 campsites, West Beach Resort has 70 summer sites, and the Washington State Department of Natural Resources has 9 sites at the island's only public beach at Obstruction Pass.
Services: Full services in Eastsound, the island's commercial center, and limited services in the villages of Orcas, Deer Harbor, and Olga.
For more information: San Juan County Parks, San Juan Island Chamber of Commerce, San Juan Islands Visitor Information Service, Moran State Park, Washington State Ferries, Doe Bay Village Resort, West Beach Resort, Department of Natural Resources (see Appendix A).

 The drive

Since the Washington State Ferry system is an extension of the state highway system, start the "drive" to Orcas Island at the busy Washington State Ferry dock in Anacortes. From Interstate 5, take Exit 230 at Burlington and turn west onto Washington Highway 20. Follow WA 20 for 16 miles to Anacortes. From there, signs will direct you the last 5 miles to the terminal, which is 84 miles from Seattle and 90 miles from Vancouver, British Columbia.

The state ferry system was established in 1951 when the state bought Puget Sound Navigation and replaced the Mosquito Fleet of small private boats with state ferries. Ferries leave Anacortes for the four ferry-served islands about sixteen times per day. Some carry up to 175 cars and 2,000 passengers. Even with that large capacity, long waits to board are inevitable in the summer.

Drive 3: Horseshoe Highway on Orcas Island

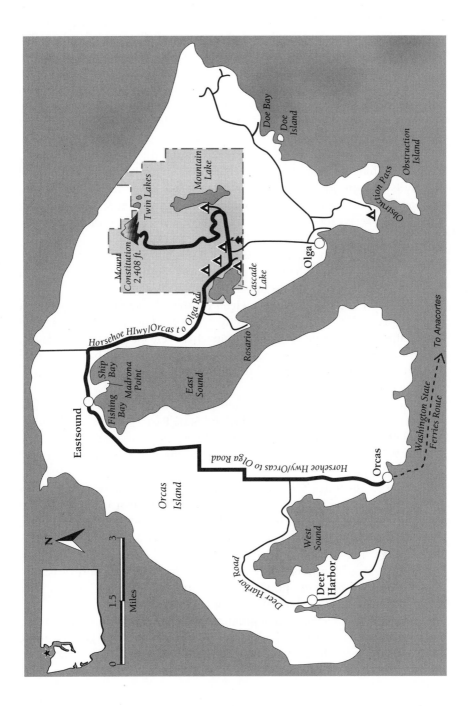

Pay round-trip passenger and car fees before embarking. Once snugly parked on board for the sail to Orcas Island (about one hour and twenty minutes), passengers are free to roam the ship's upper decks. There are wide outside walkways on both sides of the large cabins. Inside, the cafeteria serves full breakfasts and lunches, and there is a small gift shop with books, newspapers, and magazines. The lounge area has racks with travel brochures for Washington and British Columbia.

Once underway, the ferry turns west and passes Shannon Point, site of a marine research lab for students of Western Washington University. The two large islands to the north side are Guemes (served by its own ferry) and Cypress (no ferry service).

After passing west out of Guemes Channel, the ferry crosses Rosario Strait into Thatcher Pass. The pass separates Decatur Island on the left and Blakely Island on the right. The boat then heads north into Lopez Sound and passes Lopez Island's Spencer Spit on the left. Spencer Spit Marine Park is frequented by great blue herons, geese, kingfishers, and a host of migratory birds. The park is also home to rabbits, deer, and raccoons.

Lopez Island, population 1,500, is a flat island preferred by bicyclists. It is so much in the rain shadow of the Olympic Mountains that a profusion of cactus actually grows on the south part of the island.

The ferry rounds Humphrey Head on the left before making its first stop at Upright Head at the northern tip of Lopez. The second stop is Shaw Island, after a pass through Harney Channel between Shaw and Orcas islands. Franciscan nuns operate the only business enterprise on Shaw, the Little Portion Store at the landing, and they also help secure the ferry lines (the rope ones) during docking.

The ferry landing on Orcas Island at the village of Orcas is just a few minutes away. The boat passes Blind Island State Park (good bottomfishing) on the left, at the entrance to Shaw's Blind Bay, then crosses to Orcas at the head of West Sound. Orcas Island was named for a late eighteenth-century viceroy of Mexico.

At 54 square miles, Orcas Island, with a permanent population of about 2,600 people, is the largest, and hilliest, of the San Juan Islands, and the only one with four zip codes, one for each of the villages: Orcas, Deer Harbor, Eastsound, and Olga. It also has the most services for tourists. The island is shaped like a horseshoe, so getting around can take some time without a boat to zip across the fjords. This is a three- and four-gear sort of island. And, as you have no doubt noticed on the ferry, bicycling is a very popular way to get around. Orcas has 70 miles of paved road.

The village of Orcas has a population of one hundred. The Orcas Hotel, built in 1900, is a prominent landmark. The three-story Victorian sits atop a knoll of bedrock overlooking the busy ferry landing and Shaw Island beyond the channel. There are also some cafes, a wine shop, a small grocery, and a post office.

Upon disembarking, turn left at your first and only opportunity. This is the Orcas to Olga Road, popularly known as the Horseshoe Highway because for the 13 miles to Moran State Park it follows the horseshoe shape of the island as it goes around East Sound.

Going north from Orcas, once past West Sound on the left, the road keeps well to the east of Turtleback Mountain and the 1,028-foot Orcas Knob. On the road north from Orcas, and Crow Valley Road to the west, is Crow Valley, with Turtleback Ridge on the left and valley pasturelands to the right of it. Until settlement by whites in the 1800s, the island was the summer shellfishing grounds of the Lummi Indians. They now use the beaches of their waterfront reservation on the mainland near Bellingham.

For pioneers, the main economic activities were farming, fishing, and logging. Fruit orchards were big on all the islands until the Columbia River was dammed. Much of East Sound was taken up by plum tree orchards. There are still many different kinds of fruit tree to see along the Horseshoe Highway, some still tended and some lost to the overgrowth, but tourism now provides the largest island income.

The road continues to the head of East Sound, the commercial center of the island. Nine miles north of the ferry landing, Eastsound is the biggest community on the island. It has a population of 1,100, and some of the oldest buildings date from the 1870s.

This part of Orcas Island is considered the "saddle." There are several old resorts just to the north on the water overlooking Sucia and Matia islands, which are a few miles offshore. Both islands are marine state parks with campgrounds.

The Orcas Historical Museum in Eastsound is open from mid-May through the summer. It features exhibits on fruit farming in the 1930s and resort life in the 1940s. The museum is on North Beach Road and is open noon to 4 P.M. Monday through Saturday.

Waterfront Park is a short walk from the business district. Small, with picnic tables and grass, it has a full view of East Sound. When the tide is low enough, it is possible to walk across the tidelands to Indian Island just offshore.

Madrona Point, the point of Eastsound land, juts into East Sound between Fishing Bay and Ship Bay. Early in the 1990s a property developer sought approval to build condominiums on the point. The plan was halted by the Lummi Indian Tribe, which considers the peninsula to be a sacred burial site. The point is owned by the Lummis and is treated by islanders as a very special place. To get to the point, turn right (south) on Prune Alley.

Madrona Point is a preserve open to the public for daytime use. This forest is mostly madrona trees, through which trails meander to several small coves on the water. The bright red and orange trees are permanently bent from the southerlies that barrel up East Sound.

From Madrona Point the Horseshoe Highway rounds Ship Bay and turns south along the east side of East Sound. Before the turn, Crescent Beach is on the right. There are two oyster farms on the tidelands. If the crews are working, stop and have a look through the binoculars. When the tide is on its way out, there may be some blue herons patiently waiting for breakfast. A rare treat is watching sea gulls try to eat seastars (starfish). Sea gulls do not have enough on the ball to be puzzled by the creatures. Seastar rays distend the sea gulls' cheeks, while the birds wait to feel satisfied. They can't be swallowed, of course, so the gulls finally disgorge the seastars and look for something else to eat.

On Ship Bay, little plastic kayaks, looking a bit like Tsunami Ranger surf kayaks, rent for ten dollars per hour. From here it is just a few miles to Moran State Park.

East over the hill from Eastsound, still on the Horseshoe Highway, the road forms a T near a stone gate and a tank that is covered with community messages. The tank was a gift from the Lions Club to the teenagers of Orcas Island as an outlet for their late-night artistic callings. It has evolved into an island bulletin board. Turn right here. The next 2 miles of the Horseshoe Highway is named Coon Hollow, but bicyclists call it Hell's Highway. The

A view of Mount Baker from atop Mount Constitution in Moran State Park.

road has been widened a bit, but it is still narrow, with no shoulders, very busy, windy, and steep. Hell's Highway loses its intimidation factor after the climb up Flaherty's Hill, about 1 mile before the state park entrance. For bicyclists, this is about the toughest road in the San Juan Islands.

On the downhill side, 0.5 mile before Moran State Park, the entrance to Rosario Resort on Cascade Bay is to the right. It is well worth a side trip to see the Moran Mansion there, built in 1906 by the man who donated his parklands to the state. Be sure to look into the Music Room, with its twenty-six-rank (1,972-pipe) Aeolian player pipe organ (*circa* 1913) and a nearly one-hundred-year-old Steinway grand piano. Mini-concerts are still performed for the resort's guests.

Moran State Park is 0.5 mile beyond the turnoff to Rosario. The road to the eastern part of the island runs through the park. Cross the one-lane bridge under the arch that says "Moran State Park." The park's registration booth is just past the North End Campground, inside the park's west entrance. The turn-off onto Mount Constitution Road is 1.1 miles ahead on the left, and from there it is 5.3 miles to the mountaintop and the stone tower.

Here, the narrow road parallels Cascade Lake, the largest of the five Moran Park lakes. It covers 171 acres. A woodsy path goes around the 2.5-mile perimeter and links with the 1-mile trail around Rosario Lagoon. The lake is a natural spawning ground for native trout and is stocked with rainbow trout, cutthroat, and kokanee salmon. The lake's fishing season is April 29 to October 31, and a public boat ramp is available. Swimming is allowed in the lake, which is also home to ducks in the winter.

Moran is Washington's fourth largest state park and is considered by many to be the state's finest. Albert Moran, a ship builder and former mayor of Seattle, donated three thousand Orcas Island acres to the state for the park. Since the original donation in 1920, the park has expanded to over 5,000 acres. With its 151 year-round campsites (24 on the water), the park is not often crowded. Its busiest times are summer weekends.

The north end of the park has fifty sites on a wooded slope above the road across from Cascade Lake. Midway in the park are fifty-seven sites, some at the lake's edge. At the south end of Cascade Lake there are seventeen sites, and up at Mountain Lake there are eighteen more on a small peninsula. This is a reservoir lake, so there is no swimming, but fishing is OK. There are no RV hookups. Some restrooms have twenty-five-cent showers. There are also concessions and boat rentals. Park hours are 6:30 A.M. to dusk.

There are 30 miles of foot trails in Moran State Park, including gentle, moderate, and strenuous hiking terrain. Most trails are in the woods, but there are places where they open to views of Lopez, Lummi, Blakely, Matia,

Barnes, Cypress, and Clark islands. Many of the park's hiking trails inter-connect, so the length of a any given hike is flexible. Within Moran State Park's 5,000 acres are 300 acres of old-growth forest. Cold Springs is a particularly nice picnic spot in isolated timber area.

Twenty-one of the park's facilities were built by the Civilian Conservation Corps (CCC) during and after the Depression. Much of the construction used hand-cut local quarry stone and big timbers.

Just past Cascade Lake, the Orcas-to-Olga Road turns south toward Olga and the eastern part of the island. Straight ahead, as indicated by a crowded little sign, are Mount Constitution (4.7 miles), Twin Lakes, Cold Springs (picnic spot in isolated timber area 3.7 miles), Cascade Falls (0.4 mile), Mountain Lake turnoff (1 mile), a scenic viewpoint (2.2 miles), and Little Summit (3 miles).

The park has 45,300 feet of waterfront on 5 lakes. Between the two largest, Cascade and Mountain, it is worth a stop to see the 75-foot Cascade Falls in a grotto packed with ferns. The falls are located off the main park road 1 mile past the recreation center, just past the turnoff to Olga. It's well marked, and the hike in is 0.25 mile long. Beyond Cascade Falls, the largest, are two more waterfalls.

Mountain Lake is 198 acres nestled in the hills at the end of the park road and has crystal-clear water. The loop trail around the lake is 3.9 miles. This is a reservoir lake, so swimming is not allowed, but you can rent row-boats for some peaceful exploration or fishing. If the river otters are not too close, expect to hook brook trout and cutthroat, but kokanee is the usual catch. There are a few tiny islands with places to beach the boat.

The one road through the park ends at Mountain Lake. It is impressive to see a 4-foot diameter tree that fell over the road. A section as long as the road is wide was cut away for traffic. Mount Constitution Road veers to the left (north) just before the lake. Access is controlled by a gate, which is closed at 10 P.M. in the summer and 5 P.M. the rest of the year. A sign warns that Mount Constitution Road is not suitable for buses, vehicles with trailers, or large motor homes.

The drive up to Mount Constitution is a constant climb on a second- and third-gear sort of road. It is often very windy. The terrain alongside the climb starts as a thick forest, but before long it begins to seem more like a grove, with the trees more widely spaced. The grass under and among the trees is reminiscent of California's rolling hills, and just as lovely. But there is one big difference here—the big rocks are completely covered in moss and everything is green, so much so that the grasses look like marsh grasses growing in wetlands.

In the late afternoon, stop for a moment and enjoy the effect of horizontal sunlight on the trees. The afternoon sun lights the trees brightly from the side. As good as Chuckanut Drive (Drive 4) is for the water views, Mount Constitution Road is just as stunning for views of the woods.

All along the road, on the fill slope, are log barriers—logs cupped on each end by rock pylons, or bollards. A thick moss covers these logs. At the overlook halfway up Mount Constitution Road, looking west toward the sun, it is difficult to tell just where one island stops and the next one begins. The islands present an endless series of lumps and bumps receding out to sea. Little Summit, on the east side of the road, is 2,200 feet high.

As you continue up, the thick second-growth forest is interspersed with grassy meadows. Walking between the trees is possible, especially since the forest floor seems to have no brambles or other undergrowth. It is mostly moss, grass, logs, and pine needles. Shortly before and to the right of the observation area parking lot lies long and narrow Summit Lake. Lily pads nearly cover the surface.

From the parking lot, where there are public restrooms, it is just a short wooded walk to the top. The summit is forested by hardy stands of lodgepole pine. Western redcedar, western hemlock, and Douglas-fir dominate the forest at the lower elevations. The views from the top of Mount Constitution are spectacular. Some people consider it to be the finest marine view in North America.

Mount Constitution is a remnant of an ancient mountain range connected to the Cascades. It is the highest point in the San Juan Islands. Directly east, Mount Baker stands out in all its nearly 11,000 feet of glory. On a clear day you can also see Vancouver, British Columbia, Vancouver Island, Mount Garibaldi north of Vancouver, Mount Rainier, and the Olympics. Dozens of islands fill the mid-distance of your vision.

In late summer, smoggy air drifts south from Vancouver, British Columbia, visible over Bellingham as far south as Skagit County. The bad air flows up British Columbia's Fraser Valley during the day and sinks at night. If the wind blowing down the Fraser Valley persists, the smog has nowhere to go but south across the international border and beyond. It is no wonder that Skagit Valley farmers are concerned about its effects.

The tower at the top of Mount Constitution, 52 feet high, is one the park's CCC-built structures. Sandstone blocks from an island quarry were used for the tower, and workers forged and shaped the decorative wrought-iron gates, railings, and barriers. The tower was patterned after twelfth-century watchtowers of the Caucasus Mountains in southeastern Europe. Designed by the famous architect Elsworth Storey, the tower has cell-like rooms, winding stairs, and narrow window slits.

During the summer, a volunteer park interpreter is stationed at the top of the tower. Be sure to take the time to chat and gain some historical perspectives not otherwise available.

Just ahead of the tower, where people like to sit and picnic, there is a 1,000-foot drop-off. It is quite something to watch eagles soaring beneath you. From here, you can hike down to Twin Lakes, a distance of just over 1 mile. Elevation loss is 1,200 feet. From Twin Lakes it is a 2.5-mile hike to Mountain Lake.

From the parking lot there are trailheads to Twin Lakes (1.5 miles) and Mountain Lake Landing (3.6 miles). A more serious trek is the Mount Pickett Traverse. Or for a real excursion, a hike around the entire park perimeter can take a whole day.

4

Chuckanut Drive

General description: Twenty miles of the state's original Pacific Highway, half of it cutting a straight line through Skagit Valley farmlands and half clinging precariously to bayside cliffs.

Special attractions: Fossils, including palm fronds, are visible in exposed Chuckanut sandstone, Fairhaven Rose Test Gardens, Fairhaven Park, Taylor United Samish Bay Shellfish Farm, Larrabee State Park.

Location: Northwest coastal Washington, paralleling Interstate 5 between Bellingham and Burlington.

Highway number: Washington Highway 11.

Travel season: The road is open year-round.

Camping: Larrabee State Park, with 87 sites, lies about 7 miles south of Bellingham on Chuckanut Drive.

Services: Four restaurants, two bed and breakfasts. Full services are available in Bellingham in the north and Mount Vernon in the south.

For more information: Larrabee State Park, Bellingham-Whatcom County Convention and Visitors Bureau, Bellingham Parks and Recreation (see Appendix A).

 The drive

This drive has been called the Wizard's path through Oz, Washington's Big Sur, and a landmark coastal drive. Much of it hugs the cliffs over Chuckanut and Samish bays, before it straightens out to cross the rich delta farmlands of Skagit Valley. Visitors linger to watch the ever-changing seascape from high above the shoreline, hope for a sunset, and take advantage of the drive whenever they are in the neighborhood. **Caution:** Chuckanut Drive is a narrow highway built to 1920s standards. RVs of all sizes can navigate safely if drivers are not in a hurry and yield to bicyclists and other motorists.

Begin Chuckanut Drive in the South Bellingham village of Fairhaven, by driving 1.5 miles west on Old Fairhaven Parkway from Interstate 5 exit 250. At the intersection with 12th Street, turn left across the bridge and begin the *official* Chuckanut Drive. This scenic drive starts at the next traffic light on the south end of the short bridge, between Fairhaven School on the right and the beautiful Fairhaven Park on the left.

The most attractive feature of this Bellingham city park is visible from the road: A large experimental rose garden covers an expanse of groomed

Drive 4: Chuckanut Drive

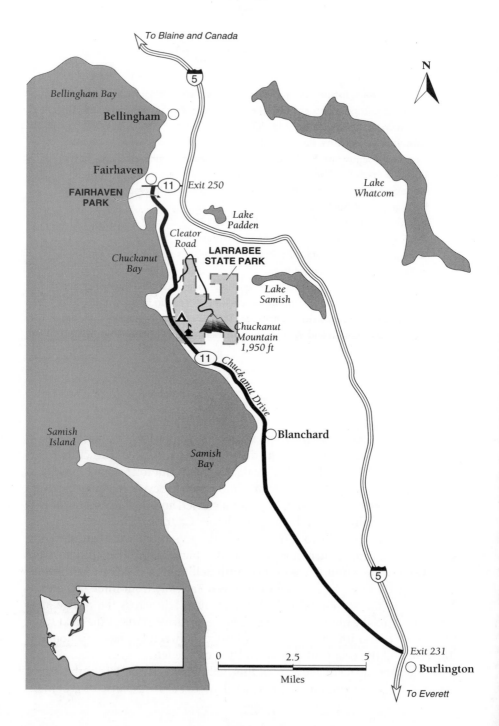

To Blaine and Canada

5

N

Bellingham Bay

Bellingham

Fairhaven

11 *Exit 250*

FAIRHAVEN PARK

Lake Padden

Cleator Road

LARRABEE STATE PARK

Chuckanut Bay

Lake Whatcom

Lake Samish

Chuckanut Mountain 1,950 ft

11 *Chuckanut Drive*

Samish Island

Samish Bay

○**Blanchard**

5

Exit 231

○ **Burlington**

0   2.5   5
Miles

To Everett

park grounds. The garden blooms from mid-June through September, if the deer don't eat the buds first. Weddings take place in the garden nearly every summer weekend. The former park caretaker's house, which faces the rose garden, is now an American hostel. Just beyond the garden, the entrance to Fairhaven Park is marked by tall brick posts. The park has some very pleasant strolls alongside Padden Creek. There are also wooded picnic areas, tennis courts, lots of grassy areas, a playground, ballfield, basketball court, and a children's wading pond.

Prehistoric animals once lived in the Chuckanut Drive region. It was sub-tropical, and the evidence is fossilized in rocks along the way. The fossilized vertebrae of two animals can be seen at the north end of Chuckanut Bay, in the rocks on the east side of Natural Dry Dock above the high-tide mark. This is just north of Governor's Point and Rock and Dot islands.

All along the first half of this scenic route, for about 10 miles, roadcuts and blasted rock reveal fossilized glimpses into the far past of the Chuckanut Mountains. Dinosaurs roamed here, leaving only their skeletal impressions in the stones along the roadway. The Chuckanut Mountains are an exception to the otherwise general glacial debris route along the 140 miles between Vancouver, B.C., and Seattle. The mountains of the Chuckanut Formation are much older than the north-to-south deposits of glacial till and east-west Cascade Mountains outwash.

The thick (10,000 feet) sequence of sedimentary rocks along Chuckanut Drive was named the Chuckanut Formation in 1927, by R. D. McClellan. The Formation is arkosic and graywacke sandstone, conglomerate, shale, and coal. Chuckanut sandstone was used to build many of the major early civic buildings on the West Coast.

The formation includes most of the Cascade foothills bordering the lowland of coastal Whatcom County. There are carbonaceous shales full of leaf fossils, and even whole fossilized tree trunks can be found standing upright. This is all from a vast alluvial floodplain, deposited by ancient streams—so there are no marine fossils, but rather palm fronds mixed among the many plants.

Chuckanut Drive crosses two folds in the thick sediment bed, one an anticline (arch) and one syncline (trough). The axis of the Chuckanut Mountain anticline lies at Chuckanut Village. The village can be reached by turning right, about 1 mile south of Fairhaven Park, at the base of a long hill.

Continuing south from there on Chuckanut Drive, the road parallels the beds on the formation's western flank. Near the junction with Chuckanut Point road, at the sharp bend in the road, the beds swing sharply around and form the Chuckanut Mountain syncline. Its axis heads northwest toward Chuckanut Island in the bay. South to Oyster Creek, the road is again nearly parallel to the beds.

What follows is a short mileage guide to some of the interesting geological features that can be seen along the road. Consider it a mini-geologic/geomorphologic Chuckanut Drive.

Mile 0: Fairhaven Park, driving south from Fairhaven Village. Opposite the park is an outcropping of Chuckanut sandstone.

0.6: The somewhat overgrown roadcut on the right, just after Viewcrest Road, reveals pebbly clay deposited by floating ice eleven thousand years ago.

1.2: The glacial outwash gravel pit on the left is now a parking lot for the Interurban Trail and Teddy Bear Cove.

2.1: Overgrown Chuckanut sandstone dips steeply on the southwest limb of the Chuckanut anticline.

4.7: Chuckanut sandstone and shale can be seen here, near the axis of the Chuckanut syncline. The viewing is good, but there is no place to park.

5.0: Chuckanut sandstone and shale are evident at this parking area for the 1.9-mile trail up to Fragrance Lake.

5.3: Chuckanut sandstone can be seen in the road cut.

5.4: This marks the Larrabee State Park northern boundary, just before a parking area for hikers on their way down to the beach.

5.6: This is the north entrance to Larrabee State Park.

5.7: Here at the south entrance to Larrabee State Park, near-vertical sandstone and interbeds of shale can be seen on the west flank of the syncline.

5.9: This marks the Whatcom/Skagit county boundary.

6.3: At this roadside park, view Chuckanut shale with lots of leaf fossils.

7.2: Parking area at Milepost 13.

7.4: Here, cliffs of Chuckanut sandstone, shale, and coal dip to the north.

7.7: At this roadside park are plant fossils embedded in layers of shale and sandstone.

7.9: On the Chuckanut sandstone and shale here are fossil palm fronds 2 to 3 feet in diameter. (Please look at them only; they are fragile and easily destroyed. There are more fossil leaves in carbonaceous shale beneath the fossil palms.)

8.2: At this parking area there are beds of Chuckanut sandstone. Look on the left for a memorial plaque placed by the Ladies Improvement Club of Edison, Washington.

8.5: Look for Chuckanut sandstone, shale and, coal in the cliffs on the left. There is a local synclinal flexure near the bend in the road.

8.8: There are outcrops of Chuckanut sandstone at this roadside park.

9.3: From here to Oyster Creek are outcrops of green basic igneous rock.

9.6: Here at Oyster Creek, blue-green schistose serpentine can be seen at the south end of the bridge.

9.9: There are outcrops of quartz-sericite phyllite at numerous places on the left.

10.4: At this parking area, there is silvery gray, well-foliated quartz-sericite phyllite.

10.8: The quarry on the left reveals serpentinized basic igneous rock, some of it massive.

11.1: The outcrop on the left shows silvery gray to black, fine-grained foliated phyllite.

11.2: The bridge over the tidal lagoon to the Skagit Flats marks the end of the mountainous part of Chuckanut Drive.

The northern half of Chuckanut Drive is a winding, scenic, two-lane, cliffhanger of a road that clings to the mountainside above Chuckanut and Samish bays. Carved from the west-facing, fossil-laced sandstone cliffs of Chuckanut Mountain, the road affords sweeping views of the water and San Juan Islands. But remember to practice safe driving: 7 miles of the drive have no straightaway. This section is also very popular with bicyclists, many of them in training for races. So it's not a good road for making up lost time. It requires its own pace.

Along the Chuckanut Drive.

Year-round, cars, motorcycles, and recreational vehicles pull into the many overlooks and picnic spots, and motorists watch the sunset. Even on the rainiest of Pacific Northwest days, there is usually a colorful sunset over the San Juan Islands. Wildlife along Chuckanut Drive includes foxes (rarely seen), raccoons, porcupines, and deer. Rumors of Sasquatch in the mountains have persisted for years.

The southern 10 miles cuts between farmlands of the Skagit Valley.

U.S. military engineers built the first road through the Chuckanut Mountains in the 1860s, in order to connect the town of Whatcom in the north with military posts in the south. Called the Military Road, it is not known for sure if it went over Chuckanut Mountain or if it followed the present highway. Whatever its route, it was eventually abandoned.

Most Puget Sound travel was done on steamers in the early days of this century, but as the population in the northern regions continued to build, there was pressure for a through road to the south. The drive was first conceived of in 1891, but it remained a crude path for years. During early construction, convicts stockaded at Oyster Creek were used for labor. The road was finished in 1921, when there were only seven cars registered in Whatcom County. Chuckanut Drive eventually became one of the more famous links on the International Pacific Highway.

Originally, it was just a gravel road from Bellingham to the county line at Clayton Bay. From Clayton Bay to Blanchard, the road followed the water's edge and was known as the Blanchard Road. At high tide, Blanchard Road was impassable. The right-of-way to Blanchard Road was bought by Great Northern, which built a railway that left no public access. Eventually the Skagit County Commissioners built a road on the present route of Chuckanut Drive.

The road was taken over by the state highway department in 1907 as part of Washington Highway 99 and named Chuckanut Drive from Blanchard to Fairhaven. For many years the highway has been used as a backdrop for car commercials. In 1926, Chuckanut Drive was included as part of U.S. Highway 99, the Pacific Highway, parts of which still go by that name in the Puget Sound area.

Slides and washouts have always been a big problem along the mountainous section of Chuckanut Drive. It was the state's most costly highway to maintain when it was the main route between Bellingham and Seattle. There are several viewpoints scattered along the way. Several of the San Juan Islands are visible: Guemes, Cypress, Lopez, Eliza, Sinclair, big-humped Lummi, and Orcas, the highest island in the archipelago. The oil refineries seen from Chuckanut Drive are located on March Point, near the town of Anacortes.

The state has only a 40-foot right-of-way on one section of Chuckanut Drive, and the adjacent property owner was not willing to sell more land.

The state never followed through with condemnation proceedings, and it is illegal to pave any road with less than a 60-foot right-of-way. However, the highway department was persuaded to look the other way for the original paving in the 1920s. Present property owners are still not inclined to sell more rights-of-way, so the issue is not resolved.

The views of Samish and Chuckanut bays can be intriguing. Bald eagles are sometimes seen in the treetops close to shore. Blue herons look like the essence of patience as they wait out the lowering tides. Crows and sea gulls chatter and scatter in their noisy negotiation for tidbits, usually clams for the crows, which are dropped on nearby road surfaces and roofs. Sea gulls occasionally nab seastars (starfish), but usually leave them on the railroad tracks.

The Interurban was an electric railroad between Bellingham and Mount Vernon from 1912 to 1930. It was promoted and operated by the Northwest Traction Company, a subsidiary of the Puget Sound Power and Light Company. Nicknamed the "Auntie Urban," the Interurban made regular stops at nearly every milepost along the route. It served as a school bus once, though wrecks were a frequent problem, as was maintenance. Highway competition finally sealed its closure in 1929, and the tracks were torn up.

The route is now known as the Interurban Trail. Paralleling Chuckanut Drive, the 5-mile hiking and biking trail starts from Old Fairhaven Parkway in Bellingham and ends at the south entrance to Larrabee State Park.

At one time there were four means of public transportation to Bellingham along Samish Bay: the Interurban, the Greyhound Bus Line, Blackball Ferry, and the Great Northern Railroad. Now there is only Amtrak, as Greyhound sticks to Interstate 5. The ferries are long gone. They used to stop at Sockeye, where Yacht Club Road crosses the railroad tracks. Freight steamers once made Chuckanut Bay a regular port of call.

The railroad that now runs below along the water's edge is the Burlington Northern that connects Seattle and Vancouver, British Columbia.

Black Ball Ferry Company ran a ferry from Camp Perfection, a summer recreation beach on Chuckanut Bay, where the Bellingham Yacht Club was located, to the San Juan Islands and Vancouver Island. It ran between 1935 and 1941, when the boat was finally condemned.

During World War II, the yacht club's building housed an aircraft lookout and listening post as part of the civil defense system. Neighborhood volunteers operated the facility around the clock. The Yacht Club was moved to Bellingham in 1946. Nothing marks the original site today.

When November and December fogs blanket Bellingham for a week or two at a time, residents seek refuge in the sun by driving up Cleator Road. It turns left from Chuckanut Drive 0.25 mile north of Sound View road. This 3.5-mile gravel logging road climbs through Larrabee parkland to the 1,900-foot north summit of Chuckanut Mountain. An hour's bask in the winter sun makes things right with the world again. In summer, the parking area offers spectacular views of the San Juan Islands and Puget Sound. This lot is also the beginning or end of several foot trails.

Chuckanut Mountain, 1,940 feet high, was logged in the 1890s for the best of virgin fir and large cedars. Those were the only marketable timber at the time. What is now Cleator Road (starting 0.25 mile north of Sound View road) was the original logging road to the top, 1 mile northwest of Fragrance Lake. In 1955, it was extended to Fragrance Lake, Lost Lake, and down to the park and Chuckanut Drive. The road was given to the park in exchange for logging rights to a stand of timber within the park's boundaries. Much of Chuckanut Mountain's timber burned in a wildfire in the 1960s. An excellent locally produced map to the Chuckanut Mountains is available in Bellingham bike shops.

Continuing south on Washington Highway 11, Larrabee State Park starts just north of the Whatcom/Skagit county line. It hugs the seaward side of the Chuckanut Mountains and extends down to 8,100 feet of shoreline that has sandstone sculpture formations and tide pools galore. Some are shaded by a forest canopy of madrona trees and evergreens that lean over the water's edge.

The park contains 2,500 acres, with 87 campsites, including 26 with full hookups, and 40 picnic sites. From April 1 through September 30, the park is open from 6:30 A.M. to dusk. The rest of the year, park hours are 8 A.M. to dusk.

This is Washington's oldest state park. The first 20 acres was donated to the state by the family of Charles Xavier Larrabee in his honor in 1923. Additional donations, purchases, and land swaps have increased it to its present size. There are several freshwater lakes above and a boat launch below. More than 8 miles of trails meander through the woods and valleys, not counting the 5 miles of interurban trail that run north to Bellingham. In fall, the bigleaf maples show their magnificent colors.

The park has an amphitheater used for concerts by the U.S. Air Force Band. It's also the awards stage for the annual Chuckanut Foot Race, an early July 7-miler with several hundred participants.

At the Oyster Creek Inn, there is a one-lane road to the right, a very sharp right, that goes down to the Taylor United Samish Bay Shellfish Farm. It is open daily, and it is a good spot to access the water to watch great blue herons and bald eagles do their daily grocery harvesting just beyond the water line. Oysters are for sale here, either in the shell or freshly shucked. The company also grows and sells manila clams and mussels. From the live tank, April through October, Dungeness crab and pink scallops are available. Visitors can see the operation first hand. At nearly 48 degrees north latitude, Taylor's Samish Bay Pacific oysters benefit from the cold waters of Rosario Strait. Spawning season is delayed, resulting in a late firm oyster for serving raw on the half-shell.

Back on Chuckanut Drive, roadcuts just south of Oyster Creek reveal phyllites with well preserved relict sedimentary structures. At Oyster Creek, where the formation lies upon serpentine, a laterite was found. It is former iron-rich soil, made by intense tropical weathering of the underlying serpentine.

Some of the phyllites are black because of the graphite in the rock. Originally these rocks were shales rich in organic material. During metamorphism, carbon in the organic material was converted to graphite. Some greenschist, serpentine, and metagraywacke can be seen at the south end of Chuckanut Drive in Skagit County.

The phyllites are older than the overlying Chuckanut Sandstone, which is late-Cretaceous to early Tertiary. Actual phyllite age is hard to tell because the geologic time clock was reset by the metamorphism of the parent rocks.

Upon crossing the Colony Creek Bridge near the town of Blanchard, the road takes one more curve and then it runs straight as an arrow through the Skagit Valley to the Interstate 5 interchange at Burlington.

This whole area is nearly at sea level. Samish Island off to the right is not an island at all. The road to it goes over a permanent, low-elevation land bridge. There is a pasture on the left, at the intersection with Colony Road, where horses prance and dance under the full moon.

Look upward for hang gliders that take off from a site on the west side of Blanchard Hill. The site is a clearcut. Pilots land alongside Chuckanut Drive on the flats.

Both sides of this drive show off Skagit County at its agricultural best. Rich delta soil, sometimes flooded during heavy winter rains, grows peas, berries, and rich pasture lands that feed the dairy industry.

In the distance nearly 1 mile to the right, it is possible to make out the Edison School that journalist Edward R. Murrow attended as a boy.

5

Mountain Loop Highway

General description: A 78-mile drive along 3 forested river systems between the towns of Granite Falls and Arlington in Snohomish County.

Special attractions: 300 miles of trails, Glacier Peak, Jackson and Boulder river wilderness areas, historic mining districts, fishing, hiking, views, lush vegetation, camping. Wildlife includes eagles, beavers, black bears, mountain goats, black-tailed deer, and barred owls.

Location: Snohomish County in northwest Washington, 15 miles northeast of Everett.

Highway number: Washington Highway 92, Forest Road 20, Washington Highway 530 (collectively called the Mountain Loop Highway).

Travel season: The road is open year-round to Deer Creek just beyond Silverton, but snow accumulation normally closes the road by December from that point to just before White Chuck, a distance of 15 to 20 miles. The road usually opens during April or May.

Camping: Many campgrounds with RV and tent sites, but no hookups or dump sites. Seven Forest Service campgrounds, with picnic tables, fire grates, toilets. Drinking water is available in Verlot, Rutlo, and Gold Basin.

Services: Darrington and Granite Falls have lodging, restaurants, and gas, but the only services on the loop itself are at Milepost 10 east of Granite Falls near Verlot. The Mountain View Inn, 1 mile west of Verlot, is open year-round. It has a restaurant, six-room motel (forty dollars per night for up to three or four people), and a general store. Gas is available two blocks east. The inn is located at 32005 Mountain Loop Highway, Granite Falls, WA 98252; (360) 691-6668.

Nearby attractions: Mount Pilchuck, Pacific Crest National Scenic Trail, North Cascades National Park, Puget Sound, Seattle, Wild & Scenic Skagit River, steelhead fishing on both rivers, either from the bank or in a boat. Summer fish include steelhead, rainbow, cutthroat, and Dolly Varden.

For more information: Monte Cristo Enterprises, Inc., Darrington Ranger District, Verlot Public Service Center, Mount Baker-Snoqualmie National Forest, Granite Falls Chamber of Commerce, Darrington Chamber of Commerce (see Appendix A).

 **The drive**

The Forest Service has designated the 50-mile stretch between Granite Falls and Darrington the "Mountain Loop Scenic Byway." This Mountain

Drive 5: Mountain Loop Highway

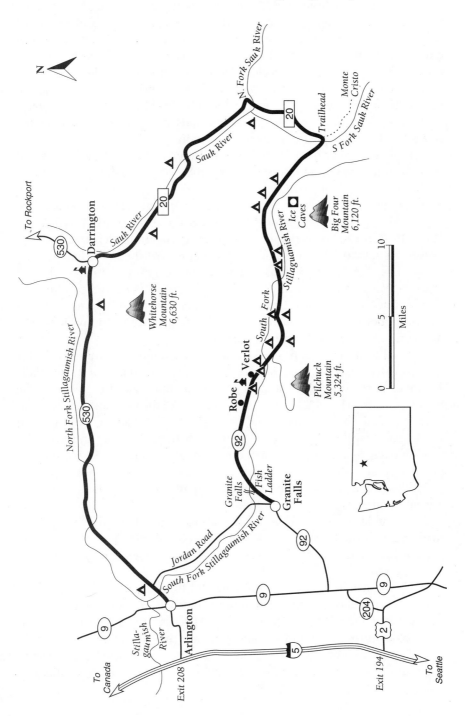

Loop Highway, one of the state's most popular weekend drives, travels into the heart of the western Cascade Mountains. It passes through the heavily wooded Darrington Ranger District of the Mount Baker-Snoqualmie National Forest, looping almost entirely around the Boulder River Wilderness. The road follows three river systems. The Forest Service designated this drive as a Scenic Byway in 1992, one of eleven in Washington State. Close enough to Seattle to easily cover in a day, it is a good loop drive on which people can get an idea of what it must have been like a hundred years ago when everything was just grown over. The roadside woods are thick and lush along the rivers and the route goes over a low mountain pass.

Begin the scenic drive at the town of Granite Falls, which can be reached from the north by taking Interstate 5 exit 208 east on Washington Highway 530 to Arlington. Just past Arlington, still on WA 530, cross the North Fork of the Stillaguamish River and turn right onto Arlington Heights Road, then right again to Granite Falls on Jordan Road. From the south, take I-5 exit 194 at Everett and go east on U.S. Highway 2. Stay in the left lane over the causeway that crosses Eby Island and go left onto Washington Highway 204 toward Lake Stevens. In 3 miles, at Washington Highway 9, turn north for 2 miles to Washington Highway 92. Turn right onto WA 92 and continue for 9 miles into Granite Falls. Granite Falls has Railroad and Reunion Day in early October, with a parade, crafts booths, food vendors, pony rides, and miniature railroad and logging displays.

Local trout fisherman go no farther than just north of Granite Falls for the first cascades of the Cascades. The town was named for the striking falls 1.5 miles north of town. The falls go over a smooth granite ledge to the boulders below. They are located on the left side of the road, about an eighth-mile walk down a gravel path. The Granite Falls Fish Ladder, when built in 1954, was then the world's longest vertical baffle fish ladder in the world. Salmon navigate a 280-foot tunnel dug through the granite. In season, it is possible to stand over the fishway on the grate and see coho, pink, and chinook salmon working their way up to spawn above the falls. Expect to see bald eagles from October to March.

Beyond this point, locals call the Stillaguamish River the "Stilly." The road passes through second-growth dense woods of bigleaf and vine maple, alder, fir, and Western redcedar. The forest floor is covered in moss and lush undergrowth.

Nine miles from Granite Falls, the Old Robe Trail is an easy walk for less than 1 mile to the abandoned townsite of Robe. Park on the right shoulder by the sign for Old Robe Historic Trail. The trail starts in an old clearcut then passes through the forest and down onto the river's flood plain.

To continue on foot past Robe, follow the trail downstream through alder and brush to the white water canyon, with its slick rock walls and

Stillaguamish River.

flourishing greenery. The path crosses the stone and mortar roadbed, built out from the canyon walls by early railroad workers, and passes through two tunnels. They are dark, damp, and creepy. Signs warn that you enter the train tunnels at your own risk. Shortly after the tunnels, the path disappears under a heap of rubble, probably a collapsed tunnel. The railway line was completed in 1892, but the river reclaimed its territory long ago. The flood of 1897 (the year of the Klondike gold discovery) took out three trestles, caved in two tunnels, and filled all the others. Several sections of track were washed away.

The railroad was rebuilt in 1900, and again in 1915 when an excursion train began its fifteen-year run to the mining town of Monte Cristo. Torn asunder by flooding again in 1930, the owners dismantled what was left and sold it as scrap iron to Japan.

As you continue east on the Mountain Loop Road, a sign near the entrance to the Mount Baker-Snoqualmie National Forest announces that all RVs must be street-legal and that drivers must be licensed to operate on all mountain roads.

The route, especially on the eastbound section, is like driving through a long tent of trees. Canopies from both sides of the road meet overhead nearly the entire way. The abundant trees include second- and third-growth Western hemlock, Douglas-fir, Western redcedar, black cottonwood, red alder, vine and bigleaf maple, plus some Sitka spruce. With an average annual rainfall of 140 inches, this forest has no problem staying green. In the fall, however, this is a very colorful drive. Flowers frequently seen are dogwood, trillium, and queenscup beadlily. Mountain goats can sometimes be spotted, and at Gold Basin Pond, there are osprey and great blue heron.

The forest Service's Verlot Public Service Center, 11 miles east of Granite Falls, is a good place to check for local maps, road conditions, and campsite availability. Just inside are booklets that explain the self-guided tour of the facility and paved interpretive trail. On display are more than twenty identified trees and plants common here, a cross-section of a 700-year-old Douglas-fir, an ore cart from the Monte Cristo mines, and firefighting equipment.

The mountain just southwest of Verlot (pronounced Ver-LOT) is Mount Pilchuck, elevation 5,324 feet. Two good hikes are possible on the mountain: one to the top and a slightly easier one to Heather Lake. To hike to the top of Mount Pilchuck, with its 360-degree view of the Cascades and Puget Sound, drive 0.5 mile past the Verlot Ranger Station, cross the bridge over Benson Creek and turn right onto Forest Road 42, 7 miles from the former Mount Pilchuck Ski Area, elevation 3,100 feet. Park near the trailhead sign. With a 2,300-foot elevation gain, the 4-mile, round-trip hike should take about 4 hours.

Heather Lake is also a 4-mile round trip, but should require only 3 hours because the elevation gain is only half as much. However, some of the trail is steep and traverses rough scree. The long and narrow lake sits at the foot of a huge cirque cut deep by a glacier into the side of Mount Pilchuck's rock. Rock walls rise steeply hundreds of feet on three sides of the lake. A subalpine forest clings to existence on parts of the walls.

This is a popular trail, and it passes through both old-growth forest and old clearcuts. There is one tree near the lake whose roots poke 15 feet into the air before connecting with the tree trunk. Its nurse log was probably dissolved a hundred years ago. The trailhead is on the road to the now-closed Mount Pilchuck Ski Area. Take FR 42 for 1.5 miles to the trailhead parking lot, then hike 100 yards up the logging road to the trailhead.

As you continue east on the Mountain Loop Highway, it seems that about every 0.5 mile several cars are parked along here, with people playing near the water and having a good time. Around the Fourth of July expect to see American flags flying on tents and sandbars.

There is a photogenic bridge, called Red Bridge, where traffic crosses to the north side of the river. The Red Bridge Campground is here, where people swim and float on both sides of the bridge. All along here are remnants of the area's mining days—abandoned town sites, old mine tunnels, and grown-over railroad grades.

The little town of Silverton looks like a tiny version of Roslyn, the Washington town featured as Cicely, Alaska, in the TV series *Northern Exposure*. The buildings have old peaked roofs made of metal so the snow will slide off.

Three miles beyond Silverton is Big Four, named for Big Four Mountain. The Big Four Ice Caves are a very popular side excursion, just a 1-mile hike from the road. The trailhead is 22.5 miles from Granite Falls at the Big Four Picnic Area. The trail starts at a beaver marsh, goes through thick forest, and over the South Stilly Fork up to the base of an ice field. The caves form here in late summer from the melting ice. It is not recommended to actually enter the ice caves, for fear of falling ceiling ice. They are normally visible from August through October. From here, hikers get a remarkable view of 6,135-foot Big Four Mountain.

On the drive toward Barlow Pass, traffic can be quite thick on a summer weekend. When you cross Perry Creek, at Milepost 26, you'll see why. Many colorful tents fill the woods near the water's edge as people enjoy an old-fashioned wilderness in a national park, but without the regimentation of a state park closer to a freeway.

On the way to Buck Creek, just a few miles farther, the beautiful overgrowth on both sides of the road is a big surprise to newcomers. It is not possible here to see the forest for the trees, nor can any mountains be seen.

Just trees and the river are visible. But stay alert to other drivers who are just as astounded. Be prepared when the car ahead of you puts on its brakes and pulls over to the right, thinking it polite to let you pass. That's if you put your brakes on in time to avoid a rear-end collision.

The paved portion of the drive ends just ahead at Barlow Pass, elevation 2,351 feet. Cars are parked willy-nilly in this area, their drivers having taken the 4-mile hike up the gated road on the right to Monte Cristo. Monte Cristo is a ghost town, a short-lived boom town alive with gold and silver miners near the turn of the century.

Ore was discovered in 1889. It was called the Seventy-six Lode, on the side of Wilmans Peak overlooking Seventy-six Gulch. The ore proved to contain not only galena (lead sulfide), but worthwhile amounts of gold and silver. At its height between 1894 and 1897, Monte Cristo served about a thousand residents with hotels, restaurants, saloons, churches, a school, a hospital, a drug store, barber shops, butcher shops, and a newspaper. The miners usually stayed in bunkhouses up in the mountains and came to town only on their days off. Some mine tunnels were 3,000 feet deep. There were 247 mining claims registered. A quarter of them have been patented and are still privately owned. But within twenty years of the strike, Monte Cristo became a ghost town because the quality of the gold and silver ore was low.

Monte Cristo is now privately owned and operated, maintained to remind visitors of the toil and courage of the miners and pioneers who created

Display at Verlot Public Service Center.

its history. What was once a 40-foot-wide street in Monte Cristo is now just a path. There are several mountain peaks near here around 7,000 feet high.

On the loop from Barlow Pass, on what is now called Forest Road 20, it is 23 miles along the Sauk River to Darrington. Drivers are warned that the gravel road is a single lane with turnouts. What follows are 14 unpaved miles: the loop may be bumpy with chuckholes, but grading is normally good. Most RVs can navigate this road, but anything bigger than a Class C would be hard to turn around. Four-wheel-drive is not remotely necessary: even Corvettes make the drive without incident.

First-time visitors to the Northwest might be surprised to learn that dirt roads can be dusty. The expectation is for muddy ruts, mist, rain, and soggy, boggy terrain. But even here, where 12 feet of rain falls each year, there is a dry season. On a clear sunny day, when it has not rained for awhile (usually in late August), dirt roads are dusty roads. The trees are coated with dust too.

Winter storms in November of 1995 swelled the South Fork of the Sauk River along this section and washed away 150 feet of the road. The flooding closed the Mountain Loop Highway for seven months, until it was repaired and reopened in July of 1996.

The posted speed limit is 25 mph; reasonable, perhaps even generous, for this single-lane road with occasional pullouts. It was built in 1938 by the CCC and follows the South Fork of the Sauk, then the Sauk itself, for the 29 miles between Barlow Pass and Darrington.

In some sections the river is not visible through the woods, but the sight of granite walls on the right is sobering. In many places people have pulled off the road and into the woods to a clearing, parked, and camped. Just 20 feet off the road good parking, good camping, and good access to the Sauk River can be found, but none of this can be seen from the road itself. People nail paper picnic plates with arrows pointing to their particular campsite onto roadside trees.

The drive's popularity may have to do with its proximity to Everett and Seattle and its location at the base of the Cascades. Anyone would feel a bit of awe at the uncivilized landscape. It has been mined, fished, logged, and paved, but it has not been tamed. A few steps off the road in the dense growth, you can visualize the women described in Annie Dillard's novel, *The Living*, turning sideways and compressing their hoop skirts to pass between the trees.

It is not hard to see how early prospectors became lost following rivers that headed away from where they were trying to go. For us there are road signs with binoculars and camera symbols on them, indicating wildlife viewing spots.

The Mountain Loop Highway crosses the Sauk at the point where the

White Chuck River joins it, and from here on the road is paved.

The valley of the Sauk flattens and widens before Darrington. There are enough clearcuts close to the road that you can see some distant vistas.

From Darrington, the Sauk River flows north to feed the Skagit River. The scenic loop drive ends technically at Darrington, but it is very nice to continue for 32 miles west via WA 530 from Darrington to Arlington and I-5.

Darrington is a small town in the flatlands among three wild and scenic rivers, the Glacier Peak Wilderness, the North Cascade National Park, and the Mount Baker-Snoqualmie National Forest. Its elevation is 540 feet. The town is famed for its annual July Bluegrass Festival (always the third weekend). It also hosts the National Field Archery competitions, not to mention annual summer snowmobile races on grass. Darrington was the home of Sauk and Suiattle Indians until early in this century, when gold and silver miners overran the area. It was largely settled by people from North Carolina, and it is their descendants who stage the annual Bluegrass Festival. There are also whitewater rafting opportunities with several outfitters. Darrington provides access to the Glacier Peaks Wilderness Area and has a shortcut north to the North Cascades Highway at Rockport.

From Darrington to Arlington on WA 530, the highway follows the steelhead-rich Stillaguamish River. There are good panoramic views, with a whole mountain range to the left that features Whitehorse Mountain across the meadows. The country smooths a bit after the town of Hazel—the peaks are less sharp, and the countryside seem a bit tamer.

To reach I-5 from Arlington, continue west on WA 530 for 4 miles.

6

Whidbey Island

General description: This 60-mile drive stretches across one of Puget Sound's flat islands. It is reached by ferry in the south and connected to the mainland by bridges in the north.

Special attractions: Ebey's Landing National Historical Reserve, hiking, bicycling, picnicking, bird and wildlife watching, scuba diving, fishing, kite flying, boating, photography, beach activities.

Location: Puget Sound.

Highway number: Washington Highway 525 and Washington Highway 20.

Travel season: The drive is open year-round.

Camping: Camping is available in several state parks.

Services: Full traveler services are available in Oak Harbor.

For more information: Ebey's Landing National Historical Reserve Trust Board, Cascade Loop Association, Hatzoff Productions, Oak Harbor City Hall, Washington State Parks, Island County Fairgrounds (see Appendix A).

 The drive

This island drive includes rural turn-of-the-century towns, shoreline, and pastoral landscapes, but it begins with a twenty-minute ferry ride. Catch the Washington State Ferry from Mukilteo (from Interstate 5 north of Seattle via Washington Highways 525 or 526) to Clinton on Whidbey Island. Ferries leave every half hour until midnight. You might want to stop at the town of Langley first. Head 3 miles north of Clinton on WA 525; turn right onto Maxwelton Road. Langley is a 2-mile drive north from here. With its numerous antique shops and boutiques, Langley hugs the water of Saratoga Passage. It has a nice waterfront park, and campers are welcome at Langley's Island County Fairgrounds, 819 Camano Avenue.

Have a look at the sculpture on First Street, created by the same woman who did the bronze pig for Seattle's Pike Place Market. The life-size bronze sculpture depicts a boy looking out over the railing to the Saratoga Passage, while his dog holds its head up with a ball in its mouth.

Seawall Park in Langley is a good place from which to watch bald eagles, sea lions, otters, great blue herons, and sometimes a visiting pod of

Drive 6: Whidbey Island

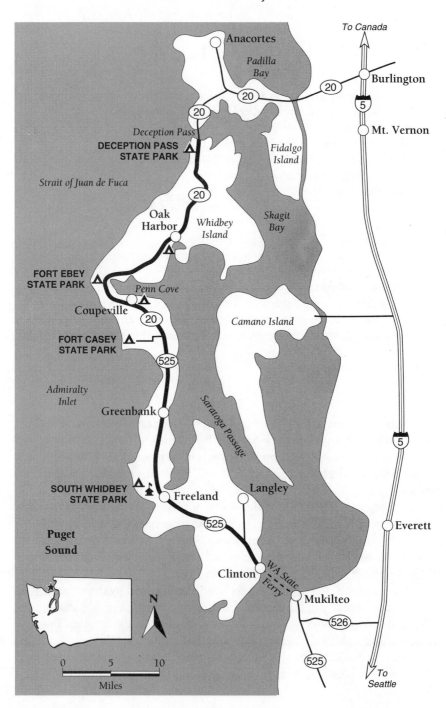

To Canada

Anacortes

Padilla
Bay

20 Burlington

20

5

20

Mt. Vernon

Deception Pass

DECEPTION PASS △
STATE PARK

Fidalgo
Island

Strait of Juan de Fuca

20

Oak
Harbor

Whidbey
Island

Skagit
Bay

△

FORT EBEY △
STATE PARK

Penn Cove

△

Coupeville

20

Camano Island

FORT CASEY △
STATE PARK

525

Admiralty
Inlet

Greenbank

Saratoga Passage

SOUTH WHIDBEY △
STATE PARK

Langley

Freeland

525

5

Everett

Puget
Sound

525

Clinton

WA State
Ferry

Mukilteo

N

526

525

To
Seattle

0   5   10

Miles

orca whales that often travel to Saratoga Passage for early fall feeding.

After returning to WA 525 and turning right, the scenic drive passes mid-island farms and woodlots, interspersed with newer homes belonging to people who either commute to the mainland or maintain them as weekend and summer homes.

Whidbey Island's width varies from 1 to 8 miles. It is a delightful string of tiny towns that just charm the dollars off visitors. The island's population is about sixty thousand people. It is also the longest island in the country, now that New York's Long Island is considered a peninsula. People surf its western shores under the flight path of jets from the Whidbey Island Naval Air Station.

Whidbey Island's shorelines are mostly steep bluffs, with beaches of stone and sand littered by the tidal wash of logs. The island lies dead ahead of the Strait of Juan de Fuca, the 17-mile channel that separates the Olympic Peninsula and Vancouver Island and brings the tides of the Pacific Ocean into Puget Sound. The island was named for Joseph Whidbey, the sailing master of explorer George Vancouver, in 1792.

The town of Freeland is 10 miles north of Clinton, sited at the south end of Holmes Harbor. The town originally built itself around a cooperative sawmill nearly a hundred years ago.

About halfway between Freeland and Greenbank, but 1 mile to the west, is South Whidbey State Park. It has 54 campsites and 2 miles of beach. The Wilbert Trail is a really nice loop trail through an old-growth cluster of Western red cedar and Douglas-fir. Some of the trees are more than 250 years old. The park is 4 miles north of Freeland and 3 miles south of Greenbank on Smugglers Cove Road.

A bit over 1 mile before Greenbank, Resort Road on the right leads to the Meerkerk Rhododendron Gardens. The 53-acre gardens are maintained by the Seattle Rhododendron Society. There are more than one thousand native and exotic rhodies. The gardens are open from March through Labor Day.

Alongside WA 525, 7 miles north of Freeland, Greenbank Farms is the country's largest loganberry farm. Actually a vineyard, the 125-acre farm is owned by Whidbeys, who distill the berries into Washington's only liqueur. The farm is open for self-guided tours. It also has a tasting room, gift shop, and picnic tables.

Continuing north through the gracious farmlands, 5 miles north of Greenbank, WA 525 joins WA 20. A worthy sidetrip branches left here on a spur of WA 20. In just over 3 miles, Keystone Harbor is the focal point of Fort Casey State Park, Camp Casey, an underwater marine park, and the landing for the ferries to the Olympic Peninsula. After the first mile, however, at the left turn onto Keystone Road (still on WA 20), the drive parallels a southeastern border of Ebey's Landing National Historical Reserve.

This is the first reserve of its kind established by the National Park Service in 1978. It is 22 square miles of rural historic district that includes farmlands, beaches, parks, trails, ninety-one nationally registered historic buildings, and the entire town of Coupeville. Private owners still work the historic farms under an agreement with the Park Service to preserve the prairies as they are.

The purpose of the reserve is both to commemorate and preserve the rural communities as a living museum to demonstrate how this land was explored, pioneered, settled, and farmed since Captain George Vancouver first arrived in 1792.

The reserve, bisected by WA 20, extends from shore to shore, starting below Coupeville and extending northward around Penn Cove on the east side of the island to within 2 miles of Oak Harbor. Much of the scenic drive is through the reserve.

At Keystone Spit, adjacent to the ferry landing breakwater, there may be scuba divers enjoying the underwater marine park. The beach is steep gravel, and tough as anything to navigate while wearing heavy diving gear. Nothing compares, though, with coming face to face with a wolf's head eel 30 feet down.

Washington State ferries cross back and forth across Admiralty Inlet from here to Port Townsend on the Olympic Peninsula.

Just on the other side of the ferry landing is Fort Casey State Park. The park has thirty-five campsites, some along the beach, but no RV hookups. Beyond the campground is the old arsenal and defense facility. This is still part of the state park. It is co-administered with Seattle Pacific University. Coastal gun emplacements are displayed here, and there is a museum in the fort's old lighthouse. The west-side beach is fine for walks and exploring. Whales can be seen on occasion from Fort Casey and Ebey's Landing. Orca pods that stray from their usual waters around the San Juan Islands are the most fun, but there are always plenty of river otters, harbor seals, and California sea lions. More rare are sightings of dolphins, minke whales, and humpback whales. In late spring and early summer, gray whales migrating from California to the Arctic may be seen.

A trail extends north along the beach for 4 miles to Fort Ebey.

Return to the drive, taking WA 20 north toward Coupeville. The highway parallels the edge of a U.S. Naval Reservation, a branch facility of the Naval Air Station north of Oak Harbor. When you pass the north of the airfield, Rhododendron State Park is on the left. The park has a 1.5-mile loop road through stands of wild rhododendrons, many of them 10 feet tall. The peak viewing season is during May and June. The park is 1 mile east of Coupeville on WA 20. The only sign at the entrance is a blue and white campsite sign. The park has campsites, hiking trails, and picnic spots.

Take a side excursion into Coupeville. The town is an old island seaport dating from 1875. It now nets more tourists than fish, enticing them with unique variety shops, restaurants, bed and breakfasts, and bookstores. Most of the architecture is Victorian. Free pamphlets guide visitors on a walking and driving tour of the town's many historic buildings.

For a good side trip from Coupeville to Ebey's Landing, start at the intersection of Coupeville's Main Street and WA 20. Drive south on Main Street, which becomes Engle Road, for 1.7 miles. Turn right (west) onto Hill Road. Hill Road ends, in about 1 mile, at Ebey's Landing. Rumors of good surfing here claim that the waves make it all the way in through the Strait of Juan de Fuca from the Pacific. It could happen. The sandy beach here is backed by 200-foot sandstone bluffs. Look closely for cactus. It is not planted as a joke; it actually grows naturally in the rain shadow of the Olympic Peninsula. Washington State Parks maintains a day-use parking lot, and owns and manages a nearly 1-mile strip of coastal bluffs between the sea and the farmland, directly north of Ebey's Landing. At Ebey's Landing proper, there is a nice bluff trail and plenty of beach to explore. The beach trail goes all the way from Ebey's Landing to Fort Ebey State Park, a distance of nearly 3 miles.

WA 20 from Coupeville follows the contour of Penn Cove, home of the famous Penn Cove mussels. A 1-mile detour onto Madrona Way will take you to the Captain Whidbey Inn. The inn is a 1907 vintage madrona log resort, loaded with the quaint charms of yore. Don't miss the sagging second floor of the main building, and take a peek into the tiny rooms. Perusers of the upstairs library may stay longer than intended.

One mile west of Penn Cove, across the narrowest part of the island on Libbey Road, Fort Ebey State Park rests on high bluffs above the Strait of Juan de Fuca, where it is joined by Admiralty Inlet. There are some good hiking trails and picnic sites in the day area. Take the curving plank boardwalk to the beach. The beach can be hard to navigate because of all the monster driftwood logs, but check for glass fishing floats from Japan, or maybe some Nike shoes from the latest overboard cargo container. Leftovers from the old fort days include gun batteries and bunkers. They are fun to explore. The park has fifty campsites but no RV hookups.

Instead of returning to Penn Cove and WA 20 to get to Oak Harbor, a drive up the west island coast road, West Beach Road, to Joseph Whidbey State Park would be more interesting. It is about 6 miles from the intersection of Libbey Road and West Beach Road north along the bluffs of West Beach to Joseph Whidbey State Park.

This day-use park has more than 0.5 mile of beachfront on the Strait of Juan de Fuca. This beach was known as Civil Service Beach back when the

Navy used it for a rifle range. Log steps lead down to one of the best places around for watching waterfowl, marine birds, and other wildlife. There is a 0.5-mile trail through a freshwater wetland. In the summer, orcas can sometimes be seen offshore.

To get to Oak Harbor from here, take Swantown Road southeast. It intersects with WA 20, joining West Pioneer Way in 3 miles.

Oak Harbor was named for the white oaks in the region, known as Garry oaks. The town is preserving in perpetuity a stand of oaks estimated to be five hundred years old in Smith Park, at 300 Avenue West and Midway Boulevard. There are picnic areas in the broad shade, plus benches and a playground.

Oak Bay Beach Park has an RV and camping park plus a day-use area with a sandy beach. To get there from WA 20, turn east on Pioneer Way, go one block, and turn right (south) onto 70 Southwest Street. The park is at the end of the street.

As you continue north on WA 20, the Whidbey Island Naval Air Station is a few miles north of town. It has long been an important ingredient in Whidbey Island's culture and economy. The airborne Navy is here because of the allegedly good flying weather. A big sign at the entrance to the base proclaims the "Sound of Freedom."

This north end of Whidbey Island is more wooded and hilly than the southern portion. The drive winds more and there are fewer farms to be seen. The real beauty of the island, and the reason for most people's visits, is Deception Pass and the state park on both sides of it.

Park officials say that four million people a year come to Deception Pass State Park. Even on weeknights, the 251 campsites are often filled. The 4,128-acre park is renowned for its old-growth trees, eight islands, sandy beaches, swimming lakes, and boat launches.

Part of the attraction is the pass itself. The tidal currents that separate Whidbey and Fidalgo islands are swift and deep, a popular sight from above on the high bridge. Normally only high-powered boats try to navigate Deception Pass. Smaller craft often fall victim to the speeding, swirling currents.

Some scuba divers/adventurers are known to "surf" the currents 80 feet below sea level, but even they have power boats waiting on the other side.

The park's facilities and roads were built during the Depression, and the crowds of today have had an impact on some of the trees. The damage is caused by trampling undergrowth and compacting soil around roots, which can kill trees.

The park also has a few lakes, 30 miles of trails, marshland, sand dunes, and a few smaller islands. Black-tailed deer are common in the park, and bald eagles nest in the treetops. The park has 15 miles of saltwater shoreline, comprised of all manner of rocky bluffs, coves, tide flats, and sandy beaches. Deception Pass itself is spanned by a wonderfully photogenic bridge. It connects the northern tip of Whidbey Island with the southern tip of Fidalgo Island, which itself is connected to the mainland by a bridge.

The rushing waters are quite a sight from the bridge, 182 feet up. It is well worth parking at the convenient lot and taking a walk onto the bridge. The mid-point of Deception Pass Bridge is Pass Island. It is part of the park, as are Deception Island west of the park in the Strait of Juan de Fuca and Spy's Island, the tiny one just below Deception Island.

7

Ice Caves Route

General description: This 90-mile drive climbs north from the Columbia River on U.S. Highway 97 to Goldendale, east over the High Prairie and through Trout Lake, and heads south past the Ice Caves, through the Gifford Pinchot National Forest. You return past the Big Lava Bed and back to the Columbia River at the town of Cook.

Special attractions: Goldendale Observatory, Conboy Lake National Wildlife Refuge, Ice Caves, Big Lava Bed.

Location: South-central Washington.

Highway number: U.S. Highway 97, Washington Highway 142, Glenwood Road, Washington Highway 141 (Trout Lake-Glenwood Road), Forest Roads 24, 60, and 66, Willard Road, and Cook-Underwood Road.

Travel season: The drive is open spring through fall.

Camping: In the Gifford Pinchot National Forest (the last third of the drive in Skamania County) there are several Forest Service campgrounds both on and near the route.

Services: Services are limited on this drive, but gas and food are available in all the towns.

For more information: Gifford Pinchot National Forest, Goldendale Observatory State Park, Mount Adams Ranger District (see Appendix A).

 The drive

Begin the drive heading north on U.S. Highway 97 from the Columbia River. After a 5 to 6 mile climb up the Columbia Hills, the road reaches the relative flatness of the Klickitat Valley. From up here you can see the Cascade Range to the left. There is a good viewpoint after Milepost 7, from which you can see Mount Rainier. Straight north, beyond Goldendale on US 97, rise the Simcoe Mountains.

Goldendale offers a scenic loop tour and historic homes tours of its own. It is also the home of the highly respected Klickitat County Museum. Goldendale calls itself the Golden Gate to the Columbia Gorge. A bypass highway has been built around Goldendale, but this drive goes right through town. Turn west from US 97 onto Washington Highway 142 to reach Goldendale.

Drive 7: Ice Caves Route

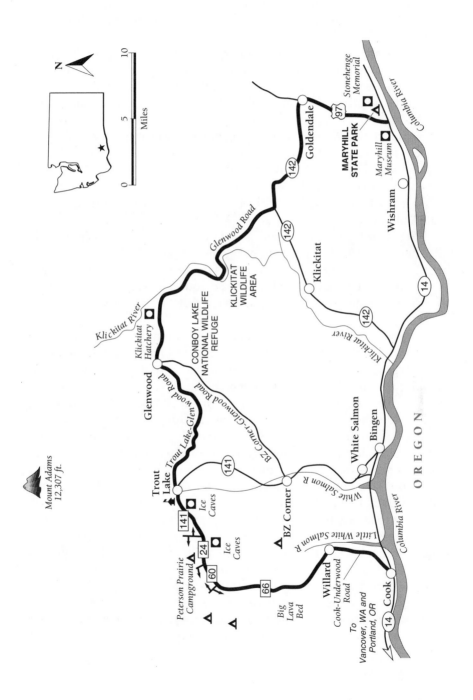

Driving through Goldendale on WA 142, watch for a brown sign to the Goldendale Observatory State Park Interpretive Center, a state park heritage area. It is a lovely uphill drive to the site through a pine forest. It's open to the public Wednesday through Sunday from 2 to 5 P.M. and again 8 P.M. to midnight.

When you leave Goldendale, going west on WA 142, gorgeous, snow-capped Mount Adams can be seen ahead in the distance, a bit to the right. The road here stretches out on the flats of the upper Klickitat Valley above the Columbia Hills to the south. Piles of volcanic rock dot the land alongside the road. It stays pretty flat for several miles, then turns north as it crosses Blockhouse Creek. After passing Blockhouse Butte on the right, WA 142 heads west across Crofton Prairie. Keep an eye out for Harris Bratton Road, because less than 0.5 mile past it the scenic drive leaves WA 142 to turn north onto Glenwood Road to the town of Glenwood. At this intersection, WA 142 branches left toward Klickitat and follows the Klickitat River to the Columbia.

The right turn to Glenwood is just at the bottom of a steep 0.5-mile hill. There is no sign for the Conboy Lake National Wildlife Refug,e nor for Trout Lake, just for Glenwood. If you pass the Double R Ranch on the right, you've gone too far—Glenwood is the road you want. Glenwood is 24 miles from here—24 miles of clear scenic views of Mount Adams off in the distance.

The road to Glenwood meanders and threads around knobby hills on its way through this Klickitat Wildlife Area. The broad vistas off to the left are in Oregon, divided from Washington by the Columbia Gorge in the foreground. Here, the planted fields are mostly flat. The paved two-lane road is good, but there are no white stripes marking the shoulders. It passes stands of pine, while the fields in between are dotted with piles of basalt. Occasionally, fields of wildflowers can be seen in the early summer. Mount Adams is in view nearly all the time. If any weather is brewing, it is easy to see that the mountain has its own micro-climate.

About 10 miles from the turnoff to Glenwood the road starts to parallel the Klickitat River. The views here are just stupendous as the road winds down ever so slowly to the floor of the Klickitat River valley. Traffic is very sparse. The Klickitat is known locally as a mean river, with its deep and fast whitewater, but it is also known as a source of big fish. Indian fishers, knowing that the Klickitat will take them if it can, secure themselves with lifelines tied to trees or rocks on shore. Every catch is shared among all the families.

This river road is absolutely stunning for its scenic qualities. The trees are grayish with rippled vertical bark. They are gnarly and twisted and look as if they were planted as an orchard. Some ponderosa pine is mixed in with them.

A Willis Canyon marker identifies this as "one of the special places in the forest. The 1,280 acres of distant canyons are part of Champion International Corporation's registry of special places in the forest." Champion oversees its land for the protection and enhancement of wildlife habitat, much as the adjoining Washington Department of Wildlife lands are managed.

The road continues to descend in twists and turns until it crosses the bridge over the Klickitat River. A public fishing area and a game range are found to the left, and the road climbs up the other side of the canyon. Keep an eye out for quail.

The route proceeds on a straight course over a mildly flat yet gentle hill. This plateau is high above the water. Pass a big lumber yard on the right, piled high with milled logs. Even in the middle of summer, traffic is light, and most of the big rigs on the road are stock trailers.

Just after the turnoff to the Klickitat Hatchery the road passes between two narrow lakes. The wide flat area ahead is the Camas Prairie, dotted with cattle and irrigated hay fields. There are no lines on the road at this point. It is a bit bumpy, but serviceable. Mount Adams continues to loom closer on the right. Even this far up from the Columbia Gorge, there can be a stern headwind, sometimes blowing strong enough to force driving speed down by about 7 mph.

Glenwood has a few closed storefronts, but there's also an open tavern, a grocery, a gas station, and the Shade Tree Inn. At the turnoff for BZ Corner, keep straight, following the sign to Trout lake.

At the subsequent Y, turn left onto Trout Lake-Glenwood Road, still following the signs to Trout Lake, the Conboy Lake National Wildlife Refuge headquarters, and the Forest Service ranger station at Trout Lake (18 miles).

To the right, the road goes to a Bureau of Indian Affairs ranger station on Bird Creek Road, to Bench Lake, and to Bird Creek Camp.

Trout Lake–Glenwood Road passes the Glenwood Rodeo Grounds, with Mount Adams in the background. The road is rough-paved with no painted lines, but there are little yellow reflectors down the middle. Stay alert for unfenced livestock, which includes bulls.

After passing Cemetery Road to the left there is an entrance to the Conboy Lake National Wildlife Refuge on the left. The road here is basically flat, cut among the forests.

The route descends through a forest and comes into another broad sweeping valley, half forested and half farmed. It stretches for miles to the west and north. Even this far from the hubbub of civilization, there is a sign for a llama ranch and bed and breakfast on Sunnyside Road. Residents of Trout Lake and the western Columbia seem to feel their interests are better served by the *Oregonian* newspaper, as the paper boxes along the road

View of Mount Adams from Glenwood Road.

indicate, even though their community is in Washington.

This area is sometimes called West Klickitat, the westernmost part of nearly 100-mile long Klickitat County. The people of Klickitat County have never been fond of governments farther west, state or otherwise, interfering in their lives. As for the government in Washington, D.C., the county is out of compliance with the Columbia Gorge Scenic Area and loses federal monies because of its staunch stance. In a sense, these rural people have always been too busy trying to survive to be bothered with formal organizational procedures. The Act of 1853, which established the Washington Territory, mandated that counties organize their own governments. At that time only about fifteen families lived in Klickitat, or as they said at the time, "passed the winter." The people did nothing, so the Territory ordered a local election in 1860. The election aborted for lack of interest. Even appointees the following year refused their duties.

Klickitat County is a psychological and physical outpost, and Washington media does not suit the residents's needs. Daily news and entertainment via television and radio come from Oregon stations. The people even shop in Oregon when they can, as Oregon has no sales tax. Lucky for them that Washington has no income tax.

Trout Lake–Glenwood Road and Sunnyside Road intersect at a stop sign with Mount Adams Road. It is considered a Forest Service road and runs for about 7 miles to the foot of the A. G. Aiken Lava Bed, at about 1,100 feet in elevation. Nearby, Mount Adams climbs steeply to 12,307 feet.

Even today Mount Adams is an out-of-the-way site, somewhat of a forgotten mountain. It is the second highest in Washington and Oregon, but it was not even mentioned in the journals of Lewis and Clark. They saw Mount Adams from the Columbia River, but believed it to be Mount St. Helens.

Mount Adams can only be approached via unimproved dirt roads that will never be paved. In 1942, the Mount Adams Wilderness was set aside to remain in its natural state. It was included in the National Wilderness Preservation System in 1964. The wilderness perimeter was expanded more recently, sealing off the southern and western approaches to the mountain. In 1972, the Yakima Indian Nation enforced its right to an expanded reservation boundary. This action closed most of the eastern foothills and the mountain's bulk to everyone other than tribal members. As a consequence, only the hardiest backpackers and mountaineers manage to get onto Mount Adams itself.

Take an immediate left at the Trout Lake–Glenwood Road/Sunnyside Road intersection to downtown Trout Lake. Within 1 mile is a stop sign and a gas station, where this scenic drive turns right onto northbound Washington Highway 141.

You can go straight (south) on WA 141 if you are in hurry to get back to the Columbia Gorge. This road follows the White Salmon River to the town of White Salmon on the Columbia. The Charles Hooper Winery is on this route, near the town of Husum.

Within a few blocks of the right turn onto northbound WA 141, there are stores, a post office, abandoned buildings, a fire department, and the Mount Adams Ranger Station on the left. This is the place to register before heading into the Mount Adams Wilderness.

Within 0.5 mile of the ranger station is the Berry Ridge Bed and Breakfast on the left. There are plenty of adventuresome driving options that take off from this road, but our route, still on WA 141, heads southwest toward Carson in search of the Ice Caves.

A nearby cave, known as the Cheese Cave, is on Cheese Cave Road off of WA 141 on the southwest side of Trout Lake. The cave is a 0.5-mile long refrigerator. It provided ideal storage for potatoes in the years before electrical refrigeration. Trout Lake farmers were encouraged to raise spuds in volume because of the availability of storage. Truckloads were brought from the Yakima Valley for storage in the cave. Getting potatoes in and out of the cave required a hand-operated winch. That hindrance, and the electrification of rural America, doomed the enterprise.

Later, in the 1930s, a cave study showed that its temperature and humidity were exactly the same as the Roquefort caves in France. With help from Washington and Oregon state universities in the many experiments with milk mixes, a cheese that was fully the equivalent of the famous Roquefort was born.

Racks for the five-pound wheels of cheese were built in the Cheese Caves. The curing process took six months. Hand labor included periodically scraping off the molds. The cheese became known as the best Roquefort-type (made from goat and sheep milk) cheese produced in America.

The company's promise was interrupted by a family divorce during World War II, causing a name change in the cheese brand. Also about this time American blue cheese (made from cow's milk) was coming into popularity, so there was no hope for the fledgling Trout Lake company.

The recipe had included a high percentage of goat milk in the mix. But with the business closed, there was a surplus of goats left roaming that "damn near ate the valley alive," according to an observer at the time.

Back on WA 141, the Skamania County line is 4 miles ahead, and the smaller Ice Caves (with an above-ground picnic area) are just 1 mile past that. The road climbs a bit to about 2,500 feet elevation.

WA 141 ends at the county line, and Forest Road 24 begins. This is also the western boundary of the Gifford Pinchot National Forest. The road is well-paved and heavily forested on both sides. Four-foot Christmas trees grow about two inches from the road and thick forest begins just beyond that. Keep an eye out for deer.

A little one-lane dirt road to the Ice Caves, just off FR 24, enters from the left. Any RV could navigate this short road, as it weaves around the trees, but it is wide enough to pull over and let others pass if necessary.

The Ice Caves are actually a 500-foot lava tube, an air pocket left from the volcanic eruption that created it. In winter, cold air settles into the bottom of the cave and its condensate forms ice. The ice stays year-round and was "mined" beginning about a hundred years ago to serve refrigeration needs in the town of Hood River.

There are a few places in the cave where explorers have to scrunch down, and it is very cold. Ice is constantly forming, and the cave floor is quite slippery. Wear a big hat to avoid bumping your head on the low ceilings. A hard hat would be even better. Carry a flashlight or lantern, the bigger the better. The cave is completely dark and muddy, as well.

As you continue on FR 24, the Peterson Prairie Campground is 1 mile ahead. This is a pleasant place to stop and listen to the birds chatter. The campground is one of an increasing number of Forest Service campgrounds that are managed by private enterprise.

FR 24 turns north here, but you want FR 60; follow the sign to Willard (18 miles). The scenery is absolutely beautiful here. The road is oiled and in fair condition, with wide spots to allow cars to pass. It is not steep or too winding. A comfortable speed is around 30 mph. But shortly, the pavement ends.

Two intersections follow in quick succession. At the first one, with the one-lane bridge, stay on FR 60 by turning left for Goose Lake (4 miles), Lurch (17 miles), and Carson (6 miles). The road is gravel, well-graded, and a bit wider than one lane. Local people are frequently asked by travelers about road conditions and whether the roads go through to particular towns or camps. A common response, with a twinkle in the eyes, is "Yep, it's road all the way."

There is another intersection immediately after; turn left onto FR 66 and follow it to Willard, 14 miles. (FR 60 continues on to Goose Prairie and Carson to the right.)

Just at the beginning of FR 66 (South Prairie Road), there is a lake on the left with a big beaver dam in the middle. The scene is stunningly gorgeous and almost worth the entire scenic drive. This is a two-lane dirt road, smoothly graded. Some of the signs have bullet holes through them, however. Four-wheel-drive is not even remotely necessary on this road, or on any others on the route. FR 66 supports a comfortable speed of about 35 mph.

Soon enough the road turns to pavement again, but passing zones are not marked. There is thick forest on both sides, with their canopies meeting above the road. Not visible from the road, but running alongside for miles, is the Big Lava Bed.

This is an absolutely incredible drive, one of the best. FR 66 descends past the end of the Big Lava Bed and itself ends at Willard Road. Turn right, and the town of Willard is 1 mile ahead.

There won't be much happening in Willard—some horses in the fields, kids on bicycles, beehives. In the fall, you will likely see people with chainsaws along the side of the road, cutting firewood for the winter. The Willard National Fish Hatchery, which rears coho and Chinook salmon, is about 1 mile past Willard on the left. The hatchery is on the Little White Salmon River, which this drive parallels to the Columbia.

At the intersection with Cook-Underwood Road, turn right. Continue through the town of Mill A, with its Burma Shave-type signs suggesting children at play. The wind from the Columbia can blow so hard here that clothes drying on the lines can point straight up.

Take care at the intersections to stay on Cook-Underwood Rd. Between Mill A and Cook, about 5 miles, the forests are thick. They are so dense they look black on the inside. Descending into Cook, you can smell the salt air blowing up from the Gorge. Return to WA 14 again, in the windy Columbia Gorge.

8

Columbia Gorge Highway

General description: This drive follows the north shore of the Columbia River through the Columbia River Gorge National Scenic Area.

Special attractions: Beacon Rock State Park, Columbia River Gorge National Scenic Area, Columbia Gorge Interpretive Center, Horsethief Lake State Park petroglyphs, Stonehenge Memorial, Maryhill Museum, horseback riding, hiking, whitewater rafting, windsurfing.

Location: Southern boundary of Washington, in the western half of the state.

Highway number: Washington Highway 14, The Lewis and Clark Highway.

Travel season: The road is open year-round.

Camping: There are four campgrounds on the drive. There are eight more on the Oregon side of the Columbia River along Interstate 84.

Services: Full services in Stevenson.

For more information: Gifford Pinchot National Forest, Goldendale Observatory, Mount Adams Ranger District, Washington State Parks (see Appendix A). Oregon Public Broadcasting, via Hood River radio station KOPB, is available throughout the Columbia River Gorge at 91.5 FM.

 The Drive

The entire drive is 102 miles from Vancouver, Washington, eastbound to the intersection with U.S. Highway 97 near Maryhill State Park. At the end of the drive, the Maryhill Museum and the Stonehenge Memorial are intriguing attractions; it is also easy enough to cross the Columbia via US 97 and take westbound Interstate 84 to Portland on the south shore of the river.

Begin the drive eastbound on Washington Highway 14 from Interstate 5 in Vancouver, Washington, or from its bypass, Interstate 205, 6 miles east of I-5. I-84 runs parallel to WA 14 on the other side of the Columbia River. From I-205, Stevenson is 38 miles. WA 14 here is a wide four-lane road with a cement barrier down the middle.

On a clear night, the city lights of Portland are something to see from this side of the river, which appears to be miles wide.

The Columbia River is the aorta of the West Coast, the blood of the lives and businesses that depend on it. The outfall of the Columbia, 17.5

Drive 8: Columbia Gorge Highway

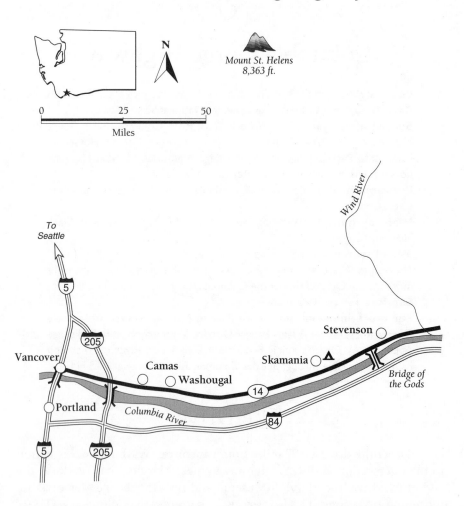

Mount St. Helens
8,363 ft.

trillion gallons of water per year, is fed by tributaries that drain hundreds of thousands of square miles in the States and Canada. Ice carved the Columbia River Gorge fifteen thousand years ago, and today many people think of the Columbia Gorge as a 90-mile, sea-level pass through the mountains. It is the one sure way to get through the Cascades in winter—between Washington and Oregon's eastern deserts and the western cities of the I-5 corridor.

During early October, the Columbia River can be entirely blanketed in fog on an otherwise sunny day. From the air it looks like a snake trying to devour cities.

The divided highway ends at Camas, where WA 14 becomes two-lane.

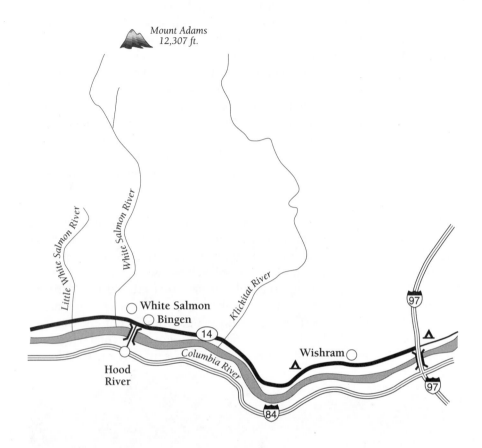

Camas calls itself the "City of Paper" owing to the immense Crown Zellerbach production and shipping facility on the waterfront. Gas and food are available in Camas.

The industrial town of Washougal, about 4 miles beyond Camas, looks like a staging area for the *Road Warrior* movies. Industry clearly is king here. But beyond what is visible from the highway, Washougal is a very pleasant riverside community. It is also home to the Pendleton Woolen Mills on the north side of the highway. Visitors are welcome, and short tours are given on weekdays. There is also an outlet store with merchandise manufactured at the mill. Food, gas, and lodging are available in Washougal. From Washougal, Bonneville is 20 miles and Stevenson is 26 miles.

Two miles east of Washougal, at about Milepost 18, the Columbia River Gorge National Scenic Area begins. It even smells better, as though the sea air mixed with river spray to produce good ions. This is away from the industrial port cities of the lower Columbia, so the terrain is much easier on the eye. The woods come right down to the road and extend below to the river.

The gorge first attracted attention when the Columbia River Highway was completed in 1915. People thought of it as the eighth wonder of the world, and they were drawn as visitors from all over the world.

The Columbia River Gorge National Scenic Area is 80 miles long and contains 292,000 acres. The Columbia Gorge Commission is in charge of reseeding native plants within a mile of the river, among other duties, to enhance the gorge's original natural qualities.

The flip side of that coin, as seen by people who live in Skamania and Klickitat counties, is the lack of economic opportunity. One mother expressed her happiness at a new McDonald's being built, because now local kids would have a place to work without leaving town.

President Reagan signed the bill into law that created the National Scenic Area, but with some reservations about government having too much to say about private property rights. Many people who lived in the Gorge at the time resisted the legislation. They preferred the environmental safeguards provided by nature, which they interpreted to be the muscular natural forces

The Columbia Gorge, looking west.

which formed, and continue to form, the Cascade Range and the Columbia River. One of their main concerns was how the political freezing of land uses would limit their possibilities of earning a livelihood.

Once you enter hilly Skamania County, the road has a much improved surface as it starts to twist and turn with the hills and the curves of the river. Keep an eye out for Sasquatch, the alleged beast of the northwest woods. In Skamania County, intentionally hurting a Sasquatch is cause for imprisonment.

The river narrows a bit after passing Salmon Falls Road on the left. Watch for logging trucks as the road continues its serpentine course. Highway speeds vary between 30 and 55 miles per hour. The fishing and camping opportunities begin to appear along this stretch near the Skamania Fire Hall. The river is still at sea level until Bonneville Dam. There is so much growth along the side of the road that mile upon mile of the Columbia remains unseen. There are some pullouts, but trees crowd the view.

Just 1 mile east of the town of Skamania, Beacon Rock looms over the highway like a monolith from outer space. Serious hikers can take the steep 1-mile trail to the 848-foot summit for a fine view of this part of the Gorge. The fifteen-percent grade trail has a handrail, but people with vertigo will want to stay below. The rock is a remmnant of the heart of an ancient volcano; sort of a basalt plug with the surrounding cone eroded away. It is thought to be the second largest monolith in the world, after the Rock of Gibraltar. (Third in size is British Columbia's granite Stawamus Chief, 37 miles north of Vancouver.) Beacon Rock was named by Lewis and Clark in 1805.

Beacon Rock State Park, with its camping facilities, trails, and swimming beach, is nearby on the left. From the state park, WA 14 passes the Pierce National Wildlife Refuge on the right. One mile farther is North Bonneville, which started in 1933 as construction housing for Bonneville Dam workers. The town was moved in the 1970s when the second powerhouse was built, which is visible on the right.

A walk through the Bonneville Dam Visitor Center, at Milepost 39, gives a good sense of the enormity of the dam and of the gorge itself. There is good seasonal viewing of the fish ladder inside. Hours are 9 A.M. to 5 P.M. daily, with the extended hours of 8 A.M. to 6 P.M. July 4 through Labor Day. Nearby is the Fort Cascade Historic Site, just to the right at Dam Access Road.

Continuing east on WA 14, look for the amazing bridge across the river to Oregon just past Milepost 41. Called "The Bridge of the Gods," it spans the Columbia River at the site of the former Cascade Rapids, which are underwater behind Bonneville Dam. The rapids were formed eight hundred years ago when a landslide dammed the Columbia and raised it hundreds of feet, flooding Indian villages in the process. River transporta-

Bonneville Dam and Beacon Rock.

tion could not make it past the rapids until the Cascade Locks were built in 1896. Indians believed, and many still do, that the rapids were formed by a collapsed stone arch that once spanned the river. In the 1880s a book titled *The Bridge of the Gods* was written by Homer Balch, the pastor of White Salmon's Bethel Congregational Church. It was a novelized version of the well-known Indian legend.

Just short of 2 miles ahead, veer to the left around Rock Cove, following the signs for The Columbia Gorge Interpretive Center and Skamania Lodge. Across the street from Skamania Lodge is the Columbia Gorge Interpretive Center. After sixteen years of planning and more than $10.5 million, the center is the showcase of the scenic area. The center itself feels like part of the gorge. It is banked three stories high, with a wall of windows overlooking the river below. The architecture is reminiscent of the sawmills that used to be here. A short movie on the future of the gorge plays every ten minutes. There are interactive displays on the geological and human histories of the area. Prominent attention-getters are the replicas of pictographs and petroglyphs, the originals of which are now underwater behind the Bonneville Dam. Very unusual are the Don Brown collection of four thousand rosaries and a Russian aristocrat's priceless furniture and art works. The center is as much about local people as it is about the Gorge itself.

It is open daily 10 A.M. to 7 P.M., from Memorial Day to Labor Day and 10 A.M. to 5 P.M. the rest of the year. Admission is charged.

Skamania Lodge is worth a side trip, The 195-room national park-style resort was partially funded by the Forest Service to help boost the tourism economy of Skamania County. The lodge, with inspiring views of the Columbia River, opened in 1993. It is a full-service resort, with a designer spa and gourmet restaurant. It also offers a golf course, hiking trails, tennis courts, horseback riding, and a Forest Service visitor center in the main lobby.

The town of Stevenson is just 1 mile farther east on WA 14, Milepost 45. A sternwheeler excursion boat stops here in the summer, recalling the days when Stevenson was an important river port. Now it may have the world's first sailboarding sign—a brown and white recreation sign with a sailboarder on it. Good visitor information is available in Stevenson at the Skamania County Economic Council and Business Resource Center downtown. Stevenson has all travel services.

On the road again, this drive is so beautiful that it lends the sense of just how wild this countryside is. Lewis and Clark, plus their twenty-six co-explorers and an Army detachment, built their own canoes for the Columbia River portion of their eighteen-month journey from St. Louis to the Pacific Coast. All but one survived the round-trip. They documented what they saw of the flora, fauna, geography, and people, but they could not have known of the forces that formed the Columbia Gorge. The most important single event, repeated up to forty times, stemmed from the flooding of ancient Lake Missoula, several thousand years ago. Glacial ice dams east of Washington broke up and gave way, releasing inland oceans of fresh water over thousands of square miles. At the present-day site of the town of Hood River, the water was 900 feet deep.

Just past Carson, WA 14 crosses the Senator Al Henry Bridge over the mouth of the Wind River, and the town of Home Valley is just ahead. The view to the right is evidence that logging is still a major employer in the region—immense piles of logs await processing.

The river is in clear sight now as you follow the bend of the railroad tracks, which parallel the river. There are stark basalt buttes to the left and mountains across the river. Between Mileposts 53 and 54, 9 miles east of Carson on the left, is a parking area for the Dog Mountain trailhead. The mountain is 2,948 feet in elevation, with exceptional views that include Mount Hood in Oregon. The 3-mile trail to the top, a former lookout site, has some steep sections, but the views and the meadows of wildflowers make this a very popular spring and summer hike.

Two miles east of the trailhead, Dog Creek enters the Columbia, and the town of Cook is 1 mile farther. From Cook, Cook-Underwood Road goes north following the Little White Salmon River for 5 miles to the town of Willard and the Willard National Fish Hatchery, where coho and Chinook salmon are reared. (See Drive 7.)

Just ahead on the main road, WA 14, Drano Lake shows its popularity with fishermen by the clusters of boats plying its waters. The lake is actually the very wide, but nearly closed, mouth of the Little White Salmon River. From the parking lot, you can see the Broughton Flume on the hillside above the lake. The flume is 9 miles long, and for over 60 years (until 1987), it floated rough-sawn lumber from the mill at Willard to the railroad below. It carried about 40 to 50 million board feet of lumber a year. The flume was patrolled on foot via a 1-foot-wide walkway.

As you proceed eastward on WA 14, tunnel number five comes up at Milepost 60. Near here on the river, sailboarders sail in neon pink and green. There is a recreational turnout at Milepost 61 that gives a good vantage point to watch. This is also the site of the Spring Creek Fish Hatchery (open 7:30 A.M. to 4 P.M. weekdays between September 1 and May 14) and the Lower Columbia River Fish Health Center. This parking lot for sailboarders is often full, and there can easily be a hundred people in the water.

The Columbia River Gorge has long been a favorite location for high-wind riders. The Venturi Effect, according to meteorologists, is responsible for the dramatically channelled winds favored by sailboarders. Eastern desert air, heated by the sun, rises and creates a vacuum that is filled by the howling winds off the cooler Pacific Ocean. The Gorge has the most consistent winds in North America, sometimes gusting up to 80 miles per hour. Sailboarders everywhere try for jobs that offer a "twenty-knot clause." When the local winds are twenty knots or more, they need to be on the water. "TOB," or "time on board," is an important factor in their particular take on the quality of life.

More sailboarders pack the Columbia at the point where the Hood River from the south and the White Salmon River from the North empty into the Gorge. The rafting and fishing are good on both rivers. Some people believe the plethora of sailboarders is causing stress on the Columbia. Some sites are in jeopardy of being closed because of the danger to the fishery. But the towns of Hood River (on the Oregon side) and White Salmon (on the Washington side) have found new wealth from tourism. Nestled between the volcanic peaks of Mount Hood and Mount Adams, this part of the Columbia Gorge offers the rural "quality of life" so sought after by Westerners.

East on WA 14, the land flattens a bit near the town of Bingen and beyond. Uphill from Bingen is the town of White Salmon with an exceptional bed and breakfast, the White Salmon Inn, and a fine view across the Columbia to the Hood River, with Mount Hood high above and beyond.

Up ahead on WA 14, note the triangular blocks of hillside on the left. They are just like the formations deep in Hells Canyon on the Idaho/Oregon border. And at about Milepost 69, the road runs right next to a straight-up wall of crumbly basalt.

The Chamberlain Rest Area is at Milepost 74, 2 miles before the town of Lyle. Here is where the Klickitat River flows into the Columbia. About 3 miles ahead is Doug's Beach State Park, a day-use area with swimming and sailboarding. WA 14 bypasses the Dalles Dam, which is nearly 3 miles south on U.S. Highway 197. In 1957 the dam flooded Celilo Falls, which, for thousands of years, was a Native American salmon fishery. The falls were actually a staircase of rapids over which Indians fished from wooden scaffolds. Celilo Falls was once one of the greatest fisheries in North America.

The drive is clearly in the desert now, as the terrain is well on the dry side of the Cascades.

Horsethief Lake State Park, the next right after US 197, has Native American petroglyphs and pictographs, which you can view with a guided tour on Fridays and Saturdays. There is good fishing here, trout and bass, and you can rent boats from the park.

Somehow the starkness of the landscape leads drivers to pay more attention to the traffic particularly all of the trucks. One of the objectives of the Columbia Gorge Commission is to persuade truckers to use I-84 on the other side of the river. This would reserve WA 14 for tourists, residents, and recreational drivers.

Columbia Gorge Interpretive Center.

At Milepost 90 is the town of Wishram, a Burlington Northern Railroad division point. It looks like a ghost town, half empty, with no road signs identifying it. It brings to mind the popular local saying that, "Klickitat County is the best place in the world to live if you can figure a way to make a living."

As you continue, lava boulders look as if they have been plopped all over the hillsides to the left, ready to roll. Some on the right side *have* rolled!

The Lewis and Clark Highway leaves the Columbia Gorge National Scenic Area a few miles after Wishram, just before Milepost 98. From above, you get fine vistas of the river.

Look for the turnoff to the right for the Maryhill Museum, well above the river with great views. The tree-shaded grounds are a welcome sight on a hot summer day. The museum is a historic site, built in 1926 by Sam Hill for his wife Mary. She didn't take to its location, and his friends convinced him to turn it into a museum. One of those friends was the Queen of Romania, and some of her belongings are exhibited in the museum. There are also many Rodin sketches and sculpture replicas, plus Native American artifacts.

Hill, who owned 7,000 acres here, also tried to establish a colony of Belgian Quakers between the World Wars. His plan failed, but one of his accomplishments was the building of a full-scale model of Stonehenge between 1918 and 1929. It sits 3 miles from the museum overlooking the Columbia, adjacent to Maryhill State Park. Hill was a Quaker who was appalled by the carnage of World War I. He had visited the real Stonehenge, which he considered to be a sacrificial monument, and built his own Stonehenge here to honor the fallen soldiers of Klickitat County.

Maryhill State Park has fifty campsites with hookups and twenty standard campsites, plus a boat launch and an unguarded swimming beach. The 100-acre park has nearly 1 mile of waterfront.

9

Olympic Peninsula Loop

General description: This drive is a counter-clockwise loop around the wild and woolly Olympic Peninsula.

Special attractions: Olympic National Park, Olympic National Forest, Dungeness National Wildlife Refuge, river rafting, llama trekking, guided berry picking, horseback riding, beachcombing, clam digging, kayaking, windsurfing, hiking, biking.

Location: The northwest corner of the state.

Highway number: U.S. Highway 101, U.S. Highway 12, Washington Highway 8.

Travel season: The drive is open year-round.

Camping: There are many state park, Forest Service, and National Park Service campgrounds on the peninsula. Some campgrounds are open year-round, accessible only to cross-country skiers and snowshoers in the winter. There are also many private RV parks and campgrounds.

Services: Full services at towns and cities along the way.

For more information: Forks Timber Museum & Visitor Center, Hoh Rain Forest Visitor Center, Hoh Valley Adventures River Rafting, Makah Tribal Museum, North Olympic Peninsula Visitor & Convention Bureau, Ocean Shores Chamber of Commerce, Olympic National Forest, Olympic National Park Headquarters (see Appendix A).

 The drive

This drive traverses farmlands, follows the placid west bank of Hood Canal, enters thick, dripping, temperate rain forests, follows wide rivers and rushing creeks, and offers refreshing stopovers on sandy beaches and in small towns. Expect to spend about 10 glorious hours driving the 454-mile loop, which includes 100 miles on three side trips to Hurricane Ridge, the Hoh Rain Forest, and the beach town of La Push.

On maps of the Peninsula, the huge, dark green area in the middle (and another thin piece down the coastline) represents the 900,000 acres of Olympic National Park. The lighter green area, nearly surrounding the park, is Olympic National Forest.

The rainfall may be more than you can imagine. Places like Quinault Lodge measure it in feet, up to 12 in a year. Ferns, trees, and everything else

Drive 8: Olympic Peninsula Loop

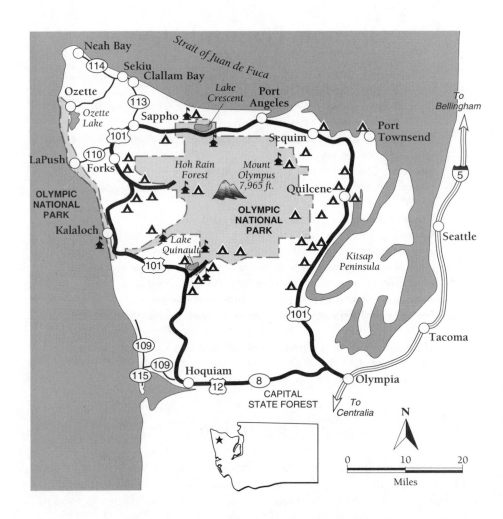

grow to monster proportions. Where does all that rain go? The peninsula has twelve major rivers and two hundred smaller streams, renewed almost daily.

The park is open year-round, but some roads and facilities close in the winter. Much of the Olympic Peninsula's topography consists of sharp, steep ridges over 4,000 feet high. The mountains are a beautiful mass of folded and metamorphosed rock, never-melting snow fields, and several small glaciers.

Begin the drive from Interstate 5 exit 104 for the Olympic Peninsula and Ocean Beaches. **Caution:** Don't take exit 101; take exit 104 to U.S. Highway 101. US 101 is the only way around the peninsula. It makes a loop, starting just west of Olympia, but there are enough side trips to keep curious travellers busy for days.

City life is really left behind as the highway heads by saltwater marshes, farms, green fields, and wooded hills. Just after crossing Eld Inlet, a lesser arm of Puget Sound, the highway turns right toward Shelton, the Olympic Peninsula, and Hood Canal. Washington Highway 8 continues straight, to the stormy Pacific Ocean beaches.

Primitive forests line both sides of the drive here, but after a while, water can be seen through the trees on the right. The salt air smells refreshingly good. The drive travels next to Eld Inlet for a couple of miles before bearing west across Schneider Prairie alongside Schneider Creek, then the highway enters the woods again. The clearcuts are obvious, but the farms in the valley are pleasant distractions. The world here is green as far as the eye can see. The road enters Mason County near Milepost 356.

Schneider Creek flows into the southern end of Totten Inlet's Oyster Bay. US 101 swings around the bottom of the bay, crossing the lush delta and then Kennedy Creek. Shorebirds are plentiful here.

From Kennedy Creek, and continuing for another 15 miles to the Skokomish River and the Skokomish Indian Reservation, the main sights visible from the highway are tree farms, largely owned by timber companies that can harvest a new crop of trees every generation.

US 101 continues north toward the town of Shelton, situated on Oakland Bay. Shelton's economy depends on logging and the waterfront. On the south side of Shelton (taking a side trip through town on Washington Highway 3) there is an interesting overlook. Look on the right for a giant old wheel and a log monument. They indicate the pullout. The 11-foot wheel, one of the biggest ever built, was originally used to run bandsaws to cut spruce to build World War I aircraft.

Visible below is the Shelton waterfront, Oakland Bay in particular. Log booms await processing in the local plywood plant for loading onto the train for another mill. Some are towed to Tacoma to be made into paper. The Tacoma tow is a 24-hour round trip, with a 3-man tug that pulls 250 truckloads of logs at a time.

Log broncs—spiffy powerful mini-tugs that can turn on a dime—sort the logs by size and species, then bundle them into rafts. Shelton also ships between two and three million Christmas trees around the world every year.

About 2 miles past Shelton, the highway passes Turtle Lake on the right, then Munson Lake and Johns Lake. In another few miles the highway passes the George Adams Hatchery on Purdy Creek. The creek joins the Skokomish River 1 mile downstream, which in turn flows into the bottom of Hood Canal at The Great Bend. For several miles past the creek, US 101 traverses the Skokomish Indian Reservation. Beaches along the Great Bend have some of the best shellfishing on Hood Canal. Potlatch State Park, just ahead on the water, and the community of Potlatch are both named for the Indian tradition of celebrations wherein valuable gifts were bestowed on friends and relations.

Here the drive enters the Canal Zone, as the 80-mile Hood Canal area is called locally. US 101 passes through 40 miles of the zone. The road always remains within a few miles of the western boundary of Olympic National Forest, which itself serves as a buffer zone around much of Olympic National Park.

Much of Hood Canal's fame comes from its oyster production. Plenty of restaurants and diners along the way give travelers a chance to try them out. Around Hoodsport there also are wineries with tasting rooms.

US 101 hugs the shore for most of the drive along Hood Canal. Life here walks at a slow, purposeful pace. Many of the homes belong to people on the busier side of Puget Sound, the Seattle area. They come here to refresh and enjoy themselves on weekends and summer vacations.

Populations are sparse in the Olympic Peninsula's four counties: Clallam, Jefferson, Grays Harbor, and Mason.

The logging and fishing industries have taken a serious downturn, requiring out-of-work loggers and commercial fisherman to learn new skills as tour guides and travel hosts.

Hoodsport, 2 miles north of Potlatch, is nestled between the canal on one side and steep wooded mountains on the other. The area's seasonal ranger station can be found at the drive's intersection with Lake Cushman Road. Eleven-mile-long Lake Cushman, about 5 miles west up Washington Highway 119, has good camping and fishing. The state park's 81 campsites lie 2 miles up the western shore.

On US 101, between Hoodsport and Lilliwaup, look for scuba divers, easy to spot by the little colored flags floating on the water. If you spot a crew getting ready to enter the water, stop to watch them put on as much as one hundred pounds of gear and lead weights. The divers try to achieve

Kalaloch Beach.

neutral buoyancy in the water, enabling them to either move or remain motionless with minimal effort.

At the town of Lilliwaup, Hood Canal extends a mile across to the Kitsap Peninsula. The village has some tourist services and a post office. The tidelands here provide an abundance of clams and oysters.

The next small community, Eldon, sits near the mouth of the Hamma Hamma River. "Hamma Hamma" is a corruption of the Twana Indian name for their village, *Hab'hab*, itself named for a reed that grows in the swampy parts of the river. The small estuary here serves as a good feeding station for great blue herons and migrating sea birds.

Brinnon, near Dosewallips State Park, looks to be an average sort of Hood Canal town. Small, with a few businesses and a senior center, its marine workers live by the tides. Lots and lots of geoducks (long, heavy clams) are harvested here and sent to Japan, where they are considered a delicacy. May is shrimping month all up and down Hood Canal, and the waters off Brinnon are particularly good. Look for the distinctive shrimp boats, with their net-hauling cranes hanging out the sides of the boats.

Just after Brinnon, starting on the north side of Dosewallips Road, the drive parallels the boundary of Olympic National Forest for a few miles and then passes through an extension of the park. A 5-mile access road here leads to the Mount Walker observation area. The graveled road, Forest Road 2730, begins just inside the park boundary and climbs steeply up to Mount Walker's 2,804-foot summit. The parking lot is 0.25 mile from the Mount Walker trailhead, and the trail is 2 miles to the south viewpoint. The views are spectacular, covering 5 million acres. On a clear day you can see the Seattle Space Needle, 28 miles away. The Trident Submarine Base can be seen directly across the canal—the deep bay directly below the lookout provides enough room for the submarines on practice maneuvers. A number of forest campgrounds on Mount Walker attract the faithful.

Back on US 101, the 5 miles of road to the town of Quilcene leave the national forest and descend to the shores of Quilcene Bay. At the south edge of town there is an Olympic National Park ranger station, the biggest building around. What boggles the eye in Quilcene are the piles of oyster shells, mounds actually, that demonstrate a healthy sea-farming enterprise. Quilcene oysters have an international reputation among restauranteurs, and they are always in demand. The harvest continues year-round here. A new museum in town offers a historical perspective on the area.

From Quilcene, the drive on US 101 goes due north for 9 miles from Quilcene Bay to Discovery Bay (a town and bay).

The road first follows the course of Leland Creek and then Snow Creek. At the town of Discovery Bay, the opportunity presents itself for a 26-mile, out-and-back side trip on Washington Highway 20 to Port Townsend. This town is second only to San Francisco in its collection of Victorian gingerbread houses. Many thrive as bed and breakfasts, and others open for tours held in May and September.

From Port Townsend, Washington State ferries run across Admiralty Inlet to Keystone on Whidbey Island.

On the bluffs above Port Townsend sits Fort Worden State Park, a thriving community of specialty schools, conferences, and symposia. A drive down Officer's Row gives a good idea of the scale of the fort. Portions of the film *An Officer and a Gentleman* were filmed here because it looks so much like a working fort. It's one of three forts in this part of Puget Sound, built to protect Navy bases and shipping ports during World War II. Its big guns were never fired in hostile action, and Fort Worden closed in 1953.

Continuing north on US 101 from its intersection with WA 20, the drive parallels the southern curve of Discovery Bay for 6 miles. The views east across the bay to the Quimper Peninsula inspire photographers the whole way. As the drive turns west across the Miller Peninsula, it cuts through woods to the southern tip of Sequim Bay. The views here rival anything near the water, as the drive rounds the bottom of the bay and follows its coast in a northwesterly direction for about 3 miles.

The town of Sequim lies just ahead at the southern edge of the dry Sequim Prairie. Farmers need to irrigate here because it only rains an average of 17 inches per year. That is half the rain of anywhere else around Puget Sound. The Olympic Mountains easily get a hundred inches more rain than that every year, casting Sequim and several of the San Juan Islands in their "rain shadow." The term "banana belt" is spoken with pride locally.

The community holds an Irrigation Festival for a week in early May to celebrate the opening of the floodgates of the 1896 flumes built to carry water from the Dungeness River to the fields on the Sequim Prairie. The festival enjoys its reputation as Washington's oldest.

From Sequim, a side trip 5 miles north on Sequim–Dungeness Way to the Dungeness Spit could provide some interest. The sand spit, actually the Dungeness Spit National Wildlife Refuge and a county park, is the longest natural sand spit in the nation. Currently 6 miles long, it grows about 15 feet each year. The spit, used by about twenty-five thousand shore birds, thirty thousand migrating ducks and geese, and up to five hundred harbor seals, shelters a bay with one of Puget Sound's last undisturbed eelgrass beds. Black brant geese depend on this eelgrass for food.

US 101 west from Sequim to Port Angeles is 15 miles of straight highway through low-elevation woodlands. Notice, however, the frequency of creeks that pass under the road. Even on the north side of the Olympic Mountains, the so-called "dry" side, a phenomenal volume of water drains into the Strait of Juan de Fuca.

One-thousand-year-old Sitka spruce near Quinault Lodge.

The deep harbor at Port Angeles is protected by the 3-mile-long Ediz Hook sandspit, a natural jetty with a path, road, and picnic tables. The road to the Coast Guard station at the end of Ediz Hook allows for one of the best views of the peninsula. As you look toward the mountains, Port Angeles fills the foreground from nearly 2 miles away.

There's another great view from Hurricane Ridge above Port Angeles, looking down into the park itself. It is oftentimes hard to see the forest for the trees in the national park. Most of the 38 miles of road within its borders follow valley floors. The road to Hurricane Ridge affords a rare chance to get up high (5,329 feet) and have a good look. To get there from Port Angeles, a distance of 18 miles, follow the signs from US 101 downtown or go south on Race Street, which becomes Hurricane Ridge Road.

At the entrance to the national park, the Heart O' the Hills Campground is open, even through the winter, on a restricted basis. But the road beyond is plowed to Hurricane Ridge itself. The Civilian Conservation Corps built this road in the 1930s. Construction halted at a steep talus slope that defeated further effort. The drive up, a dramatic vertical climb with steep drop-offs and a dearth of guardrails, stirs the blood. It can even divert your attention from wildlife-spotting. Lookout stops on the way up, however, offer breathers to look for black-tailed deer and the occasional black bear. On the ridge itself, tame deer may come close to see what you have to offer, especially at the picnic tables. Please do not feed them, as feeding wildlife human food can eventually lead to a dead animal.

Winter weather gave Hurricane Ridge its name, the result of 80-mile-per-hour winds and 45 feet of snow. The small downhill ski area here operates on weekends and holidays only, with a poma lift and two rope tows. On weekends, the feature attraction is snowshoe walking with a forest ranger.

The visitor center has park information and sells sandwiches, light meals, curios, and gifts. The center opens daily from late April through September, and on weekends and holidays during the ski season.

West on US 101 from the log-sorting yards of the business end of Port Angeles, the road turns inland through wooded areas and follows the eastern shore of Lake Aldwell into Olympic National Forest. The Elwha River feeds the lake year-round. The drive crosses the Elwha to follow the course of Indian Creek west along the national forest's northern border. About 6 miles from the river, US 101 goes along the northern shore of Lake Sutherland and meets the western end of Lake Crescent.

The drive travels through Olympic National Park for a while, and this section is officially the park's Route 11. Logging trucks also use these 11 miles of highway along the south shore of Lake Crescent. There is no other route to or from the northern Olympic Peninsula; therefore it must accommodate all vehicles. This includes bicycles, but caution signs warn both drivers and bikers about the hazards of this winding narrow road.

Glacier-scoured Lake Crescent, 650 feet deep, has a brooding look, like a Scottish loch. Two species of trout unique to the lake provide some of the best fishing in the state. The boat you may see plying the waters is the Storm King, an excursion boat and mock paddle wheeler, modeled after lake ferries of the 1920s. It offers ninety-minute tours guided by a park naturalist.

Take a detour through the scenic grounds of Lake Crescent Lodge. The lodge, open from late April through October, includes a dining room and gift shop, guest rooms, and cottages on the grounds.

Continuing west on US 101, the drive soon enters Olympic National Forest again and follows the course of the lush Soleduck River Valley to the small town of Sappho. The river visibly swells in size as it is joined along the way by creeks from both the north and south. East of Bear Creek, US 101 passes from Olympic National Forest into the Olympic Experimental State Forest until it reaches the Olympic National Park coastal strip at Ruby Beach.

One mile west of Sappho the drive twice crosses a wide oxbow of the Soleduck River. The highway turns a bit southwest and passes below Lake Pleasant, in the Soleduck River Valley, before arriving in the town of Forks.

Just over 1 mile before Forks, Washington Highway 110 (La Push Road) takes off 14 miles westward to the town of La Push at the mouth of the Quillayute River. The fishing community here is home to the Quileute Indian Tribe. On the way from US 101, WA 110 splits. Northern WA 110 (Mora Road) goes north of the Quillayute River to Rialto Beach, the only direct access to Olympic National Park's coastal strip between the Hoh River and Neah Bay. The rock headlands and the offshore sea stacks appear as stark reminders of the wildness of this coast. Southern WA 110 (La Push Road) goes to La Push. First Beach in La Push is a mile-long sandy crescent popular with surfers and kayakers. March and April at La Push are the best months to watch gray whales on their coastal migration.

Back on US 101, heading south, the road passes between clearcuts, crosses the Calawah River, and enters the Forks Prairie. The historically untamed logging town of Forks sits in the middle of the prairie. Community spirit and pride have kept the town populated with those determined to rise above the downturns in the logging industry.

In 1991 volunteers, using donated materials, built the Forks Timber Museum. It displays the best quick-study course on logging anywhere on the peninsula. The museum is next door to the Chamber of Commerce Visitor Information Center, right on US 101 as it leaves the south of town. With all the rivers and creeks draining west from the Olympics, Forks earned its reputation as the outfitting center in the area. Fishing guides are available for backcountry treks or short trips to ocean beaches.

Leaving Forks, the drive passes Mill Creek, the Forks Airport on the right, and then Grader Creek before turning southeast to follow the Bogachiel (Muddy Waters) River to Bogachiel State Park, the only developed campground on the peninsula.

The next 7 miles to the Hoh Rain Forest turn-off follows a level course through inland Olympic Experimental State Forest. You can choose to visit the rain forest, the only coniferous one in the world, by turning left onto the Upper Hoh Road where it crosses Hell Roaring Creek. From here the drive goes 18 miles up the valley to the visitor center.

Much of the drive parallels the Hoh, a wild and scenic river with a swift-moving, but gentle flow. It is one of the main peninsula rivers, fed by four tributaries from Mount Olympus. Rafters commonly see river otters, herds of grazing elk, bald eagles, and harlequin ducks. Along the Hoh River you can stop and walk to a high bank over the wide gravel bars and sometimes see elk.

Temperate rainforests are a rarity. There are three on the western side of the Olympic Peninsula in the river valleys of the Quinault, Queets and Hoh rivers. Other temperate rainforests are found in western British Columbia, New Zealand, and southern Chile. As much as 145 inches of rain falls annually on the Hoh.

At the Hoh Ranger Station and visitor center you'll find the Hall of Mosses Trail, a 0.75-mile loop. It is easy going and self-guided, but it can take a few hours if you dawdle in wonder at the cathedral-like setting. The Hoh Rain Forest is the only intact coniferous rain forest in the contiguous United States. The 600-year-old Sitka spruce trees grow to 200 feet or more, dwarfing the surrounding Douglas-fir and Western hemlock. Club moss dangles from the branches, and the sunlight that filters through the canopy is actually green. The moss underfoot feels squishy. The trees have a green shell of moss and epiphytes, which are nourished by airborne moisture and rain. These plants are eaten by Roosevelt elk. The elk, because of their eating habits, sculpt the landscape and leave incongruous open areas to be warmed by the sun. The elk herd includes the Hoh campground in its home range. The big animals are often seen on the trails near camp, and they sometimes wander past the picnic tables. Please resist the temptation to feed them.

It rains 132 inches a year here, so wear rain gear. Daily guided walks, which include full interpretive programs, are offered from mid-June to Labor Day. The center is open all year, but in January and February it is self-service only.

Six miles from the national park boundary, and 6 miles before the Upper Hoh Road ends at US 101, you'll find the Hard Rain Cafe & Mercantile, with twelve RV sites: six with full hookups and six with only water and electricity. For llama treks into the national park, call (360) 374-9288.

In 1976, Olympic National Park was recognized by UNESCO as a biosphere reserve for its striking temperate rainforests and the large protected ecosystem. The park was also selected as a world heritage site in 1981.

Back on the highway, US 101 crosses and then parallels the Hoh River for about 9 miles. Two miles farther it hits the coast at Ruby Beach, where Sitka spruce grow to the cliff's edge. Some grow horizontally over the crashing waves below. There are great bluff views here of the ocean and the long, flat beach named for the garnet colored sand. A parking lot here serves beach walkers. If you witness a sunset here, you will never forget it.

As US 101 emerges from the forest and runs alongside the coast, you may realize that nearly all the northern half of Washington's coastline, from the very northern tip to the Quinault Indian Reservation below Kalaloch and Queets, is phenomenally natural in a way that most coastlines are not. The wild Pacific Coast abounds in steep rocky bluffs, pristine beaches, endlessly pounding waves, and whole groves of trees are bent from ocean storms. The coastline stays natural and protected for two reasons: Quinault Reservation beaches are off-limits to the public and Olympic National Park's coastal strip has co-opted roads to the beaches.

This part of the drive, about 7 miles between Ruby Beach and Kalaloch, looks out toward Destruction Island and the Quillayute Needles National Wildlife Refuge. The park's beaches are numbered, in reverse order, from Beach 6 to Beach 1 between Ruby Beach and the northern border of the Quinault Indian Reservation 1 mile south of Kalaloch. You can access these beaches by trails. A bit south of Beach 6, a 0.25-mile-long road to the east leads through a grove of huge Western redcedars. The world's largest, 61 feet in diameter, grows at the end of the road.

Kalaloch Lodge, right on the ocean side of US 101, is one of the favorite Pacific getaways for Seattle people, even in the winter, when storm-watching takes over as the favorite pastime. It seems like the waves start breaking on the horizon and take forever to get to the beach. The park beach is long, flat, and hard-packed, bordered on the bluff edge by driftwood logs accumulated over many years. The digs here consist of eight rooms in the lodge, a motel unit, and forty housekeeping cabins on the bluff above the beach.

The Kalaloch Ranger Station is just past Kalaloch Lodge. During the summer, rangers lead low-tide beach walks on Beach 3 and Beach 4, north of the ranger station.

Continuing south, just inside the northern boundary of the Quinault Indian Reservation, US 101 passes through the town of Queets at the mouth of the Queets River. The Queets Rain Forest is the least accessible of the peninsula's forests because of its remote location and lack of commercial development in the area.

Between Queets and the turn off to Lake Quinault, the drive seems to cross a multitude of streams and creeks as it traverses 27 miles of the reservation. The tribe owns the lake itself, in which it rears fish, but only owns a southerly portion of the land that abuts it. The north side of the lake is Olympic National Park, and most of the southern side is Olympic National Forest. The drive passes Quinault North Shore Road and an elbow of the lake before crossing the Quinault River. Soon after, turn left at the little town of Amanda Park onto the road that presently joins South Shore Road. Lake Quinault Lodge is 2 miles from Amanda Park. The road follows the shoreline to the lodge, but the views are mostly of the forest from the inside. The Quinault Rain Forest is the state's second-largest, and this portion of the drive shows you just how dense the forest is.

The lodge, built in 1925, is a grand national park-style affair overlooking the lake. The lobby can be a bit of a hubbub with people coming and going from the restaurant, the front desk, and the gift shop. But its beauty and comfort more than make up for it.

The 4-mile Quinault Loop Trail goes along the south shore of Lake Quinault and deep into the rainforest. It takes two or three hours of walking at a reasonable pace. For scenic value and exciting terrain and flora, this is probably second best to the Hall of Mosses Trail in the Hoh Valley. The woods here are absolutely primordial, full of swamps, trees standing on their own stilt-like roots (their nurse logs having finally rotted away after a few hundred years), ferns bigger than seem possible, and columnar trees that stand taller than a Paul Bunyan tale. You can start the loop trail from several places, including the Quinault Ranger Station, Lake Quinault Lodge, Willaby or Falls Creek Campground, and the Quinault Rain Forest Nature Trail parking lot.

The 0.5-mile Quinault Rain Forest Nature Trail gives the short version of life in the rain forest, where it can rain 160 inches per year. The walk passes a bog, nurse logs, thick undergrowth, and towering trees, plus a narrow gorge cut by a cascading stream. Interpretive signs are provided. The trailhead is 1.4 miles from US 101 on Lake Quinault's South Shore Road or 0.5 mile south of the ranger station.

Back on US 101, as you head south again, the first 8 miles to the southern border of the national forest will complete the public lands portions of the drive. The Quinault Ridge on the left and at the southern end of the Colonel Bob Wilderness is an impressive sight. Receding in the distance, ten fingers of 700-foot-elevation ridges point toward Lake Quinault from Quinault Ridge, and each is separated by a creek that flows either into the lake or its outpouring river.

After leaving the national forest, this drive still feels very much like an Olympic Peninsula environment. There are dense woods as far as the eye can see, but clearcuts and young stands are noticeable.

The drive to Hoquiam follows the course of Stevens Creek to the town of Humptulips (the name means "hard to pole") on the Humptulips River, then passes over several creeks before joining with the West Fork Hoquiam River and eventually the Hoquiam River itself.

The drive continues briefly on US 101 east through Hoquiam to Aberdeen, then picks up U.S. Highway 12 to Olympia. (US 101 turns south and crosses the Chehalis River.) The great piles of lumber along the drive into Aberdeen show that logging is still very important to the local economy.

Aberdeen's Grays Harbor Historical Seaport is the home port of the tall ship *Lady Washington*, a full-scale reproduction of the first ship to visit the West Coast. Signs direct drivers from downtown on the west side of the bridge over the Chehalis River to view the ship.

As you continue east on US 12 along the Chehalis River near Montesano, there is a wildlife viewing site and fishing access. Called Friends Landing, it was designed specifically for wheelchair users, but everyone is welcome. A barge dock was converted into a two-level fishing pier next to a superb sturgeon hole. Pacific tides cause water levels in the river here to change as much as 11 feet. The current is slow and peaceful and the atmosphere is very relaxing. The Chehalis may be the only river in Washington that is open twenty hours per day for fishing. In the nearby spruce swamp you might see deer, bears, geese, beavers, and eagles.

To get to Friends Landing, just west of the town of Central Park, turn right onto Alder Grove Road. Continue straight through the one intersection and over Peels Slough. Alder Grove Road ends at Friends Landing, a distance of about 2 miles.

Back on US 12, the drive goes through the town of Brady just before crossing the Satsop River. Another 5 miles through the green valley and the drive picks up Washington Highway 8, continuing straight. (US 12 turns south.) It passes through low-elevation woodlands, by the town of McCleary, and in another 15 miles connects with US 101 just 6 miles from I-5.

10

Neah Bay and Ozette

General description: This 84-mile drive follows the rocky shore of the Strait of Juan de Fuca to the Makah Indian village of Neah Bay near the tip of the Olympic Peninsula.

Special attractions: Makah Tribal Museum, deep-sea charter fishing, scuba diving, beach walks, tidepooling.

Location: Northwestern-most tip of the state.

Highway number: Washington Highway 113, Washington Highway 112, Hoko-Ozette Road.

Travel season: The road is open year-round.

Camping: Clallam River Campground (state owned) has sites for tents and RVs 1.5 miles south of Clallam Bay on WA 113. Olympic National Park's Ozette Campground, at Lake Ozette, has a total of fourteen sites for tents and RVs and is open year-round.

Services: Gas, groceries, restaurants, and lodging are available in Clallam Bay, Sekiu, and Neah Bay.

For more information: Olympic National Park Headquarters, Makah Cultural and Research Center, Clallam Bay-Sekiu Chamber, Makah Tribal Museum, Neah Bay/Makah Tribal Council, Neah Bay/Ozette Chapter of Clallam Bay-Sekiu Chamber (see Appendix A).

 The drive

Begin the drive at the town of Sappho where U.S. Highway 101 and Washington Highway 113 intersect. Turn north toward the Straight of Juan de Fuca on WA 113, known locally as Burnt Mountain Road. Within 1 mile, WA 113 crosses a creek fed by runoff from Deadmans Hill ahead on the right, elevation just over 700 feet. Loaded logging trucks on the road are clues to what happened to the hillsides on this part of the drive. Keep an eye out for beaver as the drive passes Beaver Hill, Beaver Creek, and Beaver Falls on the left. Those are all within 2 miles of Sappho. Beaver Lake is 1.5 miles past Beaver Falls on the right. Both fall with the boundaries of Olympic National Forest, which extends to 2 miles north of Beaver Lake.

This is a lonely, peaceful part of the drive, as it twice crosses yet another Beaver Creek and goes down the north slope alongside the West Fork Pysht River. Just after crossing the river WA 113 ends, and the drive picks up Washington Highway 112 northwest to Clallam Bay and Neah Bay. WA 112

Drive 10: Neah Bay and Ozette

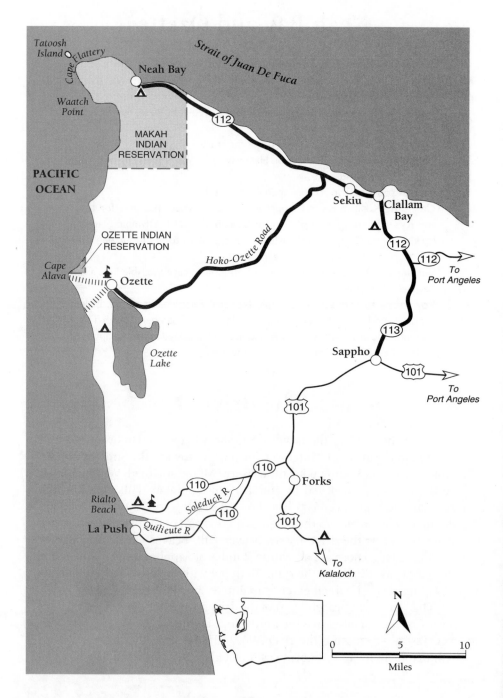

descends several hundred feet in elevation in just under 3 miles. It then follows the Clallam River for 3 miles into the town of Clallam Bay on the straight.

In the center of the town of Clallam Bay there is a waterfront park with a footbridge over the Clallam River. It is still possible to find agates on the pebble beach, and during low tide near the Slip Point Lighthouse, you'll get a good close-up look at the intertidal marine life. A bit east along the shore there are fossil beds where some of the world's oldest and rarest marine fossils have been found, typically named after those who found them.

Sekiu is Clallam Bay's twin city on the western end of the bay. In Sekiu you can visit One-Mile Beach; park near Olson's Resort. This level trail on the bluff above the shoreline is actually an old railroad grade and allows several accesses to scamper down to the sandy beach.

WA 112 runs inland for about 4 miles west of Sekiu. Note the pleasant lack of activity at the Sekiu Airport on the right. From the road crossing over the Hoko River you can see Kydaka Point and the river mouth with its large tidal lagoon.

This drive is located under the Pacific Flyway, the migratory flight path of more than two hundred kinds of birds. An albino bald eagle lives near Neah Bay, and a local grapevine of bird watchers keeps track of its flight patterns. Farther west on the Pacific Coast, both bald eagles and trumpeter swans sometimes share the same airspace.

From Clallam Bay the drive follows the shore of the Strait of Juan de Fuca the last 13 miles to Neah Bay. There are plenty of places to stop and explore tide pools and rocky outcroppings, and enjoy the often staggering views across the strait. The rocky beaches are loaded with flotsam and treasures. The strait, gouged by glaciers, is 100 miles long and 15 miles wide where it meets the Pacific.

All along the coastline, prime fishing grounds beckon sport fishermen on the lookout for rock fish, like red snapper, ling cod, and yellow eye. Seasoned scuba divers, as well as people who want to learn, can find supplies at Sekiu. Lessons and rental equipment are available. A guided tour of the underwater shoreline is something utterly unforgettable. Some places on Earth are even more lush than Olympic National Park, as unlikely as that seems, and the intertidal region along this drive is one of those places. Because of the deep upwelling of food from the ocean floor, everything grows to surprising proportions near Neah Bay. Sea anemones can grow to 12 inches across, wolf eels 8 feet long are not unusual, and octopi can weigh more than 60 pounds.

The last few miles of the drive are on the Makah Indian Reservation. *Makah* means "generous people" in Salish, but in the Makah's own language it means "people of the cape." Tribal ancestors called Cape Flattery home three thousand years ago.

Makah Indians are not related to any American Indian nations, but rather to two Canadian tribes on Vancouver Island. Their collective identity is the Nootkan culture group. They see the Straits of Juan de Fuca as their own Berlin Wall. Land didn't matter much to the people of the cape; families historically claimed areas of open ocean for themselves. The Makah Reservation, formed by the 1855 Treaty of Neah Bay, comprises 44 square miles that include Tatoosh and Waadah islands. The islands were returned to the tribe in 1984.

The Makah heritage is shown through one of the finest collections of artifacts and Indian art on display in the Northwest. The Makah Museum and Cultural Center was built in 1979 to house ancient artifacts buried by mudslides five hundred years ago and recently recovered near Lake Ozette, 15 miles to the south. Only five or six homes were covered in the 0.5-mile-long village of Ozette, but the collection contains 97 percent of the artifacts classified as Northwest Coast, pre-contact (with whites), and perishable. There are 55,000 artifacts in the collection, but only 1 percent are on display. One ceremonial piece in particular calls out to the imagination: a representation of the dorsal fin of a whale, inlaid with more than seven hundred otter teeth.

Ozette is one of five ancient villages known to the Makah people, and only one of two to be excavated. Tidal erosion at Ozette required excavation to save the artifacts. Visitors are not allowed at the excavation site.

The Makahs were granted American citizenship in 1924, an event celebrated every August during Makah Days with canoe races on the bay, a salmon bake, foot races, and a parade.

From Neah Bay it is well worth continuing on 8.5 miles of dirt road and walking a 0.5-mile trail to the tip of Cape Flattery. Follow the signs to the Makah Air Force Station west of town and take the right-hand fork to reach the trailhead to Cape Flattery. This drive is mostly low elevation alongside the Waatch (pronounced WHY-atch) River to its mouth, from where it turns upland through dense woods along the southwestern edge of the cape. The hike descends among towering trees, around swampy ground, and suddenly arrives on the scrub-covered bluffs overlooking the vast Pacific Ocean.

To stand on the most northwestern tip of the lower forty-eight states could be a personal geographical achievement. Not even Lewis and Clark made it here. They surely would have been struck by feelings of awe by looking 200 feet down into coves with swirling tidal currents, thundering waves, and rocky outcroppings.

The cliffs are undercut by big sea caves, which can be seen by looking across the coves. Birds soar both above and below. Immense waves crash into the rock walls, sending spray up toward where you stand. It feels much like the end of the world. The views of Vancouver Island and the Pacific coastline are breathtaking.

The 0.5-mile-long volcanic outcropping, just 0.5 mile out to sea, is Tatoosh Island, with its resident sea birds and hundred-year-old lighthouse. During May and June the bluffs of Cape Flattery are a good place from which to watch the grey whale migration.

Recognizing the richness and grand scale of sea life in this part of the world, in 1994 the federal government established the Olympic Coast National Marine Sanctuary. The sanctuary is 3,000 square miles, stretching from Cape Flattery south to Copalis Beach. It extends from shoreline to as far out as 40 nautical miles. The sanctuary provides a safe environment for 128 species of birds, 30 species of marine mammals, and kelp beds of Olympic proportions.

While doubling back to Neah Bay, a low-tide exploration of Waatch Point would be a memorable experience. The tidepool shelf seems to go on forever, harboring big barnacles with black, lacy fronds, brilliant many-rayed seastars (starfish), anemones big as your fist, and piddock clams that bore holes into the sandstone for shelter.

Driving on to Ozette from Neah Bay, a distance of 40 miles, requires doubling back on WA 112 nearly to the Sekiu Airport. The Hoko-Ozette Road to Ozette turns southwest from WA 112, 4 miles west of Clallam Bay. The drive first goes along the Hoko River to the crest, and then along the Big River to Lake Ozette. The drive follows the northern shore of the lake to Ozette and the ranger station.

From the ranger station, two 3-mile trails lead through the dense forest of Olympic National Park to the ocean. The boardwalks pass through marshes, meadows, and old-growth forest. The southern walk goes to Sand Point, the northern one to Cape Alava. A traversable 3 miles of beach connect the two, thus completing the 9-mile Ozette Loop Trail. Both boardwalks access miles of beach and primitive camping areas in the woods just up from the beach. People have to pack in everything they may need, as there are neither services nor supplies of any kind.

On the beach it is likely that you'll see sea otters peeking out of the kelp, or migrating whales. Sea stacks stand at attention just offshore and serve as nesting and resting sites for birds. Eagles pause on them, unnoticed by the deer nibbling at the edge of the beach.

Sand Point is one of the most beautiful and primitive beaches on the Olympic coast. Walking north along the beach toward Cape Alava, at Wedding Rocks you will see some ancient Indian petroglyphs. There are fifty-seven petroglyphs along the Ozette Loop Trail. They depict human faces, whales, and surrealistic-looking figures, but their origins and meanings remain a mystery.

Anybody can take the boardwalks to the beach on their own. Hundreds of people do it on nice summer days, and many of them find pristine camping spots above the beach log line, just into the woods. The spires of campfire smoke above the tree canopy are the only sign that anybody else is around.

The beach, which runs for miles north and south, is one of the best in the West for beachcombing. Finders keep Japanese glass fishing floats, Nike shoes, and any other flotsam, jetsam, and detritus washed ashore from Pacific Ocean storms.

Raccoons will eat any food that isn't strung high between trees, so take care to hang your stash. It's a long walk out to Lake Ozette on an empty stomach.

The camping is easy, with the right stuff—waterproof *everything* (tent, food, matches, firestarter, clothing), and don't forget tarps to string over lounging areas. There is plenty of beach wood for campfires for warming yourself between explorations.

If there's a medical problem or emergency, the ranger station has a wheeled toboggan for evacuation.

11

Hoquiam to North Beach

General description: This 40-mile drive follows the northern shore of Grays Harbor and North Bay westward to Pacific beaches.
Special attractions: Grays Harbor National Wildlife Refuge, Bowerman Basin, Copalis Rock National Wildlife Refuge, clam digging, beachcombing.
Location: Washington's central Pacific Coast.
Highway number: Washington Highway 109, Washington Highway 115.
Travel season: The drive is open year-round.
Camping: On the beach portion of the drive, Ocean City State Park and Pacific Beach State Park both have camping and hookup sites.
Services: Full traveler services are available in Ocean Shores and Moclips.
For more information: Grays Harbor National Wildlife Refuge, Bowerman Basin, Grays Harbor Chamber of Commerce, Grays Harbor Tourism Council, Ocean Shores Chamber of Commerce (see Appendix A).

 ## The drive

Leave U.S. Highway 101 at Hoquiam and turn west onto Washington Highway 109 for Ocean Shores, Ocean City, and Pacific Beach. It is 16 miles to the beach road, which extends 25 miles to the north (beyond the end of this scenic drive) and 5 miles to the south.

Two routes of WA 109 begin here in Hoquiam, connecting with US 101. One starts in town at the Hoquiam River, and the other takes off west from US 101 just north of town. They meet up again on the shoreline of Grays Harbor across from Bowerman Basin. The basin comprises an important part of the Grays Harbor National Wildlife Refuge. Take one or two hours to enjoy a close-up look at thousands of migrating shorebirds that stop to feed and rest at Bowerman Basin.

To take this side drive, 1 mile west of Hoquiam on WA 109, turn south on Paulson Road into the airport. Then turn right on Airport Way. Walk to the shore from the end of the pavement. Wear waterproof boots.

During the spring season at the refuge, shorebirds visit from as far away as Argentina. They concentrate at the muddy tide flats here at Bowerman Basin, feed and rest here, then continue their flight north to the Arctic. There may actually be a half-million shorebirds within sight at one time, since the

Drive 11: Hoquiam to North Beach

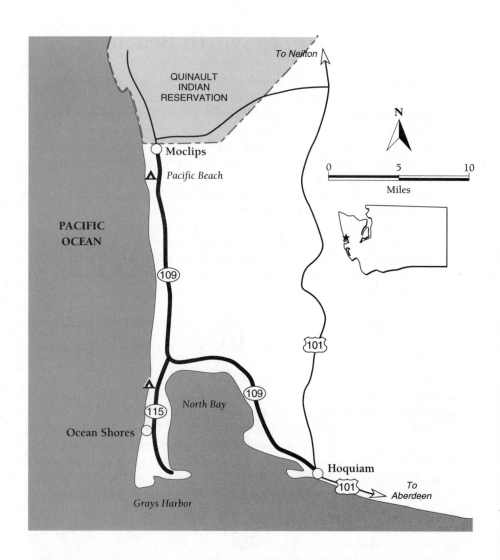

basin enjoys the United States's largest West Coast concentration of shore-birds. Western sandpipers are the most numerous, followed by dunlins, dowitchers, semipalmated plovers, and least sandpipers. People with binoculars, telescopes, and birding guides crowd on the beach to watch in awe as birds by the thousands swarm like locusts. There is no sight like a mid-air flock parting down the middle in response to the attack of a peregrine falcon.

From the mouth of Grays Harbor, miles of sandy beaches stretch away to the north and south. Reach Grays Harbor City shortly after, and from there WA 109 crosses a bit inland. It then follows the straight course of the Great Northern Railway for about 3 miles. Within 1 mile, WA 109 bears left. Two miles later it passes cranberry bogs on the left.

The flat, sandy beaches of the northern area can be reached by taking the WA 109 turnoff from US 101 in Hoquiam. It is a romantic area with a history of fur trading, shipwrecks, tough pioneers, and the ancient heritage of its Indian nations providing an atmosphere of solitude and quietness.

Where WA 109 intersects with Washington Highway 115, turn left (south) on WA 115 toward Ocean Shores. Just after passing the entrance to Ocean City State Park on the right, the drive continues for less than 1 mile between the North Bay of Grays Harbor on the left and the Pacific Ocean on the right. Ocean Shores is just ahead.

The 6,000 acres of the Ocean Shores peninsula was privately owned from 1860 until 1960, when it was subdivided into lots as a planned beach resort community with more than 100 miles of paved roads. Upon reaching the community entrance, the road becomes the four-lane Ocean Shores Boulevard. On a sunny day it seems a bit like Florida. Here you can ride go-carts, rent mopeds, play miniature golf, try out bumper boats, and ride horses. South of town is a 27-mile canal system that connects three lakes. It was constructed by developers on former marshlands.

After about 300 yards, the drive turns right, then left, and runs along the beach for about 5 miles to a parking lot at the Point Brown jetty. Along this section there are five access points to the beach, just outside Ocean Shores west of the entrance and at the ends of Chance a La Mer, Pacific Way, Ocean Lake Way, and Taurus Street.

Birding is a popular pastime for many residents here. Even though the beach is not considered particularly good bird habitat, the locals have seen flocks of six thousand or more black-bellied plovers perched during high tide. From the jetty at Ocean Shores, you can see many other species of birds, including sooty shearwaters, sandpipers, terns, and cormorants. Some visitors are inspired to begin their personal lifetime bird lists here. Migrating grey whales pass by the jetty from late February through May. Year-round marine residents include harbor seals and porpoise, sea lions, and orcas.

Continuing north to WA 109, pass the sand dunes on the left toward Ocean City and Copalis Beach. Up the beach, as the natives say, are the small towns of Ocean City, Copalis Beach, Pacific Beach, and Moclips, where the drive will end. (North beyond Moclips lies the Quinault Indian Reservation and the town of Taholah at the mouth of the Quinault River. Quinault beaches have been off-limits to the public since 1969.)

The communities and beaches along this stretch are known collectively as North Beach. It doesn't offer the kind of excitement for which San Francisco's North Beach is known, but the landscapes, seascapes, and general atmosphere are all striking in their own ways. The high forest-topped cliffs on the right stand in stark contrast to the lower sandy landscape on the left. At some points the road weaves through stands of forest and even atop the bluffs, from where the views of the beaches and ocean are inspiring.

Ocean City, the first of the towns along the way, is best known for its razor clam beds. Digging clams along here is a popular activity all summer. (Be sure to check local regulations for digging dates, times, and tides changes.) There is a reflective quality to time spent along this drive, as though the area remains untouched by the hubbub of modern times. This is NOT true on a sunny summer weekend however, when the beaches and byways are fairly teeming with flocks of tourists out to have a good time. In the

Bowerman Basin.

other seasons of the year, calm prevails. The rewards of beachcombing are greater then, too.

Just before the town of Copalis Beach, Griffiths-Priday State Park allows good walking access to the mile-long beach on the ocean side of the Copalis River. The park is day use only.

The highway crosses the Copalis River (good fishing!) at Copalis Beach, then runs alongside its south-to-north tidal drainage basin. Where the basin meets the open sea, the Copalis Rock National Wildlife Refuge begins. It runs north for 27 miles. Copalis Rock itself is 1 mile ahead just offshore.

The drive twists and turns a lot between Copalis Rock and Pacific Beach State Park, 4 miles ahead as the crow flies. The park has some popular camping areas. The largest of the one-hundred-plus sites are 50 feet long.

Pacific Beach is a pleasant little resort town. The Navy vacated a base here years ago and turned it into a recreation facility—the whole community now revolves around its holiday ambience. Beachfront resorts offer comfortable views from which to watch the inevitable fall and winter storms. Afterwards, the beach pickings should be good, since few vacationers venture this far north.

But that was not always true. Moclips, the next town north, used to welcome two excursion trains per day full of Seattleites. Those were the good old days, but Moclips still thrives as a resort town, offering full services for travelers.

12

The Columbia River Mouth and Long Beach Peninsula

General description: This 99-mile drive follows the northern shore of the Columbia River west from Interstate 5 to, and including, the Long Beach Peninsula on the Pacific Coast.

Special attractions: Julia Butler Hansen National Wildlife Refuge for the Columbian White-tailed Deer, Willapa Bay Interpretive Center, Lewis and Clark Interpretive Center, 28 miles of hard, sandy beach.

Location: Southwestern Washington.

Highway number: Washington Highway 4, Washington Highway 401, U.S. Highway 101, Fort Canby Road, and Washington Highway 103 or its beach spur.

Travel season: The drive is open year-round.

Camping: A few public and private campsites are available westward from Skamokawa to the Long Beach Peninsula. Fort Canby State Park on the Peninsula's Cape Disappointment has the drive's largest campground, and there are six more public and private campgrounds north along the peninsula.

Services: Full traveler services are available in the towns of Kelso/Longview, Cathlamet, and Long Beach. Smaller towns along the way have limited services.

For more information: Julia Butler Hansen National Wildlife Refuge for the Columbian White-tailed Deer, Long Beach Peninsula Visitor Center, Grays Harbor National Wildlife Refuge, Skamokawa/Lower Columbia Economic Development Council (see Appendix A).

 The drive

Begin the drive from Interstate 5 by taking exit 39 in Kelso and turning west on Washington Highway 4. WA 4 passes through Kelso, over the Cowlitz River 3 miles north of where it flows into the Columbia, and through West Kelso and Longview. The street design in Longview looks more orderly than most. That's because the entire city's design was laid out before anybody moved in. Only half the expected population showed up, however, so Longview never filled in. Timber may no longer be king in the Northwest, but it reigns still in Longview, as evidenced by the logging trucks and

Drive 12: The Columbia River Mouth and Long Beach Peninsula

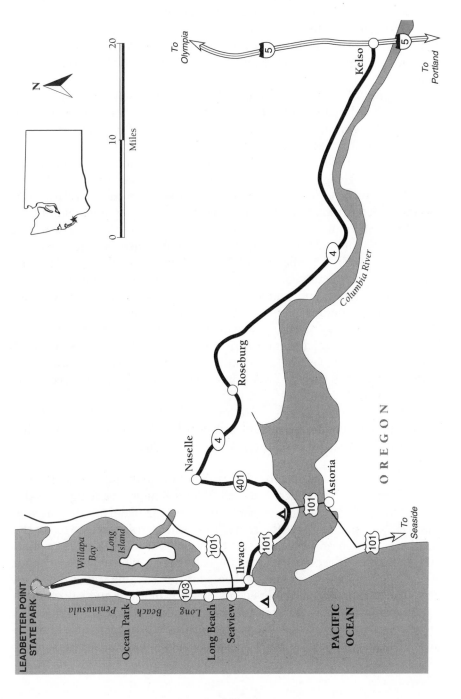

mills that produce pulp, plywood, paperboard, and other paper products.

The drive from Longview to the Long Beach Peninsula is 80 miles. The first 7 miles to Stella are largely population-free now. Ghost towns are common along this entire section of the Columbia River. Many bustling industrial centers, which could be reached only by boat, once dotted the shoreline of the Columbia. After the construction of WA 4, convenient transportation changed the entire focus of the communities. Many were simply abandoned.

Just out of Longview, Mount Solo rises on the left. The marshlands continue, interlaced by Solo Slough. WA 4 shortly becomes Ocean Beach Highway, hugging the north side of the Columbia River all the way to Cathlamet. This county seat of Wahkiakum County began its life as a trading post in the 1840s. As everywhere else in the region, the main pursuits were fishing, logging, and farming. Halfway to Cathlamet, the town of Stella proudly survived the decades of economic changes. Now the Stella Historical Society is reconstructing replicas of some of the town's original buildings.

From Stella the highway tightly hugs the shore of the river, which at one point is about 0.25 mile wide. Look for sailboarders between here and County Line Park, 1.5 miles ahead. The park is a good place to watch the prehistoric-looking sturgeons being reeled in. On the sandy beach check for washed up treasures and watch the immense ships going by. The day-use park also has restrooms, picnic tables, and barbecue pits.

The Columbia is 2 miles wide and punctuated by large islands where it reaches Cathlamet. Farther downriver it widens to over 6 miles in places. The large island just before Cathlamet is Puget Island, reached by a bridge from Cathlamet and bisected by Washington Highway 409. The road connects with a ferry to Oregon.

When Lewis and Clark passed through Cathlamet in 1805, it was home to the Cathlamet and Wahkiakum Indian tribes. Within forty years it became a trading post. The Pioneer Cemetery includes the grave of Chief Wahkiakum.

Just north of Cathlamet the drive passes through the Julia Butler Hansen Columbian White-tailed Deer National Wildlife Refuge. The refuge includes the Hunting Islands, which are separated from the mainland by a narrow channel. Set aside in 1972, the refuge has been a great success. Today the small deer graze peacefully alongside dairy cattle. In an ecologically symbiotic relationship, the cows trim the long coarse grass, which the deer cannot digest, and leave the short tender shoots for the deer. Elk can also be seen here. The best viewing times for elk are the early morning and late evening. The best viewing spots are from the road, not the trail. On the 3-mile trail the deer scatter when they sense people nearby. The refuge is also home to more than sixty species of birds, including eagles, herons, swans, Canada geese, ducks, loons, hawks, and vultures.

The northernmost reach of the refuge borders the town of Skamokawa, which has a campground where the Brooks Slough joins the Columbia. In town, on the right side of the highway, Redmen Hall is worth a look. It was originally a school, then a fraternal hall. Now it houses the River Life Interpretive Center. To make way for the construction of WA 4 in 1930, Redmen Hall was moved 30 feet up the hillside. Lewis and Clark stopped and traded in Skamokawa in 1805 when it was a thriving Indian village. Excavations show that this was a village site as far back as 350 B.C. The town is now listed on both the state and national registers of historic places.

From Skamokawa the drive heads north and inland, alongside the West Fork of Skamokawa Creek, then over the southern portion of the Grays River Divide and down alongside the Grays River. The drive bypasses the riverside cannery towns of Brookfield, Dahlia, and Altoona. These were thriving communities until WA 4 eliminated the need for the river's use as a commodities highway. When boat traffic diminished, the townsites withered and the salmon canneries folded.

Along the Grays River, WA 4 passes through the communities of Grays River (which has Washington's only currently used covered bridge), Rosburg (from which the remains of Altoona can be reached by driving south on WA 403 for about 6 miles), and Oneida, before turning northwest over the Deep River. About 1 mile after joining Salmon Creek there is a campground on the right, 3.5 miles before the Washington Highway 401 turnoff at Naselle.

For nearly 8 miles, WA 401 follows the course of the South Naselle River before once again running alongside the Columbia. The Megler Rest Area and Visitor Information Center is a good place to pick up travel brochures, watch the river traffic, and scan the 4.4-mile Astoria-Megler Highway 101 bridge to Astoria, Oregon. There is no longer a toll to cross the longest continuous-truss bridge in north America. Crossing over and back makes a fun side jaunt for a close view of the magnitude of the Columbia and a look upriver at Mount St. Helens.

The river channel's depth is maintained at 40 feet, but the pressures of the tides work against traffic as far upriver as the Bonneville Dam. When the river and the tide are pulling in the same direction, west, eastgoing tugs with log booms have to tie up and wait for the incoming tide.

Return to the north end of the bridge; the drive now takes US 101 north and hugs the riverside for about 11 miles to the town of Ilwaco on the Long Beach Peninsula. A lingering look at the shipping traffic on the river shows that the consistently deep water flows along the north shore. The ships appear to head right for the beach. There are parks and campgrounds along the way with easy access to the sandy riverside beaches.

A particularly nice park is the Fort Columbia State Park and Interpretive Center. This site preserves some of the original gun emplacements from 1898 and includes an historical museum. The self-guided historic walk allows for a good stretch of the legs.

On this part of the drive, the wide mouth of the Columbia is clearly visible. Sailors have a healthy respect, if not outright fear, for the hazards here. The Columbia Bar, the underwater sand dunes that wreak havoc on the waters above, is one of the three roughest bars in the world. This one is well-known as the graveyard of the Pacific. Crashing waves require more precautions than just high-speed windshield wipers on boats. Some boats are simply turned turtle by the forces of nature. Each river pilot who boards an incoming ship has to board the ship's pilot ladder just as the crest of a wave passes under his boat. This is a very hazardous task. Boats pitch and roll on waves up to 30 feet high. Fifteen hundred lives are known to have been lost on the Columbia Bar. The Coast Guard station on Cape Disappointment, the upper jaw of the Columbia's mouth, serves as a national training center for rescues on the water.

As elsewhere in the Northwest, community-supported murals that depict local history have been painted on many of the buildings in peninsula towns. When you drive into Ilwaco on US 101, the first mural you'll see portrays the Clamshell Railroad rolling into downtown Ilwaco in 1924. It is right near the traffic light intersection. There are several more murals about town, but a particularly intriguing one is painted on the wall of the Pacific Printing Building. It depicts horse-drawn salmon seiners.

During Ilwaco's heyday of charter salmon sport fishing, there were up to 150 working boats in the harbor. There may be only thirty-five now, and "none of them are working," said Mayor Toby Beard in 1994. Whale watching and naturalist cruises have helped the local economy since then, but the commercial boating industry is basically decimated. Sturgeon charters are available, but catch-and-release is the norm. Catching 8- to 10-foot sturgeons is not at all unusual, but fishermen can only keep fish between 49 and 66 inches, and just one at that.

Drive south from the Ilwaco waterfront for 2.5 miles on Fort Canby Road to Cape Disappointment and Fort Canby State Park, the most scenic state park on the peninsula. The Lewis and Clark Interpretive Center is here, with photos, journal entries, and multimedia displays. The Lewis and Clark expedition got as far as Cape Disappointment at the peninsula's southern tip. The park has 250 campsites and several trails to two lighthouses, beaches, and bluffs for views of the Pacific and the Columbia Bar. Columbia white-tailed deer live on Cape Disappointment. The lighthouses, Cape Disappointment and North Head, are the two oldest lighthouses on the Pacific Northwest coast.

Retrace the drive to Ilwaco; after 1 mile there is a turnoff to the North

Head lighthouse.

From Ilwaco the drive takes US 101 north to the town of Seaview. Here, drivers have the option of taking the last 28 miles right on the beach. Seaview is the starting point of "the world's longest beach drive," 28 miles of hard-packed sand, 300 feet wide (at low tide). Along the way there are numerous places to get back onto Washington Highway 103. A 1901 law stipulated the beach to be an official extension of the state highway.

The Long Beach Peninsula has much to offer its visitors, but sandy beaches—miles of them—top the list. Kids both big and little find enough amusements to stay busy all day long. The town of Seaview has a 2-story mural, 64 feet wide, on the Pacific County Transit Building. It shows local transit in the late 1800s, with a stagecoach carrying passengers on the peninsula's beaches.

From Seaview, the drive continues north on WA 103 as US 101 north turns to the right. Seaview blends right into Long Beach, where most of the commercial enterprises on the peninsula vie for tourist dollars. The options include go-cart races, bumper boats, moped rentals, and two- or four-passenger surreys (four-wheeled bicycles). Downtown Long Beach has a larger-than-life-sized bronze sculpture of Lewis and Clark, showing Clark carving his name in a tree trunk. He actually did just that in 1805, to mark the westernmost point reached by his expedition.

The Long Beach Boardwalk, accessible by ramp, offers a long walk above the sand, with good views of the dunes, beach, and ocean. The stretch of beach here is one of the Northwest's premiere kite-flying destinations. The myriads of colorful kites, including giant spinsocks, flown from the beach are a sight to behold. All conceivable shapes, sizes, and combinations stay aloft in the steady westerly winds. Rokkaku battles, where two flyers try to drive each other's kite from the sky, are a special variation. Long Beach even hosts an annual mid-August kite-flying festival, with hundreds of entrants, and the World Kite Museum & Hall of Fame. It houses the best Japanese kite collection outside of Japan. The museum points out that the Wright Brothers' first airplane was nothing more than a collection of box kites propelled by a motor.

Clam digging is also popular. On an outside wall of the Long Beach Pharmacy building, a particularly popular mural shows an activity that symbolizes the peninsula, an old-timer digging for clams at low tide.

While driving north in Long Beach, keep an eye out for Pioneer Road to the right, where the Pacific Coast Cranberry Research Foundation operates a bogside museum and gift shop on Fridays and weekends, 10 A.M. to 3 P.M.

Early in this century, cranberry plants were brought from the East Coast to some coastal areas of the Northwest. They now thrive very well in this cool, wet climate. Half of Washington's cranberries are grown here on 550 acres. The four-million-pound harvest takes place in October and early November. Bog tours are available during the annual October Cranberrian Fair in Ilwaco.

In Ocean Park, WA 103 takes a diagonal course to the east side of the peninsula, where amazingly giant piles of oyster shells present themselves in and around Nahcotta and Oysterville.

In Nahcotta, the Willapa Bay Interpretive Center (on the breakwater east of the Ark Restaurant) puts an interesting spin on its display of local history. Oystering was as big here as in Oysterville 4 miles north; in fact the center is a replica of an oyster station house. The exhibits consist mostly of walls covered with quotes from conversations with local old-timers. There are also tools of the oyster trade in a 1920s Shoalwater Bay dinghy, a double-ended fourteen-footer. The center is open Fridays and weekends May through October.

A stairway on the property leads down to the bay. Other than Leadbetter Point, this is about the only public access to the west side of the bay.

Oysterville overlooks Willapa Bay on the eastern side of the peninsula. Its turn-of-the-century character is a marked contrast to the entertainment orientation of Long Beach. Oysterville honors the indigenous oyster population. Twenty percent of the nation's oysters are harvested from the Willapa Bay beds. This is reputed to be the cleanest estuary in the country. The rich natural oyster beds were discovered, with the help of an Indian chief, in 1854. Then, much like the gold rush, the oyster rush was on—within a few months the white population swelled to five hundred fortune seekers. The concept of sustainable harvesting had not yet occurred to anybody, and the bay ran out of oysters by 1900. An infusion of Chesapeake oysters failed to thrive, but Pacific oysters brought from Japan in the 1930s did. Oysterville has been on the National Register of Historic Places since 1976. The carefully restored homes and businesses are a testament to the perspicacity of the people in this windy part of the state.

Continuing north on Sandridge Road, the drive ends at Leadbetter Point State Park. Lots of foot trails meander through the woods and over the sand dunes. No camping, fires, or beach driving is allowed. People must stay off the west beach entirely from April to August in order to protect the snowy plover nests. However, there are plenty of other birds to see during the spring and fall migrations. Look for black brants by the thousands in the marshes. The giant redwood trees seem to be an anomaly here, but they thrive and lend an almost mystical majesty to the state park.

13

Spirit Lake Memorial Highway to Mount St. Helens

General description: This 52-mile drive (each way) to Mount St. Helens is like a trip to the moon, thanks to the 1980 eruption of the volcano. The effects of its destruction increase in scale as the road ascends alongside the Toutle River Valley.

Special attractions: Visitor centers and chats with locals who frequent them, scenic overlooks of startling terrain, wildlife viewing.

Location: Southwestern Washington, accessed from Interstate 5.

Highway number: Washington Highway 504, called the Spirit Lake Memorial Highway.

Travel season: The road is open year-round.

Camping: Seaquest State Park has ninety-two campsites across the road from the Mount St. Helens Visitor Center. There are also private, state, and Forest Service campgrounds near the monument boundary. Within the monument, dispersed camping is allowed in non-restricted areas.

Services: All traveler services are available at the beginning of the drive in Castle Rock. Some of the visitor centers on the drive have cafeterias.

For more information: National Park Service, Mount St. Helens National Volcanic Monument, Cowlitz County Department of Tourism, Weyerhauser Forest Learning Center, Mount St. Helens Visitor Center, Coldwater Ridge Visitor Center, Johnston Ridge Observatory, Gifford Pinchot National Forest Headquarters, Packwood Ranger District, Randle Ranger District (see Appendix A).

 ## The drive

Eruption time for Mount St. Helens was 8:32 on the morning of Sunday, May 18, 1980. It blew two-thirds of a cubic mile off the top of the mountain. Two hundred thirty-four square miles of forest were flattened almost instantly. Volcanic ash fell for days, covering much of eastern Washington and many parts of the Inland Northwest. The Toutle River became a sweeping mudflow. It buried buildings, roads, and logging machinery 300 feet below. Six hours after the eruption, the temperature of the river water at Castle Rock, where the drive begins, was 100 degrees Fahrenheit.

Begin the drive from the busy little town of Castle Rock at exit 49 on

Drive 13: Spirit Lake Memorial Highway to Mount St. Helens

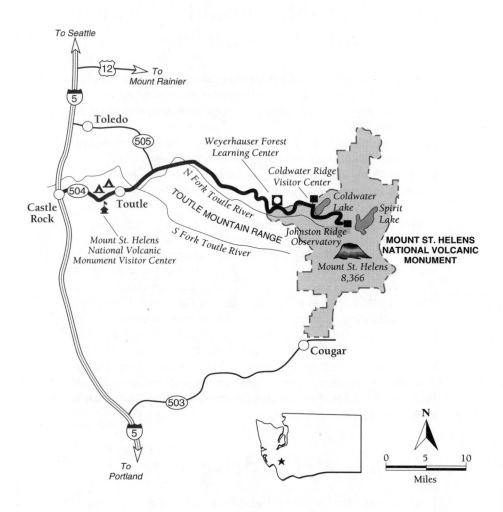

Interstate 5. With leisurely stops at each of the visitor centers, the drive could take five hours round trip.

Castle Rock is full of private enterprises, like the Omnidome movie theater, that relate to Mount St. Helens and its eruption. The first Forest Service facility is 5 miles into the drive. From Castle Rock, take Washington Highway 504 east, the Spirit Lake Memorial Highway, and follow signs for the Mount St. Helens National Volcanic Monument.

Don't be discouraged by the weather. Like any mountain-related weather system, it can be sunny in Castle Rock, completely cloudy or foggy a few miles away, and then sunny again as the drive nears the top.

Most scenic drives in this book are largely on national or state lands, so it is worth noting here that this drive to Mount St. Helens is almost entirely on private land. The vastness of the forests for the first two-thirds of the drive would suggest public ownership, but much of the land is in the hands of timber companies. Only the end of the drive is actually publicly owned.

Expect such oddities along the early stretches as yard sales that look a few months old. Towns, villages, and services rely on tourism as they did before the eruption. Even logging trucks still roll down the highway.

The first important stop to make is at the Mount St. Helens National Volcanic Monument Visitor Center. This is at the 5-mile mark on the shore of Silver Lake. The center is administered by the Forest Service in a beautiful building, and has recently begun to charge an admission fee. The new fee, starting now, is $8 each for persons 16 and older for a 3-day pass good at Mount St. Helens National Volcanic Monument Visitor Center, Coldwater Ridge Visitor Center, and the Johnston Ridge Observatory. Ages fifteen and under are free, including school groups. Persons holding Golden Age passes will pay $4. The fee is mandated by Congress as part of a three-year fund-raising study of a number of Forest Service sites around the country. This one got started first.

The visitor center's displays about the eruption and its effects are excellent. The movie and slide presentations have won awards for their comprehensive introduction to Mount St. Helens. The center also hosts a good Northwest Interpretive Association book sales area. In the diorama display, the statues look like they're made of ash. The movie lasts twenty-two minutes, and it would be no challenge to fill another half-hour milling about the displays. Outside is a short nature trail with access to the Silver Lake wetlands and its resident bird population.

Heading east on WA 504 again, the road parallels the shore of Silver Lake. The lake is 6 miles long, and it seems like lily pads cover the entire surface. In 3 miles the road crosses over the northern extension of the lake, nearly 3 miles before crossing the famed Toutle River. Surprise! There is no

Toutle River.

sign of the Toutle having ever been a mud flow. It looks just like a regular river through the woods, at least for now. Nature reclaims its own with all due speed. Weyerhauser helped the process along with the tree farm on the left, planted in 1985.

By Milepost 12, as the drive goes alongside the North Fork of the Toutle River on the right, thick mud deposits are visible. Mud and ash still wash down the mountain and get left along the edges of the water, looking much like cement.

Two miles farther is another Weyerhauser tree farm. The sign announces that it was commercially trimmed in 1992. Keep an eye out for painted rocks on the drive. A hubbub was raised in 1995 when it was discovered that the Forest Service was funding the coloring of newly exposed rocks to make them appear more natural. The practice is actually common around the country, arising out of concern for the visual quality of the National Scenic Highway System and national forests. Nevertheless, the practice was put on hold in order to study the natural weathering of newly exposed rocks.

As you approach Milepost 16, more of the wide, gravelly riverbed is exposed, with ash on the edges. Kid Valley, Milepost 18, is the last of the towns on the drive, but there are occasional dirt roads that lead into the backcountry.

At Milepost 22 there is a specially constructed facility that slows the

Mount St. Helens viewed from Coldwater Ridge Visitor Center.

river flow enough so that the ash in the water settles out. Called the "sediment retention structure," its purpose is to prevent downstream flooding and choking of the Toutle, Cowlitz, and Columbia rivers below. There is a short walk to a viewpoint overlooking the Army Corps of Engineers dam; or, to get a real sense of the debris, walk for about 1 mile to the dam itself. Go out to the middle and look upstream. It feels just like being on a beach— like you could grab a shovel and dig some clams.

The retention dam was built as an alternative to dredging the river every year, which would be prohibitively expensive. Even so, the dam will eventually fill with sediment, probably in about fifty years. Scientists speculate that the silt runoff will continue for another five hundred years.

Back on the drive, from above the river valley it is difficult to see much vegetation on the ash-covered land. The main problem with ash as a ground cover is that its composition is primarily mineral. Nothing grows in it because it has no nitrogen. To overcome this, nitrogen-fixing plants, like grasses and clover, have been planted. And when tree stands are about fifteen years old, nitrogen is sprayed over them to enhance their growth.

The river valley itself is not any bigger than it ever was before. The mountain's debris cut a wide swath during the torrent, but the valley floor is the same as it was before the eruption. Since then, silt that washes down eventually fills its channel and seeks a new route. The river seeks a lower route in the valley, leaving behind silt everywhere it goes. Getting anything to grow in the valley requires constant replanting efforts. This meandering is expected to continue for another five hundred years also.

By Milepost 24, the valley spreads out with a lush green canopy of trees. And shortly after, the mountain itself looms into view. Here you can see that Mount St. Helens has no top!

A railroad once owned the square mile on top of Mount St. Helens. Who knows why they bought it in the first place, but that square mile is now scattered all over the Northwest.

The Hoffstadt Bluffs Visitor Center, at Milepost 27, provides a deck with excellent viewing of the valley below. Early morning and late evening are good times to see the elk herd. The elk hang out there the rest of the day, too, but are hard to spot because they bed down during the midday heat.

The Hoffstadt Bluffs Visitor Center, operated by Cowlitz County, is open daily 10 A.M. to 8 P.M., May through October and 10 A.M. to 5 P.M., November through April. Admission is free.

The highway all the way up the mountain is quite good. The steepest grade is six percent. The 0.5-mile-long Hoffstadt Creek Bridge near Milepost 30 was built in 1991. The land below the bridge (it is 370 feet high) lies within the eruption's blast zone. Some scorched, dead tree trunks still stand there, but they are becoming overgrown by the trees planted after the eruption. The beginning of the blast zone was replanted in 1983, so it now just looks like a young forest.

The first road through here was a rough wagon track to Spirit Lake, on the slopes of Mount St. Helens. It was scrapped, though, in the early 1900s. In the 1930s, a paved road was built to the lake, but when the volcano blew in 1980 the upper portions were completely wiped out, and mud flows destroyed miles of the lower portions of the road. The state rebuilt and relocated the highway to a higher elevation. It was opened in 1992. The highest point of the road is 3,800 feet at Elk Rock.

Keep an eye out for deer alongside the road. They are a good sign of the health of the regrowing forests. On a clear day, you can see both Mount Rainier and Mount St. Helens.

The Forest Learning Center at Northpoint Ridge, Milepost 33, is likely the best visitor center on the drive. The effort is co-produced by the Weyerhauser Corporation, the Washington Department of Wildlife, and the Rocky Mountain Elk Foundation. The Forest Service operates the center from 10 A.M. to 7 P.M., May through October, and admission is free.

A chatty Forest Service intern stands outside on the deck with a telescope and binoculars for viewing elk in the valley below. The herd of raghorn elk is composed mostly of young males in the summer, because their harems have not yet been formed. What brings them to the valley floor

6,805-foot Pinnacle Peak ("The Chopping Block") in the Pickett Range.

are the clover and grasses planted throughout the area. Alder is starting to grow there too, which attracts the elk down from the mountains.

The dioramas inside the visitor center demonstrate human efforts to help nature's growth in the blast zone. Two films are worth watching as well.

Keep an ear open for conversations between locals and tourists on the decks of the visitor centers. They often reveal the human impact of the eruption—reminiscences and consequences that local people will feel for the rest of their lives. Everyone who was within earshot of the eruption, or who felt the rumble, can remember exactly where they were and what they were doing when it went off. You might see a couple of old duffers standing around talking about what happened, what it was all about. They must have a tape of the event in their heads that they keep replaying, over and over, because what used to be here for them is no longer.

One story often retold is of rescue crews coming into the blast zone after the eruption to search for survivors. The landscape had changed so much, there were no familiar landmarks. Lakes were gone, new rivers had formed, and the terrain bore no resemblance to the maps they carried.

As you drive closer to the mountain, you see the huge gap in the top of Mount St. Helens, revealing just where that two-thirds of a cubic mile of mountain came from.

The Coldwater Ridge Visitor Center, at Milepost 45, is nearly the end of the public road, except for a 2-mile stretch to the Coldwater Lake Recreation Area, which opened in 1994, and the 1997 addition to the observatory. The Coldwater Center is an architectural wonder and fits nicely into the surroundings, yet allows people to stare right into the yawning mouth of the volcano. Here too, there is usually a naturalist on the deck, fully conversant on the eruption and all the recovery efforts. Life is rebounding with surprising speed on this moonscape, faster than anyone expected.

Several naturalist-guided walks are offered from the visitor center. Tours leave hourly for the 0.25-mile Winds of Change trail, and there are afternoon tours and talks at the newly-formed Coldwater Lake. From the center, the drastically altered Spirit Lake is visible out beyond Johnston Ridge. Inside the building are several interactive exhibits that help explain the causes and impacts of Mount St. Helens' eruption.

The Johnston Ridge Observatory, at milepost 52, is scheduled to open in May of 1997, and is on the road 7 miles beyond the Coldwater Center. It will feature interactive displays to teach about volcanism's cyclic nature and the new landscape around Mount St. Helens.

14

North Cascades Highway

General description: High mountain peaks, deep valleys, waterfalls, rivers, dams, and spectacular vistas highlight this 132-mile drive through the Cascade Mountains.

Special attractions: North Cascades National Park, backcountry camping, hiking, mountain climbing, horseback riding, fishing, wildlife and bird watching, hydroelectric tours.

Location: North-central Washington.

Highway number: Washington Highway 20.

Travel season: Spring, summer, and fall. The mountain section of the highway closes for the winter, usually sometime in November through March. Deep snows and avalanches occur in at least seventy places. Even in summer, falling and sliding rock are likely, so be careful where you stop the car.

Camping: There are many campgrounds along the way. Park campgrounds tend to fill up on summer weekends.

Services: There are no services within the 80 miles of the park. There are limited services in towns along WA 20 before Diablo and in Mazama. Winthrop offers full services.

For more information: Mount Baker-Snoqualmie National Forest, North Cascades Visitor Center, Okanogan National Forest, Ross Lake National Recreation Area, Seattle City Light Skagit Tours, North Cascades National Park, National Park Foundation, Rendezvous Outfitters, North Cascades National Park Skagit and Wilderness District Office (see Appendix A).

 The drive

Begin the drive in Sedro Woolley, 5 miles east of Interstate 5. Sedro Woolley can be reached via Washington Highway 20, from Burlington at exit 230 or via Cook Road at exit 232. Follow WA 20 around the northern edge of Sedro Woolley to the information center operated by the Forest Service and the Park Service. It is on the left, at 2105 WA 20. This is an excellent place to buy maps, get information on highway and weather conditions, and perhaps borrow an audiocassette tape to listen to on the drive. The tape is an hour-long collection of stories and descriptions of the drive that lend an excellent perspective on the human and natural histories of this region. The tape advises drivers to stop at least a few times to get the

Drive 14: North Cascades Highway

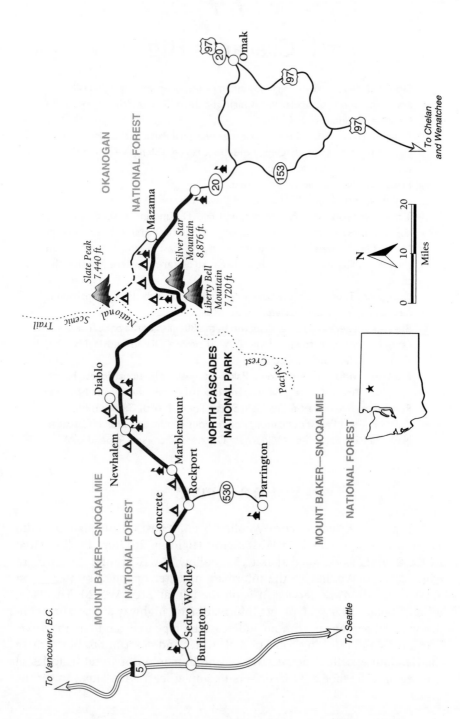

most from the trip. Return the tape at the visitor centers in Early Winters, Winthrop, and Omak, or at the ranger stations in Winthrop, Twisp, or Chelan, at the other end of the trip.

Proceeding east on WA 20, the drive travels up the northern side of the Skagit Valley. The hillsides are covered with bigleaf and vine maples and alder, a favorite local source of firewood. In the flatter sections of the valley, between here and Puget Sound, the rich delta soils provide a base for a thriving farm community. Berries and peas are the biggest valley crops, but in recent years colorful tulip fields have grown into a mainstay for farmers and a boost for tourism. Dairy farming is strong in the upper reaches of the valley.

Going toward Newhalem, the highway follows the Skagit River, passing fields of rural greenery and farmland. The highway is two-lane, and can get busy with weekenders, so plan on slow driving.

The drive bypasses the town of Concrete. Local people figure that Concrete makes most of its money from speeding tickets, issued to drivers who are going too fast to make a left turn into town. The immense structure on the left is an abandoned concrete factory that operated until 1966. The turnoff to Baker Lake is here, too. The recreational lake is 15 miles north of Concrete. The state's largest colony of nesting osprey resides at Lake Shannon, a few miles north of town.

The drive east of Concrete grows much more rural. There is still plenty of farmland between the highway and the Skagit River. Most of the forest is second-growth.

Rockport State Park, about 1 mile before the town of Rockport, is a very pleasant campground with fifty-eight campsites. Rockport has a nice park, Howard Miller Steelhead Park, on the river with rest rooms, picnic tables, a settler-style log cabin, and the ferry that used to cross the river before the bridge was built.

Just after Rockport, the drive stays consistently close to the Skagit River, and just in time, too. This is eagle country, especially from mid-December until the end of February. This 9-mile stretch between Rockport and Newhalem is an eagle sanctuary called the Skagit River Bald Eagle Natural Area. The scavengers gather here for spawned-out salmon at the river's edge. They tend to hunch in trees along the riverbank on rainy days, but during winter sunshine they can be seen flying high over the valley or bickering over a meal on a gravel bar.

As you continue on, a sign announces Marblemount as the gateway to the North Cascades. Beyond Marblemount there are no reliable gas stations until Winthrop, so be sure there is enough gas in the tank for 90 miles of travel.

The drive turns sharply to the left as it leaves Marblemount and parallels the river again. Within 5 miles, the drive passes out of the Mount Baker-

Snoqualmie National Forest and enters the Ross Lake National Recreation Area. This is technically within North Cascades National Park. There are four types of federal land programs in this part of the Cascades. At different times in the past, Congress set aside lands for a national forest, national park, national recreation area, and this highway, the first National Scenic Highway in the country.

The Washington Cascades are owned or managed by a bewildering assortment of entities. The Mount Baker-Snoqualmie National Forest extends over the western slopes of the Cascades from the Canadian border to the northern boundary of Mount Rainier National Park. But within and around this forest are national wilderness areas, national recreation areas, national parks, timber companies, other national forests, state forests, an experimental forest or two, a demonstration forest, wildlife recreation areas, watersheds, Indian reservations, a national monument (Mount St. Helens), and a national scenic area.

Both the National Park Service and the Forest Service have wilderness and recreation areas. Within North Cascades National Park the Ross Lake National Recreation Area comprises 107,000 acres along the corridors of WA 20 and Ross Lake. The recreation area corridor extends roughly 2 to 3 miles on both sides of WA 20. There are many campgrounds and hiking trails within this zone. The campgrounds are primitive and quiet, and campers

Descending Washington Pass.

sometimes see black bears on the perimeters. Some people believe grizzly bears are here too. The isolated meadows and valleys are good habitat for grizzlies, but sightings are extremely rare. Some black bears can be mistaken for grizzlies because their colors range from blond to red, and from brown to black. Other park animals include mountain goats, deer, and moose. Animals in the park that are unlikely to be seen are cougars, bobcats, coyotes, wolverines, snowshoe hares, rodents, and lynx.

The North Cascades National Park's first real visitor center opened in 1993 in Newhalem. On arriving in Newhalem, follow signs that lead up the road on the right toward the Goodell Creek Campground. The visitor center is open daily from April to October and weekends only the rest of the year. Slide presentations and other programs relate the stories of the park's creation and its delicate ecosystem and leave audiences grasping for words to describe its beauty. You'll likely have a similar reaction at scenic overlooks along the drive. The mesmerizing slide presentation took six years to produce.

The visitor center, itself a monument to fine craftsmanship, has a large exhibit room and sales area for books and maps by the Northwest Interpretive Association. From the visitor center, a 200-foot paved trail leads to a stunning overlook of the Picket Range. The Pickets are a range of peaks that are hidden from highway vantage points. This view is of the heart of the park, a section with no trails and places where few have been. A longer walk, 2 miles round-trip, leads to the Skagit River.

Continuing on the drive into Newhalem, you'll be surprised to find a traffic light. Newhalem is serious about its traffic control. The prim little village is actually a good old-fashioned company town. Seattle City Light provides housing here for its employees who work in the hydroelectric plants at the three dams. Greenhouses in Newhalem grow all the flowers for the town. They're absolutely everywhere, and you can see the greenhouses on the garden tour, one of the mini-tours, by the Gorge Powerhouse. Ladder Creek Falls and towering cedars can also be seen behind the powerhouse.

Leaving Newhalem, the drive climbs a bit more strenuously along what looks like a deep dry gulch. Gorge Dam, a few miles ahead, holds back the Skagit River waters, but along here, frequent signs in two languages warn against leaving the highway. Massive waters are released down the gorge at unpredictable intervals to serve the electrical needs of Seattle.

Once above Gorge Dam, the scene is more reassuring as the highway parallels Gorge Lake. The color of the water is an amazing green, and park rangers are frequently asked about its hue. The emerald green water is similar to some waters in the Rockies and comes from rock that is ground into powder by moving glaciers above. The powder is held in suspension in the water, and in the right concentrations, it bends the rays of sunlight to create this color.

At the head of the lake there is an opportunity for a side trip to Diablo, a very small Seattle City Light town just below Diablo Dam. From here, Seattle City Light Skagit Tours offers tours (four-and-a-half hours) from Diablo that pack in a mixture of pioneer transportation, bunkhouse meals, and views of a modern hydroelectric generator. It includes a six-minute ride up Sourdough Mountain on the antique Incline Railway, a half-hour boat cruise on Diablo Lake, a tour of the Ross Powerhouse, and a bunkhouse-style, all-you-can-eat chicken dinner. Tours operate Thursday through Monday from mid-June to September, plus weekend tours through September. They leave the Diablo Seattle City Light offices at 10 A.M., 12:30 P.M., and 3 P.M. Reservations are required.

From Diablo it's up to Washington Pass at 5,483 feet. From here, the drive is closed during winter. Even though the North Cascades Highway was built in 1972, not much has changed. The highway is just a cut through the wilderness, and since most of it passes through North Cascades National Park, it will remain a cut through the wilderness. In the novel *The Bridges of Madison County*, the main character supposedly drives this highway in 1965. He was ahead of his time by about seven years. This was the last highway to be built through the Cascade Range. It took twelve years to build and is the highest major mountain crossing in Washington.

The park was established in 1968 to honor and maintain some of America's most breathtaking and beautiful scenery. Its half-million acres, from the Canadian border to Lake Chelan, contain 318 glaciers, uncounted high jagged peaks, ridges, and valleys, and waterfalls galore. Rainy Pass, at 4,855-feet, is at the center of hundreds of thousands of acres of wilderness. This is miles and miles of wild country, with only a few trails through it. The surrounding mountain peaks rise to 8,000 and 9,000 feet.

The Pacific Crest National Scenic Trail, from Mexico to Canada, crosses at Rainy Pass. There is a picnic area here, and nearby trails lead to Rainy Lake and Maple Pass. The trail is 2,600 miles long. From this point to its end at the Canadian border, the trail is only 63 more miles.

Just 5 miles farther, 5,477-foot Washington Pass once sat on the floor of the ocean that is now 90 miles to the west. The Cascades, which may still be rising, are largely rock made from compressed sediment. Marine fossils are still found at high elevations.

The drive crosses the Golden Horn Batholith, molten rock inside the Earth pushed to the surface through the sedimentary rock. Most of the molten lava cooled and congealed just below the surface. It formed a coarse crystalline rock called Golden Horn Granite, because of its color. Liberty Bell Mountain at Washington Pass is made entirely of Golden Horn Granite. Weathered rock shows the color best. Deposits of gold were found in the cracks in the solidified granite, as was silver. Miners were the only people to stick it out in the Cascades. Although most mines did not produce rich ore, the first big payout was in 1936, at the Azurite Mine. Almost a million dollars worth of gold was mined there in a short time. But of all the money spent on gold searching, mining, and fund-raising promotion, only ten percent was recovered in ore. There are still prospectors in the North Cascades today, but they don't find much.

As you drive down the east side of Washington Pass, the difference in terrain and growth might surprise you. The 0.5-mile-long slope, on the right, is responsible for the main avalanche hazard on the North Cascades Highway. If there is any snow above, be sure to notice the plow at the ready, parked out of danger higher on the road.

The hairpin curve ahead is a good place to pull over for a look up at the subalpine larch above 5,500 feet. They turn bright yellow in the fall when their needles prepare to shed. Subalpine larch doesn't grow on the western side of the Cascades.

Once past the hairpin curve ahead, the drive makes a long slow descent alongside Early Winters Creek, which runs to the Methow Valley below. The drive is gentle now, giving opportunity to wonder at the surrounding mountains. The valley flattens and widens, providing good land for farming and grazing herds of migrating deer. There are several campgrounds along this stretch.

Gorge Bridge at Newhalem.

Two miles past the Early Winters Campground, there is a turnoff to the little town of Mazama, 0.5-mile to the left. A possible side drive, an unforgettable one, is the road from Mazama to Harts Pass. Harts Pass is the highest drivable point in Washington, at 7,440 feet, and nearby Slate Peak offers a full panoramic view of the glaciated North Cascades and the Pasayten Wilderness with its alpine tundra.

The only campground facilities are primitive campsites, outhouses, and spring water, but it is still a favorite overnight for hikers passing through on the Pacific Crest National Scenic Trail. The Harts Pass Campground is 19.5 miles from Mazama over a mostly dirt, mountainous one-lane road. The drive up is not treacherous, merely exciting, and takes a good hour. Add a half hour for possible waits for livestock and livestock trucks making their descent. No trailers are allowed beyond the 10-mile point.

WA 20 continues through the flat Methow Valley to the Western-style town of Winthrop. Along the way on this dry side of the mountains, most of the vegetation includes sagebrush, cottonwood, and ponderosa pine. The Methow, as this area is called, averages 15 to 20 inches of moisture a year, much of it snow. Near the river, stands of quaking aspen provide a good contrast in the landscape.

Winthrop, where the drive ends, was one of the first Northwest towns to reconstruct itself in an idealized version of its founding image so as to persuade people passing through to stop, look around, and maybe spend a dollar or two. In Winthrop's case, the image is a combination mining/Wild West frontier town, and that's exactly what it looks like today. Many of the goods and services follow the theme.

15

Stevens Pass Scenic Byway

General description: This 85-mile drive follows the route of the northernmost railroad over the Cascades.

Special attractions: Fishing, camping, whitewater rafting, hiking.

Location: West-central Washington.

Highway number: U.S. Highway 2.

Travel season: The road is open year-round.

Camping: Between state parks, national forests, and private enterprise, there are many campgrounds along the drive.

Services: Full traveler services are available in Monroe and Leavenworth. There are no public restrooms along the 85 miles from Monroe to Leavenworth.

For more information: Monroe Chamber of Commerce, Leavenworth Chamber of Commerce, Leavenworth Ranger District, Sultan Chamber of Commerce, Wenatchee National Forest, Mount Baker-Snoqualmie National Forest (see Appendix A).

 The drive

The route climbs gently through thick forests, then steeply climbs the last few miles over Stevens Pass. It descends the more arid eastern side of the mountains alongside the Wenatchee River through Tumwater Canyon to Leavenworth, the "little Bavaria of the Cascades."

Begin the drive by going east on U.S. Highway 2 from the town of Monroe by taking the US 2 exit from Interstate 5. Monroe is on the leeward side of a valley full of dairy farms and stockyards. In the dairy-rich Northwest the scent that you may notice is known as the smell of money. Monroe has an annual Draft Horse and Mule Extravaganza near the beginning of October.

The town is growing, as the number of fast food eateries can attest. Many who work in Seattle are moving here, as Snohomish County's growing population oozes eastward toward the Cascade Mountains. As a consequence, traffic on US 2 is often slow, especially since this is the favorite route over the Cascades to Leavenworth, Wenatchee, and Lake Chelan.

There are still plenty of farms to be seen here in the flat Skykomish Valley, but notice that the land quickly turns to hilly forest both to the north

Drive 15: Stevens Pass Scenic Byway

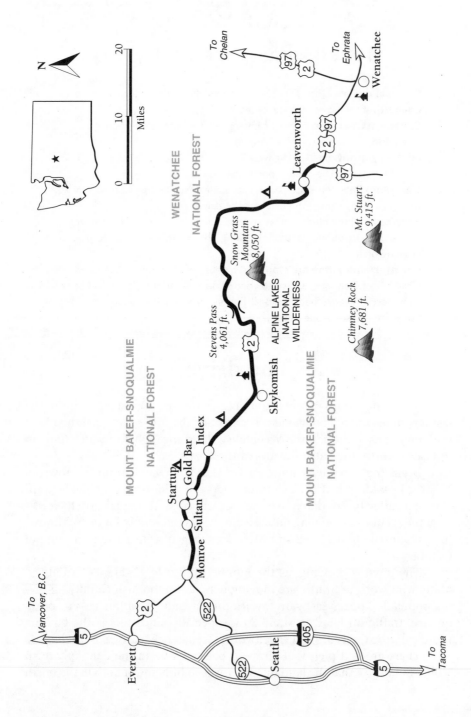

and south. The Skykomish River is broad and still along here.

Sultan, named for a local Indian chief by miners who mispronounced his name, is 6 miles from Monroe. It was originally a gold rush camp in the 1870s, but it gave way to the timber industry when the railroad arrived in the 1890s. After Sultan, the valley narrows and the farms become more scattered in favor of second- and third-growth forests of alder, cottonwood, cedar, and Douglas-fir.

Startup, just 3 miles ahead, could be thought of as the start up for the climb ahead, but the town was actually named for a mill manager. The Postal Service changed the name from Wallace to avoid confusion with Wallace, Idaho.

There is not much change in elevation yet. The rest of the drive, 69 miles from Gold Bar to Leavenworth, is designated a National Forest Scenic Byway. As with the other towns in the valley, Gold Bar began life as a mining camp and then grew into logging. It has a really nice state park about 1 mile north of the drive. Wallace Falls State Park has good hiking trails and fair primitive campsites. The falls are massive and enjoyable to watch as the water tumbles 265 feet over a series of cliffs and ledges. One trail leading to the falls is a 7-mile loop.

Above the falls you'll find a good panoramic view of the Skykomish Valley. The park is open 8 A.M. to dusk daily during April through September. From October through March it's open Wednesdays through Sundays, 8 A.M. to dusk. But it is open year-round for camping. There are six tent sites and restrooms, but no showers. In Gold Bar, turn left onto First Street and go about 0.5 mile to McKenzie (Ley) Road. Turn east (right) and follow the signs to the park.

From Gold Bar, the drive follows the South Fork of the Skykomish River 21 miles to the Skykomish Ranger Station. The jagged peaks of the Cascades reveal their youth as they now become visible. Civilization is left behind as the drive enters the dense Northwest woods. Directly south, Mount Index comes into view. At 5,979 feet, it towers over everything else.

Within the Mount Baker-Snoqualmie National Forest there is the Henry M. Jackson Wilderness to the north of the drive and the Alpine Lakes Wilderness to the south. The Skykomish River begins to show a lot of whitewater at this point.

The town of Skykomish, invisible through the trees on the other side of the river, offers the lodging closest to Stevens Pass. It gets plenty of snow, as the metal roofs in town can attest. Winter skiers lend a party ambience to the surroundings. During other seasons, hikers and backpackers use Skykomish as their mountainside headquarters. Eight thousand people lived here during construction of the New Cascade Tunnel.

The river waters rush through here nearly year-round, but the drive's climb into the Cascades is still gradual at this point. The forest seems to grow even thicker, if that is possible. Within a few miles of Skykomish, the drive picks up the Tye River. Its source is little Tye Lake, just north of the Stevens Pass summit.

Up high on the mountainsides, perennial avalanche chutes are visible. Nothing grows in them because of the scouring that occurs repeatedly during the winter snows. In 1910, an avalanche wiped out two passenger trains that were waiting outside the old tunnel, which burrowed north of Stevens Pass, killing 118 people. A new tunnel was built south of Stevens Pass by 1929 and is still in use today. At 7.8 miles, it is the second longest railroad tunnel in the Western Hemisphere.

Scenic, basically a railroad siding, is the western portal of that new tunnel. It comes out on the other side at Berne, a town reclaimed by the forest. One mile east of Scenic, US 2 rounds a sharp curve and begins its steep 4-mile climb to Stevens Pass. This section of highway is extra wide to provide room for overheated vehicles and to allow passing of slow traffic. In winter, deep snowbanks are created by snowplows.

Near the summit are the remains of tunnels, snowsheds, switchbacks, and construction towns and camps. The area is called the Stevens Pass Historic District and is listed on the National Register of Historic Places. A group of concerned citizens, called the Stevens Pass Greenway, is working to preserve the entire route between Everett and Wenatchee. Eventually, they hope to link the three mountain passes of Stevens, Blewett, and Snoqualmie in one continuous scenic loop.

The summit of the pass is 4,061 feet, and its main feature is the ski area on the right. This is a very popular day hill for skiers and snowboarders from both sides of the mountains. Just a few miles ahead, you'll find cross-country ski trails.

The drive down the east side of the pass begins alongside Stevens Creek, but within 2 miles the creek joins Nason Creek flowing down from Lake Valhalla. The drive stays with Nason Creek until the water turns north with Washington Highway 207 at Coles Corner, home of the Squirrel Tree Inn. Lake Wenatchee State Park is 5 miles up WA 207 on Lake Wenatchee.

As you head down the east side of Stevens Pass, Douglas-fir gives way to ponderosa pine. That indicates that this is the dry side of the mountains, but there is still enough moisture for quaking aspen.

The drive turns straight south from Coles Corner and in about 5 miles, meets up with the Wenatchee River at Tumwater Canyon. The Tumwater Campground is also here. Tumwater Canyon is one of the most dramatic whitewater rapids in the state. Its churning rapids cascade through the gorge fed regularly by waterfalls from above. Twelve hundred acres of the Canyon are set aside as the Tumwater Botanical Area. Its purpose is to preserve a rare May-blooming flower, *Lewisia tweedyi*.

On leaving Tumwater Canyon the drive enters the town of Leavenworth. Note the first right turn onto Icicle Canyon Road—it may be something to see later on. The fish hatchery on Icicle Creek raises chinook salmon, and shortly past the hatchery the Sleeping Lady Conference and Music Center shines as a rehabilitated Civilian Conservation Corps camp. Icicle Canyon Road continues for miles into the forest below Icicle Ridge, and there are at least eight campgrounds on the river.

Leavenworth itself is pretty much surrounded by Wenatchee National Forest lands, and the woods are riddled with hiking trails that go in all directions. The town is almost a Bavarian theme park. The architecture of the hotels, motels, restaurants, and stores will all make you think you've landed in Europe for the weekend, but without the airfare. Leavenworth has more shopping opportunities than you could do justice to in a day, and the beauty of the natural surroundings will convince you you're on vacation. Leavenworth has succeeded so well at becoming Bavarian that some town services have occasionally required German translators.

The Washington Autumn Leaf Festival has been going on for more than thirty years in Leavenworth. It takes place over the last weekend in September and the first weekend in October. The first Saturday afternoon features a Grand Parade with a "who's who" of marching bands. Oompah music in City Park bandstand gets people dancing, and an accordion player wanders the village.

City Park is where most things happen in Leavenworth, or at least start. The band gazebo is here, and it is well-used by bands and other groups. Even the dogsled pulling contests take place here in winter, as do the arts and crafts shows in summer. The park closes at dusk and is located on Front Street right in front of the main business block between Eighth and Ninth streets, next to US 2. To get there from eastbound US 2, simply turn east (half-right) onto Front Street as you near the center of town.

Riverfront Park has a very nice path for strolling along the Wenatchee River. The whole loop is about 2.5 miles. There are some sandy beaches tucked away and part of the trail explores Blackbird Island. From the island another bridge connects with the trail to Enchantment Park. Access the Riverfront Park trailhead by going south on Ninth Street to the end, then left to the parking area. The trail is well marked.

16

Peshastin to Ellensburg
via Blewett Pass

General description: This 54-mile, north-to-south drive traverses the Wenatchee Mountains between Stevens Pass and Snoqualmie Pass highways.
Special attractions: Historic mining sites, hiking, camping.
Location: Central Washington in the eastern Cascade Mountains.
Highway number: U.S. Highway 97.
Travel season: Year-round.
Camping: There are several Forest Service campgrounds along the drive.
Services: Very limited traveler services are available on the drive. Leavenworth to the north and Ellensburg to the south offer all services.
For more information: Leavenworth Ranger District, Cle Elum Ranger District, Wenatchee National Forest (see Appendix A).

 The drive

This route incorporates the 48-mile Forest Service Scenic Blewett Pass drive. The first 21 miles climb through rugged, wooded terrain to Blewett Pass. From there, the drive descends to a plateau that overlooks the Swauk Prairie and Kittitas Valley, then descends through rolling farmlands to Ellensburg. In the winter, traction devices may be required.

Begin the drive by turning south on U.S. Highway 97 from U.S. Highway 2, about 5 miles east of Leavenworth. Soon after, the road climbs from the Wenatchee River Valley, starting south on US 97. The highway winds up to Blewett Pass alongside Peshastin Creek in the midst of rugged terrain. Steep, rocky slopes border each side of the road, as you climb into the Wenatchee Mountains and the Wenatchee National Forest.

The landscape on the right (west) side of the canyon is a staggering reminder of the power of lightning. The damage from the 1994 wildfires that burned this part of the state is high up and away from the road, orchards, and homes. Firefighting crews brought in from all over the West battled blazes to save homes and businesses in the Leavenworth area and near Chelan. The crews became part of the families whose properties they were protecting, joining them for meals, swapping stories, and promising to keep in touch after the fire season was over.

Drive 16: Peshastin to Ellensburg via Blewett Pass

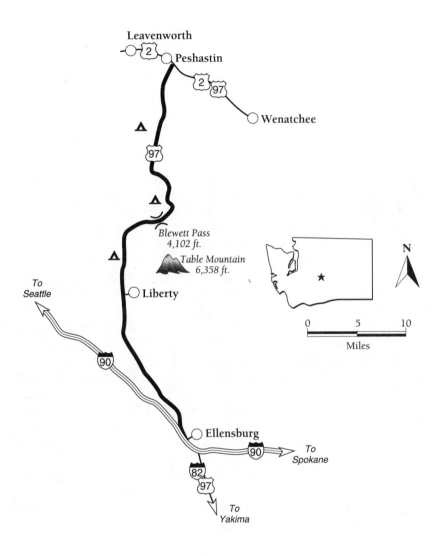

This route over Blewett Pass is lower in elevation than the road over Stevens Pass on US 2. US 97 is a well-paved, newer highway with long, wide pullouts and sufficient passing zones. By connecting with Interstate 90 to the south, this drive provides an alternative way to cross the Cascade Mountains during winter, since Stevens Pass and Snoqualmie Pass are sometimes blocked by avalanches.

Nine miles south of US 2, Ingalls Creek Road on the right leads to a campground and Hansel Lane, which parallels the other side of Peshastin Creek. Along Ingalls Creek, a 4-mile trail goes to Ingalls Lake. The gentle hike is especially nice in the spring for wildflowers and in the fall for the changing forest colors.

Continuing the drive, way up on the right is the Stuart Range, which provides the southern buffer for the Alpine Lakes Wilderness. From Ingalls Creek, the road goes pretty much straight south for about 5 miles to Sheep Mountain where the Old Blewett Pass Highway leaves the drive.

By Milepost 177, the steep canyon walls show no fire damage. A one-lane dirt road leads to Ruby Creek on the left. It is a steady climb through this section. By Milepost 176, the elevation is 2,000 feet. What look like rock buttresses to the right are actually old bridge supports for the original Blewett Pass Road. Traces of it are visible through the trees.

About 1 mile before Peshastin Creek and where the Old Blewett Pass Road leaves US 97, sits the old townsite of Blewett. It became the local center of commerce when gold was discovered in Peshastin Creek in 1860. Nearly three hundred people lived near the mining areas at the height of placer mining. Buildings included a school, a two-story hotel and boarding house, stores, a saloon, a telegraph office, and both frame and log homes.

Within fifteen years the stream was panned out, but gold veins were found soon after and hard rock mining began. In 1879, a wagon road south to Cle Elum was completed, and a road north to Peshastin was finished in 1898. Stage lines ran three days a week. But within twelve years the population had dwindled to about forty people. There was more mining activity during the 1930s, but Blewett finally dissolved into the forest in the 1940s. US 97 now runs through it. Even today along the highway, gold and silver miners work the surface. Old mining tunnels bored into roadside rock can be seen from time to time on the drive. The drive climbs steadily and there are many access points to the Peshastin Creek from the old highway.

About 1 mile past King Creek, the Old Blewett Pass Highway offers an alternative, more narrow drive that is closed in winter. It leaves US 97 here to follow Peshastin Creek, rejoining at Swauk Creek. The Forest Service maintains the old road as Forest Road 7320, and it feels like an endless series of switchbacks. However, there are several turnouts along the way. Five miles in from the start, the sedimentary hill to the right contains fossils and impressions from a time when the region was tropical. Old Blewett Pass is just ahead, at 4,064 feet, and the return to US 97 is 4 miles beyond the pass. The views from the edge of the road are exciting. This was the old highway, whose treacherous path required a new route over Swauk Pass, which is now popularly called Blewett Pass. Many call the new route "the road over Blewett Pass," and map makers are finally giving in as they refer to Old Blewett Pass and Blewett Pass.

On the newer Blewett Pass Highway, by Milepost 166, the drive climbs to 3,500 feet as it nears the pass. The forest is a lush, dense green along here. This is clearly one of the more gorgeous mountain passes in the state. In places there seems to be more birch than Douglas-fir. For fall gold, the sub-alpine larch trees at 4,000-foot Blewett Pass put on quite a show. Larch is a deciduous high-elevation conifer whose soft, bright yellow needles stand out in contrast to the darker evergreens. After it blazes gold, it then drops its needles. The viewing is best in mid-October.

At the summit between Mileposts 164 and 163, at 4,100 feet of eleva-tion, find parking areas for winter snow enthusiasts, like cross-country ski-ers and snowmobilers. Snopark permits are required to park here in the winter, but not during other seasons. From this point, a 0.25-mile-long road leads east to the trailhead for the Swauk Forest Discovery Trail. It loops around Swauk Ridge for 2.5 miles. With a self-guided brochure from the trailhead kiosk, this is a good chance to learn about modern forestry prac-tices, see seasonal wildflowers (like lupine, penstemon, and Indian paint-brush in July), and wander through stands of both ponderosa and lodgepole pine.

Heading down from the pass, the drive enters Kittitas County, with its occasional range areas for livestock. By Milepost 162, the drive is low enough in elevation that the larch has disappeared. The forest here resembles that on the northern side of the pass, being mostly pine and Douglas-fir trees.

The Swauk Campground is on the left at Milepost 160, and at Mile-post 159 the old Blewett Pass Highway joins US 97. A few miles beyond the Swauk Campground, the drive straightens a bit and goes due south, paralleling the Teanaway Ridge on the right and crossing and recrossing Swauk Creek.

The Mineral Springs Recreation Area, near Milepost 156, has a restau-rant, camping, and a parking area for cars and trailers. This area is great for hikers, backpackers, and trail riders.

On this side of the pass there are more open meadows among the stands of trees. Elk are semi-plentiful in this part of Washington and can be seen in the meadows at feeding times.

Eight miles from the summit is a marked turnoff on the left for the still-inhabited Liberty townsite, the oldest mining town in Washington. The buildings, many of them log cabins, are on the National Register of Historic Places. At the turnoff there is a reader board with information on the Wenatchee National Forest.

As the drive comes out of the Wenatchee Mountains, the glacier-scrubbed Swauk Prairie can be seen to the right with the Kittitas Valley straight ahead. The drive descends through range area and rolling farmlands to Ellensburg.

The tip of Mount Rainier can be seen to the right, and the countryside makes a transition from mountains to near-desert in a short distance. Irrigation makes farming here economically viable.

The scenic drive ends at Ellensburg, but US 97 bypasses it to the south. Ellensburg has full traveler services and good museums, especially the downtown Clymer Museum and Gallery with its emphasis on western art.

17

North Bend to Ellensburg via Snoqualmie Pass

General description: This 76-mile drive crosses eastward over Snoqualmie Pass and follows the course of the Yakima River from Keechelus Lake to Ellensburg.

Special attractions: Hiking, camping, sweeping mountain vistas, Snoqualmie Pass ski areas.

Location: Cascade Mountains of Western Washington.

Highway number: Interstate 90, Washington Highway 10.

Travel season: Year-round, but avalanches close the pass for a day or two once or twice each winter.

Camping: There are several campgrounds, including state parks, along the drive.

Services: Limited services are available on the drive, but full traveler services are offered only at towns on each end of the drive. There is a Best Western motel with a restaurant at Snoqualmie Pass Summit.

For more information: Mount Baker-Snoqualmie National Forest, Wenatchee National Forest (see Appendix A).

 The drive

Begin the drive at North Bend, going east on Interstate 90. North Bend is the gateway to the Cascades. Most of the land around North Bend is owned by the Weyerhauser timber company, whose forests are in their second or third cycle of growth. The younger clearcuts are identifiable by their lighter shade of green. North Bend was called Ranger's Prairie at the time of the first white crossing of Snoqualmie Pass from the west in 1856, when Seattle was but a little village.

Contrast the flatlands of the Sallal Prairie, between the South and Middle forks of the Snoqualmie River on the left (the forks meet about 2 miles north of North Bend) and the steeply ascending Harmon Heights on Rattlesnake Mountain on the right. At the eastern end of the prairie, an unlikely airstrip sits below Grouse Ridge.

The large prominence on the left is Mount Si, the most-climbed mountain in Washington. Its top is 4,160 feet high, in the midst of the 8,019-acre Mount Si National Resources Conservation Area. The trailhead for the

Drive 17: North Bend to Ellensburg
via Snoqualmie Pass

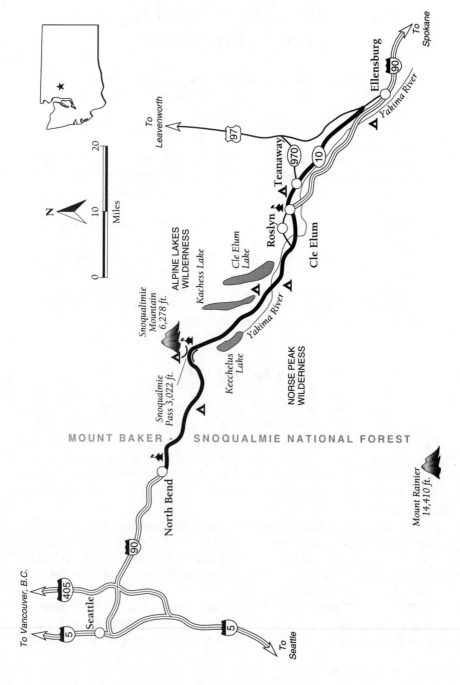

4-mile, round-trip hike to the top can be reached by following North Bend Way east of North Bend. The Department of Natural Resources has developed a public-use plan in an attempt to protect Mount Si from overuse.

The drive climbs rather slowly, leaving the golf courses behind as the canyon walls begin narrowing the valley. Nine miles from North Bend, the Tinkham Campground is nestled next to the river. It has forty-seven sites for tents or trailers. Take the Tinkham Road exit, I-90 exit 42, cross the river to the right, and drive on the gravel road for 1.5 miles.

The last landing site for many miles is 1 mile ahead on the right. Although they cannot be seen from the highway, there are dozens of small lakes up to the left in the Alpine Lakes Wilderness. The wilderness, set aside by Congress in 1976, is a part of both the Mount Baker-Snoqualmie and Wenatchee national forests. Craggy peaks dominate its skyline, the tallest being Mount Stuart at 9,415 feet. The area has one of the highest concentrations of glaciers in the continental United States. Later in the drive, there will be some good viewing opportunities.

This drive was not always considered an easy venture. The first transcontinental family car vacation crossed Snoqualmie Pass in 1911. The car was pulleyed up the steepest grades and barged across Lake Keechelus. The first 300 miles, from Puget Sound to Spokane, took almost a week.

In 1915, the road over the pass was christened the Sunset Highway. It was a dirt road, closed by snow every winter, and would remain so for decades, but at least Puget Sound was connected with the Inland Empire. Its final completion as a section of interstate highway took place in 1978.

Interstate 90 is now one of the most heavily used mountain highways in the country. Sections of the old wagon road are still visible, and even traces of the original Indian trading route can be seen. But logging and newer road construction have erased most visible traces of the original routes.

For a taste of driving the pass in earlier days, Forest Road 58 is available. Originally the Snoqualmie Pass Wagon Road, this narrow winding pavement parallels I-90 between exits 47 and 52 for 5 miles on the other side of the river. It is quite negotiable by ordinary passenger car.

Still following the course of the Snoqualmie River's north fork, the drive turns north for the serious climb to Snoqualmie Pass. On the other side of the pass the highway turns straight south. These changes in direction are a serious flight hazard for pilots of small planes who try to use the highway as a guide when the mountains are obscured by clouds.

For drivers, though, interstate highway designers did their job well on Snoqualmie Pass. It is never too steep or too twisty through forests and rocky slopes. At the pass, the drive crosses from King County into Kittitas County at an elevation of 3,010 feet. While the elevation does not seem high, winter storms can dump a lot of snow here in a hurry. That makes

Seattle skiers happy, since it's only an hour's drive to the pass from the city.

The Pacific Crest National Scenic Trail crosses I-90 at the pass. To the north, the trail enters the Alpine Lakes Wilderness. Southward, the trail traverses open ski slopes and woods before reaching Lodge Lake, 2 miles from I-90. Where the trail crosses the pass, the drive leaves the Mount Baker-Snoqualmie National Forest and enters the Wenatchee National Forest.

At the summit, follow signs to the Forest Service Visitor Information Center. There is also the tents-only Commonwealth Campground nearby on Forest Road 58. Take I-90 exit 52 and cross under the freeway. Pass the westbound I-90 entrance ramp, and FR 58 is the first road on the left.

The four ski areas of Snoqualmie Pass, known collectively as The Pass, are accessible from exit 52. The three adjoining ski areas on the right of the highway are easily visible from the highway. A fourth, Alpental, is 1 mile to the south above a narrow valley. Hidden from the interstate, this narrow valley is ringed by towering peaks. In the fall here the changing colors include the neon reds of vine maple and huckleberry, vibrant in the field of dark evergreens. All this beauty is visible from the parking lot, but there are several trails that let the hiker get up close and personal with the fall season experience.

Alpental's Snow Lake Trail is packed with summer hikers whose destination is Snow Lake, the largest alpine lake in the Snoqualmie Pass area. But starting in early October the trail is more attractive to hikers who want the experience without the crowds. The first 1.5 miles pass through forest, then open up to wonderful views of Chair Peak and the Tooth. The lake, at 4,000 feet elevation, is 1 mile long and surrounded by fir trees. The round-trip hike to Snow Lake is 7 miles and the elevation gain is 1,300 feet. To get there take I-90 exit 52, bear left at the stop sign, and drive 2 miles to the Alpental Ski Area parking lot and the trailhead. The trailhead signboard suggests designated camping areas.

The Snoqualmie Pass Trail was used mainly by the Snoqualmie Indians from the west and Yakima Indians from the east. The Yakimas overwintered at Union Gap. In summer they split into family groups for food gathering as they migrated toward the Cascade Mountains. It was also a cattle trail before becoming a wagon road. The wagon road was hollowed through the forest about 1868, along an Indian trail. On the west side of the pass, 1 mile of the original wagon road is preserved by the Forest Service, with help from the Boy Scouts and other volunteers.

In the 1830s, Hudson's Bay Company herded cattle north from California, for the purpose of providing beef for their outposts and also for export. Some were taken east for Indians to raise. Annually, cowboys herded them west through Naches Pass south of Snoqualmie Pass, to Nisqually, the Hudson's Bay fort at the southern end of Puget Sound.

White explorers of the mountain passes were shown Yakima Pass (also known as Cedar River Pass—the North Fork begins near here), less than 1 mile south of Mirror Lake, but were warned of the deep snows of Snoqualmie Pass. Snoqualmie is the lowest of the passes, hence the most useful as a wagon road.

At Snoqualmie Pass, the merged glaciers from Source Lake and Commonwealth Creek split. The eastern tongue flowed eastward nearly to Thorp, gouging out Lake Keechelus and deepening the Yakima River canyon.

Three miles east of the pass, rather strange-looking Keechelus Lake appears. Just before the lake, look left into Gold Creek Valley. Gold Creek flows down from some of the Alpine Lakes into the very northern tip of Keechelus Lake, elevation 2,516 feet. From the lake flows the Yakima River, which continues for the remainder of this drive and on to the Columbia River at Tri Cities. The lake is shallow, and the tree stumps sticking out of it make you half expect to see mist rising from it, like a scene in a *Swamp Thing* movie. *Keechelus* is an Indian word meaning "few fish." This was a natural lake that was enlarged to a length of 5 miles by a U.S. Army Corps of Engineers dam. There is a nice picnic area at a boat launch, accessible by taking exit 54 and going east along the road that parallels the south side of I-90. Just before the highway department offices, turn right and continue 1.25 miles to the boat launch.

Tree stumps at Keelechus Lake.

More than a dozen former towns and work camps between Snoqualmie Pass and Ellensburg have disappeared into the forest. Mining towns and road and railroad construction camps were scattered throughout the area. A settlement of five hundred men and twenty-five families lived in Meadow Creek Camp at the base of Lake Keechelus. Their job was to build the reservoir, between 1915 and 1920. When they finished, they abandoned the town with its hospital, theater, and YMCA. All that can be seen now is forest and swamp.

A few miles farther there is an actual Swamp Lake, fed by a stream from Keechelus Ridge. Just past Swamp Lake, Kachess Lake lies out of view behind Amabillis Mountain. And behind Kachess Lake is Easton Ridge, which hides Cle Elum Lake. Both lakes are dammed, and both feed rivers that are absorbed by the Yakima River.

Driving downmountain on the east side of Snoqualmie Summit reveals a slow change in the vegetation. The forests grow thinner and the undergrowth is more grassy in the drier soil. The predominant Douglas-fir trees begin to blend with ponderosa pines. As the drive descends, pine becomes dominant on the drier east side of the Cascades.

Lake Easton State Park, 1 mile before Easton, has 2,000 feet of Yakima River front and 2,400 feet of Easton Reservoir shoreline. All the waterfront makes the park serene in spite of its 135 campsites and proximity to the interstate.

For a really fine view into the heart of the Alpine Lakes Wilderness, leave I-90 for a moment at exit 70, just before the town of Easton. From here you can see the impressive wall and the craggy summits of Three Queens, Hi Box Mountain, and the Lemah-Chikamin area. Easton is at the eastern end of the 2-mile Stampede Tunnel, an 1888 railroad tunnel that completed the first transcontinental route across the Cascades.

Just past Easton is good access to a mid-point of the most used section of Iron Horse State Park. The park is 114 miles long and 100 feet wide, a converted railroad bed. It begins at North Bend and runs east to the town of Vantage on the Columbia River, near the Gingko Petrified Forest. A trestle washout just east of Thorp limits the use of that section of trail. The more mountainous sections closer to Snoqualmie Pass go through tunnels, over trestles, and under snowsheds. Curiously, at this stop near Easton, the Iron Horse Trail serves as the trailhead for the John Wayne Memorial Trail, another railroad trail that runs from Easton to Tekoa near the Idaho border.

The town of Cle Elum is nestled between Cle Elum Ridge to the north and South Cle Elum Ridge to the south. The name means "swift water." Take the main Cle Elum exit and drive northeast for a few blocks to Washington Highway 903 & 970, where the drive turns east. Note the triple-wide streets, due to the optimism of the town founder's wife. She expected

Cle Elum to become the Pittsburgh of the west, only more beautiful because of its wide streets.

WA 970 will turn off to the left in just over 4 miles, but this drive continues straight on Washington Highway 10 through the town of Teanaway to its end at the intersection of US 97. Follow WA 10 for the final 16 miles of this drive.

Teanaway today is known as the creek and valley that lead to the Stuart Mountains north in the Alpine Lakes Wilderness. In the 1880s, plans were afoot to build Northern Pacific's headquarters here, and the community bloomed in anticipation. But the headquarters landed in Cle Elum instead, and Teanaway City was quickly abandoned.

In the plans to honor these sites, the Mountains to Sound Greenway Foundation intends to erect at least twelve interpretive signs between Snoqualmie Pass and Cle Elum.

WA 10 is higher than the Thorp Highway and I-90 below, so the views of the Kittitas Valley's irrigated farmlands are more panoramic. Paralleling the rugged canyon of the Yakima River, this drive is reminiscent of the Yakima Canyon drive. Here, however, there are some fine views of the bucolic valley below, with horses grazing in a pristine setting. Driving south, even for this short distance, the greenery becomes both less prolific and less green.

A side trip down to Thorp gives an interesting perspective on the area's history. The Thorp Gristmill is surely one of the better examples of a town rallying to preserve its heritage. Descendants of the original pioneers who built the mill in 1883, and a lot of their friends, took the sprawling building to task and refurbished all three stories. The fifteen pieces of machinery were also saved. The mill, originally powered by a water wheel, stopped production, alas, in 1946, but it is open for tours.

The drive continues above the Yakima River and next to the Burlington Northern railroad tracks to US 97. The drive ends at this intersection, 3 miles from Ellensburg.

18

The Yakima Valley

General description: This 73-mile drive weaves alongside the Yakima River through 27 miles of desert canyon and goes southwest through the agricultural Lower Yakima Valley.

Special attractions: The Yakima River with camping, rafting, boating, fishing, and hiking; Central Washington Agricultural Museum; Yakima Nation Cultural Center; Toppenish Murals; Sears kit home; American Hop Museum.

Location: South-central Washington.

Highway number: Washington Highway 821, Interstate 82, U.S. Highway 97, U.S. Highway 12, Washington Highway 22, Washington Highway 223.

Travel season: The roads are open year-round.

Camping: Camping is available in the Yakima Canyon, at the Yakima Nation Cultural Center, and in Granger.

Services: Complete traveler services are available in Ellensburg and Yakima. There are limited services in most towns along the drive.

For more information: Bureau of Land Management, American Hop Museum, Central Washington Agricultural Museum, Greater Wapato Chamber of Commerce, Toppenish Chamber of Commerce, Toppenish Mural Society, Bureau of Land Management, Von Hellstrum Inn (Sears kit house), Yakima Nation RV Park, Hispanic Chamber of Commerce of Greater Yakima, Yakima Valley Visitors & Convention Bureau (see Appendix A).

 **The Drive**

Begin the drive southeast of Ellensburg on Interstate 90 and U.S. Highway 97. At exit 110, turn south on Interstate 82/US 97. This part of the drive to the Yakima River Canyon traverses the southern portion of the Kittitas Valley in the geographic center of Washington. Within sight of the Manatash Ridge ahead, take I-82/US 97 exit 3 and follow the signs for Washington Highway 821, Canyon Road. The drive turns left at the Bureau of Land Management sign and enters the 24-mile-long canyon.

The Yakima River has not changed course as so many rivers have. Its erosion over time has kept pace with the uplift of the surrounding mountains. Geologic history can therefore be read in the basalt canyon walls with

Drive 18: The Yakima Valley

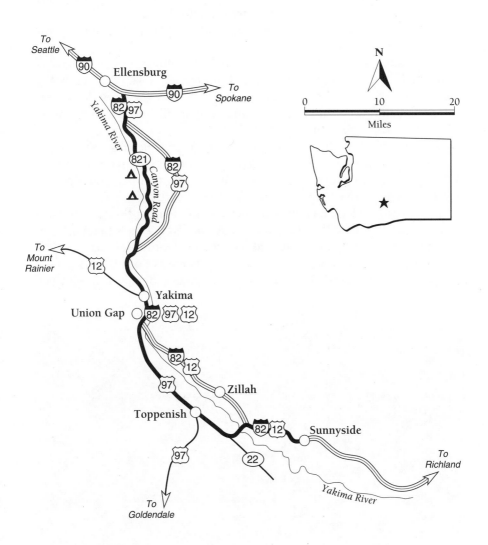

their towering ridges and stark cliffs. This is a favorite place for rockhounds who like the crumbly rock walls of the canyon. Look for bighorn sheep on the drive. On the water, catch-and-release trout fishing is very popular.

Canyon Road was built in 1924 with no banked curves. It handled the traffic speeds of the day, but in later decades, until I-82 was built in 1971, increased traffic pressure and icy winter conditions created serious driving hazards.

The surrounding shrub-steppe, which the Bureau of Land Management considers to be a vanishing habitat, hosts rare Washington birds like the sage thrasher, long-billed curlew, and sage sparrow. Springtime sees blooming wildflowers and grasses on the canyon hillsides and in the many little valleys that open onto the road.

Birds of prey, or raptors, prosper in the canyon. Nesting residents include eleven species of hawks and falcons and five species of owls. Another nine raptor species either migrate through or overwinter here. Both golden and bald eagles thrive here November through February.

The road sticks pretty close to the river on its right through this section, and shortly there is dirt road access to the river. This is the northernmost point in the canyon that provides easy access for floaters. The Yakima is an easy Class I river, and rafters can float as far as Roza Dam. Floating families lash their transports together into flotillas and make a splashy day

Yakima River.

of it. The river is often shallow enough to touch bottom, so for a cool-down from the hot summer sun, people hop off their rafts to walk or swim alongside.

The Umtanum Recreation Site is another good launch for rafts. The suspension bridge near the northern end of the site is a good place to stand over the river and watch the rafters flow by underneath. The bridge leads to the Umtanum Canyon Trail on the other side of the railroad tracks. From the trail, look for chukar partridge, quail, and woodpeckers. The rural influx of city people in search of calmer lives continues to affect places like the Yakima Valley. And although natives of the area complain about the loss of chukar hunting venues, they still hold the chukar trials in Prosser, down beyond Sunnyside.

The drive along here looks and feels like a mini-Hells Canyon, through which Idaho's Snake River flows. Happily, Yakima Canyon has a road that twists and turns, mimicking nearly every bend in the river. There are trees along the waterline and green bowls above the road. In places there is evidence of an even older road, a wagon trail.

Three homestead ranches lie within the Yakima Canyon walls. In recent years the Mahre brothers, Phil and Steve, built homes on the east side of the river, near Road Milepost 6.5. The twins are famed for their history of ski racing and now car racing.

Roza Dam, 1 mile past the Roza Recreational Site, was built for irrigation of the Yakima Valley. It diverts water into a large network of canals, part of the valley's 2,000-mile network of canals. Irrigation is the main ingredient in the valley's prosperity. Property without water rights has little value for Yakima Valley farmers. During the drought of 1994, farmers with junior water rights were denied access to the irrigation ditches. Those with senior water rights were in a good position, charging as much as $15,000 to "junior" farmers for access to ditch water. Ditch companies date back a hundred years, and the rights normally fall to Indians first and farmers second.

After Roza Dam the road climbs away from the river as both straighten out. Washington Highway 821 intersects I-82/US 97, which the drive follows south to Yakima. Bypassing the town of Selah on the other side of the river, the drive passes through the Selah Gap west of the Yakima Ridge. On the north edge of Yakima, the Naches River joins the Yakima River and U.S. Highway 12 joins the drive south to Union Gap.

Women for the Survival of Agriculture have placed crop identification signs along the highways of the Yakima region. This is for the benefit of people who zoom by on their way from one city to another, wondering about the fields of crops close to the road.

Many of the crops are cooperatively marketed. The co-op association for each crop allows its members permission to grow on a specific amount of acreage. Hop ranches are allocated in this way. Washington is also one of the world's premiere regions for growing fruit. The climate, modern growing methods, and state-of-the-art farm technology all contribute to near-ideal fruit products. Unlike rainier climates, Yakima Valley days are sunny and hot, and the nights are cool.

Restaurants and bed and breakfasts in the Yakima Valley tend to serve hearty working-people meals. It's a cultural carryover from the 5,000-calorie-per-day requirement for farmers and their laborers. One woman who came from a logging family, but married into a farming family, said nothing pleased her more than watching her huge meals disappear into the mouths of her husband and their two six-foot-tall sons.

Having passed through Yakima on I-82/US 97/US 12, the drive leaves the interstate at Union Gap. Union Gap is one of only two Washington towns that operates under territorial charter. Take exit 36 and turn west onto Valley Mall Boulevard. Very shortly turn left (south) onto Union Gap's Main Street. For a short stop at a working ranch and fruit market (open April 15 through October 31), turn left two blocks past Ahtanum Road onto Columbus Street and go straight for two blocks to Tacoma Street. Spring Creek Ranch is right there.

Spring Creek Ranch had the distinction of recording the first deed in Yakima County, in 1865. The ranch has a petting zoo, which delights kids of all ages. Not-so-wild ducklings roam the grounds in search of handouts from visitors. And about the strawberry milkshakes: they're downright chewable. If you can manage to suck a berry chunk through the straw, you'll still have to chew before swallowing. The farm has a deli and gift shop featuring gourmet preserves and dried fruit. The biggest seller in the gift shop is a $20 tin man, made entirely from tin cans by a local artist with a sense of humor. These sculptures sold so well that the sculptor was forced to buy cans of food to keep up with the demand for his artwork. He bagged and froze the food so he could use the cans in his work.

Continuing south on Main Street, the drive joins US 97 south at a confusing interchange. Stay in the left lane and go straight ahead onto the overpass. Just over the overpass there is one more short detour option, to the outdoor Central Washington Agricultural Museum visible in the park on the right. Once over the overpass, take the sharp unmarked turn to the right. This leads into Fullbright Park, a Union Gap city park that leases 15 acres on Ahtanum Creek to the museum.

The museum's tool and farm implement collection causes old-and not-so-old-timers to stare in wonder. Here are 15 acres of the hands-on and climb-aboard machinery that helped make the Yakima Valley the bread basket it is today. There are more than one hundred plows and thirty tractors, plus pea viners, combines, threshing machines, and even a portable hop-picking machine. The circa 1870, horse-powered threshing machine just about fills its own shed.

There's also a working apple sorter and a wooden tank orchard sprayer from the 1920s. And a "who-knows-when-or-where-it-came-from" lawn mower, nestled among some tractors, makes you wonder if the Stephen King movie *Lawnmower Man* might have been filmed nearby. One of the museum's keepers claims it runs.

The museum is open seven days a week during daylight hours. The premises are wheelchair-accessible, and a golf cart is available for people who have trouble walking. Visitors are free to roam around, but if you want an escorted tour, call ahead.

The drive continues south on US 97 through Union Gap itself, the passage carved by the Yakima River. It falls between the Rattlesnake Hills on the east side and the Yakima Indian Reservation's Ahtanum Ridge on the west. The drive is now on the Yakima Indian Reservation in the Lower Yakima Valley and continues to parallel the Yakima River, the reservation's eastern boundary.

The valley quickly broadens into flat ranch and farm lands, laced with irregular streams. It is also laced with very regular 1-mile-apart squares of country roads, filled in with fruit orchards, vineyards, and vegetable farms. In addition, the valley is a mix of peoples and cultures. Wapato, for example, the next town on the drive, is on the Yakima Indian Reservation. Within

Grapes in the Yakima Valley.

Wapato is the Yakima Buddhist Temple and the Filipino-American Community Hall.

Fruit and vegetable stands along the drive offer an amazing bounty of produce from local farms. Some even specialize, like the Krueger Pepper Gardens on Branch Road near Wapato. The tall trellises are for growing hops, to keep the mold-prone vines off the ground in the dry air. Hops are heliotropic; they twine around the string as the buds strive to always face the sun.

Continuing south of Wapato on US 95, in about 5 miles the Yakima Nation Resort RV Park and Cultural Center is on the right. It is perhaps unique in both the RV world and in the world of Native American interpretive programs. The RV park has fourteen full-sized tepees (they sleep up to ten people) placed artfully among ninety-five RV and tent sites. The adjacent Yakima Cultural Center contains a museum, restaurant, gift shop, library, and movie theater. The museum houses life-size displays and dioramas that show the practices of the peoples of the Yakima Nation. Displays are kept honest and accurate by the museum's sternest critics—the Yakima people themselves—who not only remember, but continue to live, the old ways.

The Yakima Reservation comprises 1.4 million acres on the eastern slopes of the Cascades and is home to eight thousand people. The entire landscape is dominated by Mount Adams.

Just over 1 mile farther on US 97, at the town of Toppenish, US 97 turns directly south, but the drive continues southeast on Washington Highway 22. A brief sojourn into downtown Toppenish will show how a declining farm town and shipping depot is regaining its economic life through tourism. Toppenish calls itself the "City Where the West Still Lives." (Toppenish is south of Yakima, at the intersection of US 97 and WA 22, just across I-82 from Zillah.)

What keeps the West alive in Toppenish is the famous murals painted on building exteriors all over town. They are larger than life and depict the lives and times of the town's early days. These outdoor murals are an ongoing project. Currently, there are forty-one completed. It has not been an easy job—about ninety percent of local citizens were against the idea at the start. But good times may come again for Toppenish because of the murals's attraction for tourists. However, the economic health of the Old West may best be indicated by what is found in the town's pawn shop: several saddles, well-worn.

Toppenish also has the American Hop Museum, dedicated to preserving the history and heritage of the hop plant that has played an important role in the Yakima Valley. This region is the second largest producer of hops in the world (the first is Hallertan near Munich, Germany). The fifteen

Hops growing in Toppenish City Park with mural in background.

varieties of local hops grow in the shadow of Mount Adams and have been shipped overseas from Seattle for four generations.

Hops in beer can be likened to the seasonings in spaghetti sauce. Hops give beers and ales their distinctive bitter flavors. Each brewmaster creates a distinctive taste from the more than one hundred varieties of hops in the world. The museum, which shows a ten-minute video of hop growing and processing, is chock full of displays. Native Americans were the first hops harvesters. They came from as far away as Alaska, paddling down the Inland Passage and up the Duwamish River.

Hop picking in the 1950s also brought Hispanics into the valley, as well as Filipinos and American Midwesterners. Today there is a Hispanic Chamber of Commerce of Greater Yakima, as Hispanics are the emerging merchant class of the valley. Businesses include small orchards, vineyards, row crop farms, and restaurants. The Hispanic Chamber's annual functions take place on traditional Latino holidays. These include the Cinco de Mayo Annual Heritage Dinner, May 5; Fiestas Patrias Celebration on the weekend before September 16; and the annual Christmas Celebration.

Proceed southwest on WA 22 for 5 miles and then turn left onto Washington Highway 223 east toward Granger. This 3-mile stretch crosses the still-meandering Yakima River and up to Granger on a bluff overlooking the river. Just on the other side of Granger, turn east onto I-82/US 12 for 8 miles to Sunnyside. This section of the drive parallels the north side of Snipes Mountain.

From I-82 take Sunnyside exit 69 and turn south onto Waneta Road for one block. Then turn east on Alexander. The Von Hellstrum Inn bed and breakfast, one of six Sears kit homes built in the region in the early 1900s, is at Braden Road where Alexander ends. This Victorian farmhouse is the only survivor. Each was pre-cut at the Tennessee factory and shipped by rail, ferry, and wagon to the homesite. Kits came complete down to the nails, and the homes typically took about a year to assemble. Kit homes were popular because Washington was still a territory at that time, and the closest architects or engineers were over the mountains in Seattle. If a family wanted (and could afford) a home that was more than a cabin, Sears was the only other choice. The Von Hellstrum Inn originally cost $1,395 FOB. Prices for the different models ranged from $725 to $2,025, and could be paid off in monthly installments of $35. Sears sold about 100,000 kits throughout the country until 1936. The Von Hellstrum land was a hop vineyard, or hop ranch, until 1947.

At last count, there were twenty-three wineries in the Yakima Valley Wine Appellation. All are within a mile or so of the Yakima River and I-82 between Yakima and Benton City. They are open for tours, and most have festivals at different times throughout the year. Tour maps are available nearly everywhere in the valley.

19

Yakima to Mount Rainier and West

General description: This 225-mile drive heads west from Yakima, ascending slowly through the dry, orchard-rich Naches Valley before crossing the Cascade Divide and the Pacific Crest National Scenic Trail on the way to Mount Rainier National Park, named a National Historic Landmark in March of 1997.

Special attractions: Mount Rainier National Park ($10 entrance fee); backcountry hiking, guided mountain climbing, snowshoeing, cross-country skiing, picnicking, winter sports, interpretive programs, and wildlife watching.

Location: Southern Washington Cascades.

Highway number: U.S. Highway 12, Washington Highway 410, Washington Highway 123, Washington Highway 12.

Travel season: The road is open spring through fall only. Mountain passes leading to the park from the east, Cayuse Pass and Chinook Pass, close in winter. The park itself is open year-round, but during the winter it must be reached from the west side. The campgrounds of Ohanapecosh, White River, and Cougar Rock are also closed during winter.

Camping: Camping in developed sites in the park is available for $6 to $10 per night. Reservations are not accepted for individual sites. There are many campgrounds along the drive on Forest Service lands and in the national park.

Services: After Yakima, only limited traveler services are available until the west side of the Cascades. Meals are served in the park at Longmire, Paradise Inn, Paradise Visitor Center, and Sunrise. Food and supplies are available at Longmire and Sunrise. Food and supplies are available outside the park in Ashford, Elbe, Packwood, and Enumclaw. No gas is available in the park. Packwood and Longmire do have gas.

For more information: Mount Rainier National Park, Rainier Mountaineering, Inc., Yakima Valley Visitors & Convention Bureau, Gifford Pinchot National Forest (Naches, Randle, Packwood ranger districts), Mount Rainier Guest Service (see Appendix A).

 ## The drive

The drive takes two eastside approaches into Mount Rainier National Park, to Sunrise and Paradise. It offers an optional side trip to White Pass (25 miles round-trip), then goes through the Gifford Pinchot National Forest to end at Interstate 5 on Puget Sound. All roads on this drive are standard

Drive 19: Yakima to Mount Rainier and West

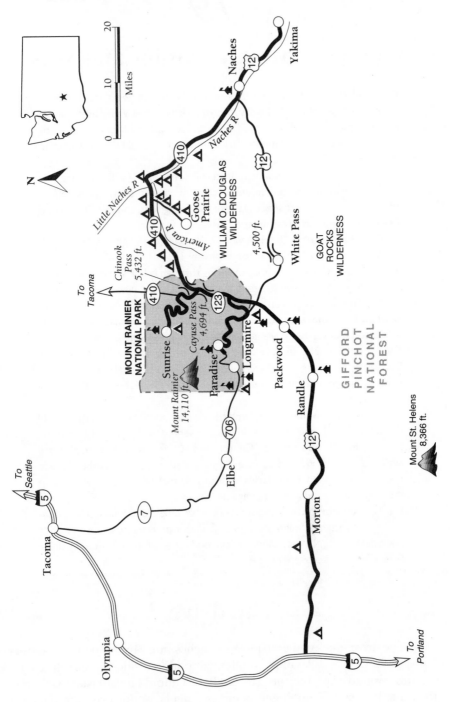

highways appropriate for any vehicle.

The drive begins on U.S. Highway 12 west out of Yakima, nearly 70 miles from Chinook Pass, into the Naches Valley. The valley is planted wall-to-wall with apple orchards, nourished by the Naches River. Umtanum Ridge parallels the highway about 10 miles to the right. At the beginning of the valley are petroglyphs referred to as Indian Painted Rocks. For a look at them, turn left onto Ackley Road at Milepost 199. Take an immediate right to the large historical marker sign. The petroglyphs are found down a short hillside trail to the sheer rock walls. The view of the two valleys below is stunning.

Approaching the town of Naches on US 12, tune in to 1610 AM radio for updates on road work, landslides, trails, and where to buy fishing licenses and Forest Service maps.

At last count Naches (population 760) had one restaurant, one tavern, one bank, one ski shop, one pharmacy, one grocery store (open to 9 P.M.), one liquor store, and plenty of churches. There are also plenty of fruit orchards.

For the next 51 miles, this drive also goes by the name of the Mather Memorial Parkway, which is a Forest Service scenic route between Naches and Enumclaw. (The total distance between the two towns is 75 miles.) It passes through the ponderosa pine-forested slopes along the American River over Chinook and Cayuse passes, and west through the Mount Baker-Snoqualmie National Forest.

Four miles west of Naches is the Y intersection of Washington Highway 410 and US 12. Stay to the right, on WA 410. Along the road for a ways, you will find Forest Service campgrounds. They tend to fill up in the peak summer season.

Along the right side of the Naches River valley, over a space of about 10 miles, is Cleman Mountain. It has thirteen named canyons descending away from the highway toward Wenas Creek on the far side. Between the highway and the mountain is Sanford Pasture, a prime range area.

By Milepost 114 (the distance of WA 410 from Puyallup, its origin), basalt columns appear on the left. The Naches River along here looks too shallow and too bumpy for a raft ride. The drive is now at 1,800 feet and climbing, cutting a slice through the mountain. The hillsides are very dry. This is lava flow country, after all, but there are clumps of trees growing near the top. The drive will be into lush growth soon enough. Below, the fishing looks good.

A few miles past the intersection with Nile Road, which has a gas station and mini-grocery, stark basalt upthrusts and volcanic cones are visible on the right. The whole hillside is composed of this old lava, which continues for miles.

Still more than 30 miles from Chinook Pass, the drive enters Wenatchee National Forest at Milepost 100. The ponderosa pine forest grows thicker as the drive ascends.

At Camp Roagunada there is a left turnoff to Boulder Cave, about 2 miles from WA 410. The cave is 400 feet long and open for public exploration. It was formed by the erosive action of Devils Creek. There is also a nice picnic area here.

Along this stretch of WA 410 there are several campgrounds, plus multiple pullouts where you can just stop and enjoy the river. Just cut through about 10 yards of woods and you're at the water's edge.

At Milepost 90, the confluence of the American River and the Little Naches River is a stirring sight. They become the Naches River, and the drive now follows the American River. This is just north of Goose Prairie, the favorite home of the late Supreme Court Justice William O. Douglas. His Goose Prairie home and Bumping Lake lie within the William O. Douglas Wilderness. Along the road to Bumping Lake are six Forest Service campgrounds. Past Goose Prairie, WA 410 is closed in winter.

On US 12 along the American River, the drive now climbs to 2,800 feet. The trees are taller, the undergrowth is more lush, and there are more campgrounds. It begins to look and feel like a wetter climate, here as the drive climbs and enters a full lush forest. By Milepost 85 it is already difficult to see the forest for the trees, which crowd the highway.

Approaching the park from the east, driving west on WA 410, though the skies may be blue, there's no promise that Mount Rainier will be visible. Even on a sunny day the view can be blocked by clouds generated by the mountain's own weather system. Approaching Chinook Pass, about 4 miles before it, the drive passes under a footbridge that serves hikers on the Cascade Crest Trail. This a subalpine zone here. Chinook Pass is at 5,432 feet, beckoning with its easy trails through mountain ash and huckleberry bushes.

After the pass, the drive descends a multitude of switchbacks as it enters the thick forest zone of Mount Rainier National Park, on its way to Cayuse Pass at 4,694 feet. The drive stays on WA 410 for another 5 miles to the right.

From WA 410, turn left toward White River Campground and Sunrise. To Sunrise from WA 410 it's 16 miles, and 16 miles back to the highway. This turnoff follows the contour of the White River. In 1 mile, stop at the ranger station/registration booth, get a map, ask about road conditions ahead, and pay the $10 entrance fee. The fee is good for entrance to any national park on the day of purchase.

The road into Sunrise climbs from 3,500 feet and passes Governors Ridge and the Cowlitz Chimneys on the left. When there is a dense cloud layer over Mount Rainier, it can be hard to distinguish what is snow and

Mount Rainier as seen from Paradise.

what is cloud. The whole lower mountain is peppered with huge rocks, but the entire top is covered with perpetually moving glaciers that descend into the valleys and radiate down the mountain. Mount Rainier is 14,410 feet high.

The drive passes Fryingpan Creek, alongside which runs a popular hiking trail. The trailhead is at 4,000 feet. This is also where the drive takes a turn to the right, with Sunrise 11 miles farther on. The drive twists and turns, climbing all the while. Even the visible mountains which merely surround Mount Rainier appear very impressive. Lupine and Indian paintbrush decorate the switchbacks. Six miles from Sunrise, the enormous scale of the glaciers ahead is hard to believe.

Fragile meadowlands are everywhere around Sunrise, interspersed by stands of trees. There are frequent signs reminding hikers to stay on the trails. This is the drier eastern side of Mount Rainier, and the elevation is 6,400 feet. Plant growth at this altitude is extremely slow. Spring and summer together may last only a month, so hearty adaptive wildflowers bloom quickly in a brief outburst of color.

A visitor center with displays and a ranger station offer information at Sunrise. A telescope is mounted on the back deck of the visitor center. Even through a telescope, climbing teams on the mountain are not easy to spot. In spite of what appears to be close proximity to the glaciers here, they are still very far away. From Sunrise, the distance to the summit of Mount Rainier is more than 7 miles.

The ranger station, a separate building, serves largely as a sign-in kiosk for hikers. Backpacks and climbing gear are stashed along a wall awaiting pick-up by mountain climbers. There are no display racks of informational brochures and pamphlets, but a variety are kept behind the desk and dispersed only in response to specific questions about the park.

Don't even think of running out of gas up here in the national park. The rangers are very clear about saying that there is no gas at the ranger station. They will, however, call for a tow truck.

The road that used to go past Sunrise for camping, now stops there. Only hikers may venture beyond this point. This is part of the National Park Service's program to close, bit by bit, roads into the wilderness.

When you return on the same road, to WA 410, the reversed direction lends an interesting perspective to the park. The afternoon light is lower and more directly illuminates the foreground. Back down around 4,000 feet in elevation the forest looks and feels tropical.

The drive turns right onto WA 410, following the signs toward Stevens Canyon, Ohanapecosh, and Paradise. In 3 miles, at 4,694-foot Cayuse Pass, continue south on Washington Highway 123, as WA 410 turns east toward Chinook Pass and Yakima. From this intersection it is 11 miles to the Stevens Canyon Entrance at Silver Falls. On the right the drive parallels Chinook Creek, a wild stream with boulders strewn about like toys. The road dips down again to 3,000 feet. The difference in elevation can be sensed in the air. It smells, almost tastes, lush and moist, like a cedar forest—it's very much an old-growth forest. Fungi hang from the sides of trees, about 20 feet off the ground. The drive passes Panther Creek a few miles before the turn-off to Paradise.

Turn right. From the turnoff, the drive to Paradise covers 21 miles. Driving toward Paradise on Stevens Canyon Road, you will soon reach a parking lot on the right for the Grove of the Patriarchs. Western hemlock, Western redcedar, and Douglas-fir tower above the forest floor to astounding heights. The interpretive trail through the grove is about 1.5 miles long.

As you enter Paradise, huge trees line this section of the drive. To cross over Cowlitz Divide, the road heads south to an extension of the park boundary and follows that loop over Backbone Ridge. It then descends the divide in a northwest direction on its way to Stevens Canyon, which is reached by crossing the Muddy Fork of the Cowlitz River above Box Canyon.

Every once in a while, when least expected, the drive takes a bend in the road, and there is Mount Rainier!

The thickest forest and the lushest growth seem always to be at the 3,000-foot level. Perhaps repeated volcanic eruptions over the eons deposited more nutrient-rich ash and pumice layers in the soil here than at other elevations. Ten miles from Paradise, in the lower canyon, the drive has all the feel of Going-to-the-Sun Highway in Montana's Glacier National Park.

Frequent dents in the paved surface, caused by crashing rocks falling from above, are reminders that this is very much the uncontrolled wilderness.

Climbing again, to 4,000 feet, Stevens Canyon is wondrous to behold. The lava origins of the terrain are evident in the towering basalt, but the near-tropical moisture and greenery are a good disguise. Out of the canyon the drive crosses Sunbeam Creek, with its very nice little waterfall. The drive's elevation is back up to 5,000 feet again. It turns southeast to follow a long contour around The Bench. After bypassing Bench Lake and Louise Lake, the drive travels right alongside the largest of several Reflection lakes. It then circles clockwise on the one-way road around the subalpine meadows of Paradise Valley to the Paradise Visitor Center. From here, the views of Mount Rainier are unobstructed by trees.

The crowds here demonstrate that this is the most frequented national park in Washington. The mountain is visible from most Puget Sound cities; that is, when it is not too cloudy and the "mountain is out." It has a magnetic draw for people from all over.

The Henry M. Jackson Memorial Visitor Center is open year-round. It has a restaurant, plus exhibits on the mountain's human and natural history and information on mountain climbing expeditions. Many Himalayan climbers train on Mount Rainier, and hundreds of climbers per year attack Mount Rainier as their main goal. Climbing courses are available locally for guided ascents. Paradise holds the world snowfall record: 72 feet fell in 1972. It is a popular winter site for snowshoeing, cross-country skiing, and snow sliding. The hotel at Paradise, the Paradise Inn, is open from Memorial Day through Labor Day.

Hiking trails take off from the main roads in all directions. Many are ideal for short day hikes. The big hike on the mountain is the 90-mile Wonderland Trail. It circles the base of the mountain and takes about a week to complete.

From Paradise it is possible to continue west to the Nisqually Entrance to the park and beyond on Washington Highway 706 and Washington Highway 7 to Tacoma. This drive, however, backtracks from Paradise to WA 123 and continues southwest through the Gifford Pinchot National Forest.

Upon returning to WA 123 via Stevens Canyon Road, turn right (south) toward US 12 and Packwood. Passing the Ohanapecosh Campground, the fragrance of campfires can be detected from the highway. The Ohanapecosh Visitor Center is just past the campground on the right. Its interpretive exhibits focus on the curiosities of Northwest forests.

WA 123 leaves the national park a few miles before the highway picks up US 12. The drive is now in a corridor of the Gifford Pinchot National Forest between the Tatoosh Wilderness on the right and the Goat Rocks Wilderness on the left. This terrain is called the Big Bottom all the way downmountain to the point where the Cowlitz River plunges into Riffe Lake. The drive follows closely to the Ohanapecosh River on the right, the source of February 1996 flooding that caused major problems on WA 123. The highway was closed for several months, then opened mid-year to one-way traffic while repairs continued.

Where WA 123 joins US 12, the elevation is 2,000 feet. At this point, a side trip presents itself. What could be the drive's third mountain pass of the day, White Pass, is 13 miles to the east on US 12. It would take about an hour's round trip to see the pass, but it's almost worth the drive just to watch Mount Rainier on the way back. The elevation of White Pass is 4,500 feet. There is an excellent ski area located there that was the training ground for Olympic skiers Phil and Steve Mahre.

Continuing the drive from the intersection of WA 123 and US 12, take US 12 west toward Packwood. Seven miles before Packwood, after the turn-off for La Wis Wis Campground, new growth on the hillsides ahead is evident. This is new growth from a twelve-year-old clearcut.

The Gifford Pinchot National Forest ranger station is in Packwood, on the left side of US 12. Even after hours, self-service registration for huckle-berry permits is available. Concessionaires manage many of the campgrounds and day-use facilities in the forest. Packwood, still 64 miles from the junc-tion with Interstate 5, has plenty of amenities for the traveler.

Continuing west on US 12, the office of the Randle Ranger District is located in Randle on the left just before the junction with Washington High-way 131. WA 131 is the "back door" route to Mount St. Helens, leading to the Windy Ridge Viewpoint. This road does not connect in any way with the western approach to Mount St. Helens, Washington Highway 504, so this is strictly an out-and-back option for the drive, about 20 miles each way. There are no interpretive centers on the way, and the scenic views do not compare well with those along WA 504 on the approach to Mount St. Helens from the west.

As you proceed on the drive west toward I-5, the countryside is de-voted to farming and logging. The Cowlitz River turned south with WA 131 back in Randle, and you won't see it again until WA 12 crosses a short stretch of it between Riffe and Mayfield lakes. This is still rugged country. Mud slides even cover the highway from time to time after heavy rains. But on a sunny day, the rolled alfalfa bales emit a wonderful scent.

As the drive nears Milepost 112 and Rainy Creek, the clearcuts are not as startling as the steepness of the logged hillsides. The national forest was left behind at Randle, so this is all private land. The clearcuts continue for several miles.

Both in and near small towns along this part of the drive, the yard sales appear to be perpetual. North of Morton is a large isolated section of the Mount Baker-Snoqualmie National Forest, a good example of the complexities of federal land administration. The forest is within the Randle Ranger District and is administered by the Gifford Pinchot National Forest. It is a very well-conserved piece of the Cascades.

Near Milepost 101, the last of the mountains on this drive lie ahead, nicely silhouetted in the evening dusk. Riffe Lake, created by Mossyrock Dam, is ahead on the left. It appears immense as the drive comes close to a corner of its northern shore. The drive follows the shore for a few miles until Mossyrock Dam. There are several fish hatcheries in the area, so lake fishing is supposed to be very good.

The Mossyrock Trout Hatchery is on Mayfield Lake ahead, to the right on Birley Road. On the Lake there are plenty of places for camping and boating. Mayfield Lake County Park is the easiest to reach, as the drive passes right by it 4 miles past the junction with WA 122. (WA 122 crosses the lake on the right, follows its northern shore, passes Ike Kinswa State Park, and rejoins US 12 several miles later.)

One mile after the county park, at Milepost 84, WA 12 crosses Mayfield Lake in a beautiful setting. Some fine views can be enjoyed across the span of the bridge.

Along the rest of the drive there are several private campgrounds and RV parks. Even though the mountains on the drive have now been left behind, this is still deer country, so be cautious on the highway during dim light. Approaching I-5, there is not the population density that you might expect. The number of businesses dedicated to travelers are on the increase, but the communities remain small and rural in nature.

20

Grand Coulee Dam Loop

General description: This 215-mile loop follows the Columbia River through the dry Columbia Plateau, visits at least 3 hydroelectric dams, traverses the Colville Indian Reservation, and returns to Chelan from Banks Lake over basalt-studded wheatlands.

Special attractions: Chief Joseph Dam, Grand Coulee Dam, Colville Cultural Center, Fort Okanogan, Colville Confederated Tribes Museum, hiking, fishing, camping, houseboating.

Location: North-central Washington.

Highway number: U.S. Highway 97 Alt., U.S. Highway 97, Washington Highway 173, Washington Highway 17, Washington Highway 155, U.S. Highway 2, Washington Highway 172, Mud Springs Road, McNeil Canyon Road, Washington Highway 150.

Travel season: The roads are open year-round.

Camping: Campgrounds dot the drive, notably near Omak and Coulee Dam. The best are Steamboat Rock and Sun Lakes state parks, just below Dry Falls.

Services: Full traveler services are available in Chelan and the town of Coulee Dam. The Four Winds Guest House in Coulee Dam was a workers' dormitory during dam construction days and is the last of the government-built homes still open to the public.

For more information: Brewster Chamber of Commerce, Bridgeport Visitor Information Center, Chief Joseph Dam Visitor Center, Colville Confederated Tribes, Grand Coulee Dam Area Chamber of Commerce, Grand Coulee Dam Visitor Arrival Center, National Park Service, Omak Visitor Information Center, Fort Okanogan State Park, Roosevelt Recreational Enterprises (see Appendix A).

 The drive

Begin the drive by taking U.S. Highway 97 Alt. north out of Chelan for 4 miles to US 97, and turn north along the Columbia River. Look into the skies southeast across the river. There may be hang gliders soaring in the air. They take off from 3,900-foot Chelan Butte, south of town, and have been known to soar for hours over the Channeled Scablands that this drive traverses. Competitions and championships are held here in the summer.

This part of the drive is also an official part of two loop drives, the

Drive 20: Grand Coulee Dam Loop

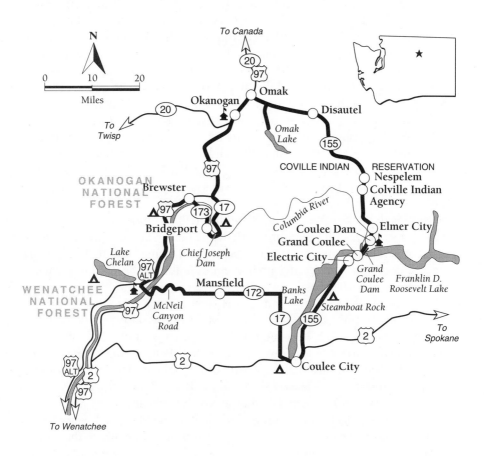

Cascade Loop that crosses the North Cascades and Stevens pass, and the International Loop that also crosses the North Cascades, then goes north into Canada and west across lower British Columbia.

The Chelan area is apple country, with orchards galore wherever irrigation water is available. There are a few apple sheds just out of town on the right. Large, refrigerated, humidity-controlled environments stall ripening until shipping time. Ahead are some stark basalt cliffs.

Exactly 2 miles out of downtown Chelan at Milepost 236, the view of the Columbia River is a feast for the eyes. The drive descends to meet the river and picks up US 97 north. Chelan Airport on the left is the end point for the triangular hang gliding competition course. Within view to the south is old Beebe Bridge over the river. This drive will return to Chelan over Beebe Bridge later.

Turn left onto US 97 north toward Pateros, Brewster, and Okanogan. Much of the land along the river here is occupied by apple orchards. The closer to the water they are planted, the easier they are to irrigate. Healthy apples need more than plentiful water and dry air, however. An immense orchard on the other side of the river, a few miles south, had such a serious soil problem that its million-dollar irrigation system did no good. There is a happy ending to the story, though: with water rights and irrigation gear in place, the area was turned into a golf course called Desert Canyon.

The drive now approaches Wells Dam on the right, the first of many dams on this drive. It has a fish ladder and a visitor center that is open daily. Just as with many other dams on the Columbia River, the retained waters behind the dam have the characteristics of a lake. This section of the Columbia is, in fact, called Lake Pateros, named after the town about 7 miles ahead, itself named for an island in the Philippines.

US 97 leaves the river for a little while before Pateros. Away from the water it is much more obvious that this terrain is an absolute desert. Some trees are within viewing range up in the mountains to the left, but the rest is little more than sagebrush and basalt.

At Milepost 253, an Okanogan Historical Society marker points out the remains of the China Ditch below. More than 100 years ago, Chinese gold miners dug the 5-mile-long ditch to sluice gold on Columbia River sandbars with Methow River water. Just before Pateros, sage honey is produced at a bee farm on the left. Washington Highway 153 enters from the left just before the bridge over the Methow River. The highway is a short-cut to Washington Highway 20 and the North Cascades Highway.

Pateros is nicely sited on the north side of the Methow River where it ploughs into the Columbia. For the next 6 miles to Brewster the road is nearly straight. The land ahead looks mighty flat. Apple orchards blanket both sides of the highway.

Indian Dan Canyon Road meets US 97 at Milepost 258. The road winds for miles through the Indian Dan Wildlife Area and into the Okanogan National Forest.

It is worth noting that the town of Brewster is the second of the Quad Cities (after Pateros) that this drive passes through. The third is Bridgeport, just before Chief Joseph Dam, and the fourth is Mansfield, 17 miles due south of the dam, in the middle of what you might call "nowhere."

Most of Brewster lies on a mile-wide peninsula that juts into Lake Pateros. From US 97, look for the right turn onto Washington Highway 173. It passes through the center of town to a bridge that crosses the Columbia River/Pateros Lake. At the south end of the bridge, WA 173 turns north while still about 100 feet above the river. The view back over the river is

Salmon caught below Chief Joseph Dam.

wonderful. The river is more than 1.5 miles wide, but from this perspective it looks like a swim across wouldn't be too tough on a hot summer day.

The drive cuts southwest between Rocky Butte on the right and the Wells Wildlife Area on Bridgeport Bar to the left. Straight ahead some wooded but dusty looking hillsides come into view. Within 1 mile the road parallels the river heading into Bridgeport. On the way, a community of automotive junkyards divides the horse pastures and young apple orchards.

Washington apple growers are trying to catch up with the tastes of the American people who might prefer Australian apples and a number of others with more fruity tastes. The usual standbys, like red delicious and golden delicious, just don't meet market demand anymore. As a result, farmers are planting new orchards and grafting a number of new apple varieties to older trees.

Brewster and Chief Joseph Dam are just ahead. A road sign suggests tuning in 1610 AM on the radio for information about the dam. Once through town, at the junction with Washington Highway 17, turn left toward Okanogan. WA 17 crosses the Columbia River Bridge and arrives on the Colville Indian Reservation. Turn right at the signs for Okanogan County State Park, Chief Joseph Dam Visitor Information Center, and Chief Joseph Dam.

The dam is named for the famed leader of the Willowla band of the Nez Perce Indian tribe. Chief Joseph was both an astute military strategist and a peacemaker in the early days of the Pacific Northwest. Chief Joseph is buried in Nespelem on the Colville Indian Reservation, about 35 miles east of the dam.

Visitor parking is right on top of the dam itself, and the views over each side are good. There are usually people fishing for salmon below. Indians may fish below the spillway because the dam inundated their traditional fishing grounds. Look over the upwater side and there may be about a dozen fish holding steady against the current, headed toward the spillway. They park for awhile in the shelter of the rocks. No fishing is allowed on this side of the dam. This 51-mile, upriver stretch of the Columbia is called Rufus Woods Lake.

The U.S. Army Corps of Engineers capitalized on the unusual dimensions of the bedrock below to construct the dam in the shape of the letter L. First built in 1956, it was enlarged and doubled in power-producing capacity in 1981. Chief Joseph Dam is the second largest hydroelectric dam in the country. Its electrical power goes to a nearby Bonneville Power Administration switchyard for distribution to public and private utilities.

Tours of the visitor center are self-guided, starting with a walk inside through the spillway. A public boat ramp is located 1 mile upstream from the dam on the south shore of the lake.

Coming back off the dam, a right turn leads to Bridgeport State Park, 2 miles away. The park is a very nice underused campground above Rufus Woods Lake. It has a swimming beach and an adjacent nine-hole golf course.

A left turn coming back off the dam leads to a junction with WA 17. Take WA 17 north toward Chief Joseph and Fort Okanogan state parks. For the next 88 miles the drive is on the Colville Indian Reservation, 1.3 million acres of mostly open range lands. At the top of the hill is a good line-of-sight view of Bridgeport to the left across the river.

The drive parallels the river, but much of its view is blocked because of the depth of the gorge and the height of the buttes rising above it. There are orchards in narrow strings along terraces on the left side. Beyond, snow is visible on the mountains even into August.

The Fort Okanogan Interpretive Center is on the left just before the junction with US 97. It was originally built from river driftwood in 1810 as a fur-trading station. Open in summer only, the center's hours are 10 A.M. to 6 P.M. Wednesday through Sunday.

At the junction with US 97, turn right. The drive will run alongside the Okanogan River for 21 miles to the town of Omak. This is a broader, flatter valley than the Columbia's, affording more room for farming. Within a few miles the drive gets into hay country, and soon the road is surrounded by ponderosa pines. This has a bit of the feel of a subalpine forest, but the elevation is only 900 feet. The pine forest seems to go for miles.

The Cascade Mountains are off to the left (the drive meets WA 20, the North Cascades Highway 5 miles before Omak). To the right is Soap Lake Mountain beyond which is, of course, Soap Lake, not to be confused with the other, larger Soap Lake 57 miles south. But there are at least a hundred small lakes beyond that one, some of them simply numbered, that are remnants of the Ice Age floods. They are also called the Missoula Floods, and they created the braided river Channeled Scablands that cover three-quarters of eastern Washington.

The floods numbered between forty and eighty-nine, occured on an average of once every fifty-five years, and lasted maybe two days to two

Chief Joseph Dam.

weeks each. One of the floods contained 500 cubic miles of water that was locked behind a glacial ice dam until the ice lost its grip and floated. This particular torrent ran wild through the Idaho panhandle, the Spokane River Valley, and most of eastern Washington. Grand Coulee is the largest of the channels resulting from the deluge. It is 50 miles long, 1 to 5 miles wide, and 900 feet deep. The Columbia River eventually resumed its original course westward along the northern rim of the plateau to the North Cascades before heading south. Many of the floodways dried up, leaving behind dry coulees with sheer walls of exposed layers of basalt. Some of the deeper basins continued to hold water and became lakes just like Soap Lake.

WA 20 joins WA 17 for the last 5 miles into Omak, home of the annual Omak Stampede and Suicide Race. The three-day event is a sanctioned rodeo with a twist: a horse race that includes a very steep descent into the Okanogan River and a swim across to the finish line in the rodeo grounds. This event has been going on for sixty years and now attracts thirty thousand people.

Coming into Omak, turn left onto Washington Highway 155 south, following the sign to Omak and Grand Coulee Dam. (The drive stays on WA 155 all the way to Coulee City at the southern end of Banks Lake.) At the first stop sign you'll see the rodeo grounds, and in front of that, the Omak Visitor Information Center. The center has one of the best selections of travel brochures in Washington. The variety covers all regions of the state, as well as Alberta and British Columbia.

Continuing the drive, go south toward Grand Coulee Dam on WA 155. The highway climbs up out of the river valley onto the plateau. Great upthrusts of rock loom on the left, looking like basalt columns stacked on top of each other.

A historical marker on the right discusses Saint Mary's Mission, 2 miles off the highway. The gate here is closed, but the main access road is just ahead.

According to the legend, in 1866 Chief Smitkin invited a French nobleman turned priest to establish Saint Mary's Mission. From a single log cabin, it grew into a junior college that served as a religious and cultural center for the region. Today it is a school for Native American children through grade eight. Saint Mary's is the last boarding school of its kind in the state.

A side trip to see the mission and school will provide some off-the-highway images that will not soon be forgotten. The drive to the mission is like a step back into another time, down a narrow paved lane, through pastoral fields, and beyond into a channeled canyon following No Name Creek to 7-mile-long Omak Lake. It is the largest body of water between Soap Lake Mountain and the forested mountains through which the drive later passes on WA 155.

Turn right from WA 155 onto the access road to Saint Mary's Mission.

The road is marked by an official green and white sign for the mission and the Paschal Sherman Indian School. Layer upon layer of basalt, sort of like huge terraces, appear amidst meadows as the drive winds slowly through groves of trees, past corrals and a stock-loading pen on the right. Get out your camera. Keep left for the mission and school. A granite marker in front of the church reads "Saint Mary's Mission Centennial 1886-1986."

The mission school is something to see, but it's not beautiful. The facilities consist of a collection of brick buildings, trailers, and an odd-looking church. School buses galore and double-wide trailers dot the scene. The setting, however, is quite beautiful.

After leaving Saint Mary's, turn left and continue down the road that goes past the mission through a bucolic green valley. At each side of this valley of No Name Creek, giant basalt rocks stand upright in great piles. This is a wondrous sight.

The winding road, sometimes two-lane, sometimes one, but all of it well-paved, continues down the valley that ranges from 0.25- to 0.5-mile wide. This looks like some of the narrower portions of the road down Baja California, and like some of the desert country in Southern California and the high Sierras.

Ponderosa pine grows in abundance here, and there is a whole grove of birch trees. Eventually you come to Omak Lake. The picnic facilities and camping area, according to a weathered sign, are for tribal members, their families, and invited guests only.

Out on WA 155 again, after the lake, the drive leaves French Valley behind as it climbs from 1,000 to 2,000 feet in elevation. There are big blocks of rocks everywhere. It looks like Earthquake Point down on Washington 97 between Chelan and Wenatchee. From here the drive descends rather rapidly through a well-forested narrow valley. This is a great drive for a sports car. There appears to be a beaver swamp on the right.

The road isn't particularly exciting, but the scenery is gorgeous. Tree stands dot both sides of the road on occasion. There are absolutely no signboards, no businesses, no towns, just the occasional ranch. No services abound for tens of miles. One business, the Bear's Den Eats, looks permanently closed.

Near Milepost 46, there is a huge hayfield on the right with those giant bales rolled up and waiting for pickup. The hillsides are brownish again with clumps of trees. The right side of the highway is still pretty wooded. Crosses dot the roadsides where people have died.

Coming out of Coyote Canyon, the drive meets the Nespelem River and the town of Nespelem. This is where Chief Joseph and some of his Nez Perce tribe spent their last years, confined to the Colville Reservation. Chief Joseph is buried north of Nespelem and there is a memorial to him along the highway.

Eleven tribal groups that were relocated here eventually formed the Colville Confederated Tribes, headquartered at the Colville Indian Agency 2 miles south of Nespelem. Colville Agency is the location of Colville Confederated Industries, the tribal business arm. The big moneymaker is the rental of forty houseboats on Roosevelt Lake, under permit from the National Park Service. The boats, both 46- and 52-footers, sleep 10 to 13 people and are normally rented for a week at a time. The Keller Ferry Marina, where they're docked, is just a few miles from Grand Coulee Dam.

The houseboats are fully outfitted with a kitchen, baths, a generous living room, and a full upper deck. The attractions include fishing, water skiing, swimming, and scuba diving in the Spokane River Arm, as well as plain old sightseeing along the 630 miles of public coastline of Washington's largest lake. There are plenty of bears, deer, and cows on the sandy beaches.

The drive continues south from Indian Agency on WA 155 and after about 8 miles meets up with the Columbia River. It goes along the shoreline through Seatons Grove, Koontzville, and Elmer to the town of Coulee Dam.

Just south of town, and before Grand Coulee Dam, WA 155 crosses the Columbia and goes right by the dam's Visitor Arrival Center. And there it is, one of the largest concrete structures in the world: Grand Coulee Dam. The dam is nearly 1 mile long and as tall as a 46-story building. There are

Silos near Mansfield.

both guided and self-guided tours offered, including a ride down the face of the dam in a glass-enclosed elevator, designed to access the powerhouses inside. Every evening, from Memorial Day through September, the world's largest laser light show is projected onto the dam's spillway. People watch from the park grounds below, and many make a picnic dinner of it.

Beyond the town of Coulee Dam and Grand Coulee Dam itself in the Coulee Dam National Recreation Area, the drive continues south on WA 155 to the town of Grand Coulee, and then, Electric City. These towns sprouted to house dam construction workers, and many of them continued to prosper after the dam was built.

A few miles south of Electric City, the drive adjoins the eastern shore of Banks Lake, which is actually a 26-mile-long reservoir, dammed to store irrigation water from the Columbia. The 27,000-acre lake is also a wildlife preserve. Steamboat Rock State Park, 13 miles from Coulee Dam, has 2 bald eagle roosts up on the butte, 700 feet above Banks Lake. At last count there were 4 or 5 eggs in one of the roosts. The park also has American white pelicans, one of our largest and most spectacular birds, according to John James Audubon. Keep an eye out for bobcats, cougars, and rattlesnakes. Steamboat is one of twelve state parks that requires advance reservations. There are no drop-in sites except for a boat-in tent area inaccessible by car. There is a large day-use area.

Toward the southern end of Banks Lake, WA 155 picks up U.S. Highway 2 and stays with it for 6 miles through 100-year-old Coulee City. Gas, restaurants, and motels are available at Coulee City. The drive crosses the top of Dry Falls Dam, which holds back Banks Lake. The feel is a bit like driving on the Evergreen Floating Bridge to Seattle, but here there is a desert on one side. As a possible side excursion, 2 miles south on WA 17 (at Dry Falls Junction at the west end of the dam) is Dry Falls and an interpretive center. It has quite a good display. The National Natural Landmark distinction honors this former cascading channel of the Columbia. The falls (they really are dry) are 3.5 miles wide and 400 feet from top to bottom.

To continue the drive, go west on WA 155/US 2 from Dry Falls Junction for less than 1 mile and turn north on WA 17, also called Leahy Road South. The highest elevations on the drive from here on are some knobs and piles of basalt. This is a plateau with little lakes, draws, coulees, and canyons channeled into the flat wheatlands between Banks Lake and the section of the Columbia River where the drive began.

Continue north on WA 17 for 14 miles. The road climbs again, to a little over 2,000 feet. Electrical transmission lines come from the right. There is plenty of sagebrush, and cactus might be expected, but not found. Little rolling hillsides seem to go forever in all directions. After Milepost 112 turn left (west) on Washington Highway 172 to Mansfield. Continue straight for

21 miles. These roads are unbelievably straight, except for the occasional deviation around a tiny lake.

Scattered at random in the fields on both sides of the highway are piles of rocks. Where there may have been one sticking out of the ground originally, farmers made a pile as more rocks were unearthed. If the light is right, along toward sunset, silhouettes of the Cascade Mountains come into view.

It seems the basalt rocks get bigger as the drive continues west. Volkswagen-sized, yurt-sized, haystack-sized, there are two or three per acre. How big can they get? There is one, right at the edge of the road, as big as a two-and-a-half-story house. Another rock is bigger by three times than the house it sits next to.

The drive passes through the town of Mansfield, zigging and zagging. While wondering what economic pressures could have brought apartment houses to a little town up on the plateau, don't neglect to turn right for WA 172 west, following the sign for Chelan.

When WA 172 turns south, about 8 miles west of Mansfield, continue straight for 0.25 mile and turn right. Drive north for 1 mile and turn left (west) on Mud Springs Road for 2.2 miles. Turn right on McNeil Canyon Road and follow it nearly 9 extraordinarily scenic miles to the Columbia River. Lake Chelan is visible from the canyon. The lake is at 1,200 feet elevation, and this plateau peaks at 3,000 feet.

McNeil Canyon Road will parallel the Columbia River south for about 1 mile. When it intersects with US 97, take it across the Beebe Bridge to Washington Highway 150. Take WA 150 past Chelan Falls and up to its junction with US 97 A and left into Chelan.

21

Chelan to Leavenworth

General description: This 62-mile drive follows along the south shore of Lake Chelan to Lake Chelan State Park, takes Navarre Coulee around Bear Mountain, follows the Columbia River to Wenatchee, and turns west along the Wenatchee River to Leavenworth.

Special attractions: Entiat Wildlife Area, horseback riding, fishing, hiking, river rafting.

Location: Central Washington.

Highway number: U.S. Highway 97 Alt., Washington Highway 971, U.S. Highway 2/U.S. Highway 97.

Travel season: The road is open year-round.

Camping: Lakeshore RV Park (Chelan), Lake Chelan State Park, Entiat City Park.

Services: Complete traveler services are available in Chelan, Wenatchee, and Leavenworth.

For more information: Chelan Ranger District, Entiat Ranger District (Wenatchee National Forest), Lake Chelan Visitor Information Center, Entiat Valley Chamber of Commerce, Lakeshore RV Park, Washington State Apple Commission Visitor Center, Washington State Parks (see Appendix A).

 The drive

Begin the drive at the Chelan Ranger District offices on the lakeside road, West Woodin Avenue, (leaving downtown Chelan). The offices are just over the bridge on the right. From here, drive southwest a few more blocks to the junction with U.S. Highway 97 Alt. Turn right on US 97 Alt. The drive will stay along the shore for 10 miles until Lake Chelan State Park.

Lake Chelan is 52 square miles in area; quite a feat for a lake that is 51 miles long. The bottom of the glacier-carved lake is below sea level, and much of it is one-third of a mile deep. It is bordered on both sides by towering mountains. Like Hells Canyon, the peaks get higher farther uplake. You may see mountain goats and other wildlife. The lake is lowered in the winter to allow for spring runoff. Lake Chelan Dam was built in 1927, but even today during "low tide," tree stumps can be seen in orderly rows.

Drive 21: Chelan to Leavenworth

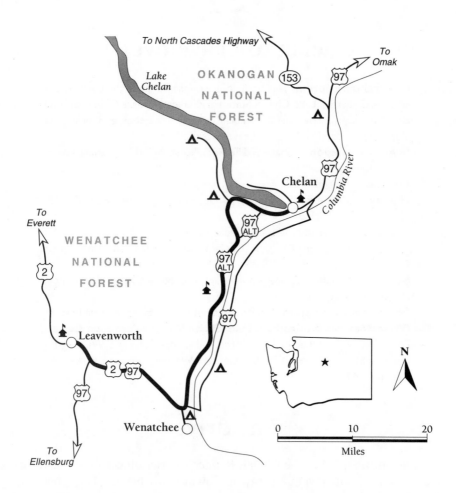

Along the drive you will see passenger ferries, "Ladies of the Lake," that serve the communities uplake. Stehekin, at the other end of the lake, is the primary destination, an easy contender for first prize among Pacific Northwest vacation sites. The only way to get there is to walk, boat, or fly.

"Stehekin is what America was" is how the one hundred residents think of their valley, originally homesteaded by many of their ancestors. The population is surrounded—some say inundated—by the Lake Chelan National Recreation Area. It is administered by the Park Service and has a visitor center and a large staff to deal with the swell of summer tourism.

Looking up and away from the lake above the highway, Chelan Butte is over the rise. The Chelan Butte Wildlife Recreation Area extends south for 4 to 5 miles to the Columbia River. Hang gliding competitions begin on the butte, triangulate over the Columbia Plateau, and end at the Chelan Airport. In the early 1990s, some hoped to annex part of the butte and build an alpine ski area. Too many agencies needed to swap too many parcels of land for the scheme to work.

After 3 miles, the drive parallels the shore. Looking over the lake, you get an idea of how serious a vacation setting Chelan has become. Condos and houses have sprouted around this end of the lake in recent years, and the number of people on the water has increased dramatically. During the summer there is a constant traffic of boats, jet skis, and sea planes.

When US 97 Alt. turns left to go up the Knapp Coulee, continue straight onto Washington Highway 971, following the signs for the recreation area, Lake Chelan State Park, and Twenty-five Mile Creek. Soon the cliffs and slopes on the left will become very steep. Signs of the 1994 fires can be seen up high ahead. Brown trees are visible on Bear Mountain on the left. The fire generated enough heat and flame to kill the trees, but they weren't consumed. There was a cross-country ski area there until fire destroyed the facilities.

The fire stemmed from three days in July of 1994, when over 10,500 lightning strikes slammed down in Washington and Oregon. They started more than 750 forest fires. The same storms maintained their northeastward course, touching off fires in Idaho, Montana, British Columbia, and Alberta. In Chelan County, which includes the Chelan and Leavenworth ranger districts, there were four major fires that burned 170,000 acres in two weeks.

The drive passes lots of slide areas on the left. Trees growing in the gullies suggest that the slides are not regular events.

Milepost 11 is a good place to pull off and enjoy the water. This is one of the wide spots on the road with signs that warn of falling rock. Sheer rock walls go straight up. Wapato Point across the lake is visible from here.

For a look at Lake Chelan State Park, pass the first turnoff for WA 971 that heads up into the mountains. The park is just ahead on the right. It is a popular vacation spot for people from all around the state. The long shoreline affords many campsites close to the water. It has a good swimming beach and plenty of boat launching facilities.

Back on WA 971, the drive traverses Navarre Coulee and passes south of Bear Mountain. The road ascends through green forests and orchards, and the views of the lake are terrific. The climb is steep as it enters the Entiat Wildlife Recreation Area. The recreation area extends in a 15-mile semicircle shaped by the Columbia River and about 5 miles inland.

The drive leaves the lake behind to become Navarre Coulee Road (as

Lady of the Lake II *heading to Chelan from Stehekin on Lake Chelan.*

WA 971 is called here) and enters some scenic terrain. There are healthy trees here, close to the road, but some fire damage is visible up on the bluffs.

This is a nice coulee, lined by tall trees and tall mountains on both sides. There are some isolated ranches and housing, plus trailers for summer vacations. At one point there is obvious fire damage down to the road, but the grasses have returned. The damage is spotty, sometimes on the left of the road, sometimes on the right.

By Milepost 2, the Columbia River valley is visible ahead. Within sight are immense irrigated orchards and faraway buttes, but there is fire damage here on both sides of the highway. From Milepost 1, the drive descends steeply to the valley and US 97 Alt.

At the intersection turn right (south) on US 97 Alt. toward Wenatchee. The railroad tracks that parallel the river are used for seasonal fruit hauling. They follow the course of the river, which is sheer rock on this side and orchards on the other.

Shortly after Byrd Canyon, the Ribbon Cliffs begin. They continue for almost 3 miles, where they culminate in Earthquake Point. Beyond the point the cliffs are well away from the highway, but they line the drive again after the Entiat River. Here, big boulders sit at the edge of the road to stop slides.

Earthquake Point is so named because of an immense earthquake here in 1872. A historical marker at the site explains what happened. A rockslide actually stopped the Columbia River's flow for several hours. Promontories of rock from the earthquake jut into the river and look like tree-covered islands. In 1995, some vehicles that were parked in a gravel pit up ahead were covered by a rockslide.

The drive enters Entiat at Milepost 217. The town has a very nice park on the river for day use. The cliffs to the right show some interesting bands of white on the black rock. Up the Entiat Valley just past town are the Entiat National Fish Hatchery, Entiat River Recreation Area, and the Glacier Peak Wilderness Area.

The Columbia River here is more properly called Lake Entiat. It is formed by Rocky Reach Dam, which the drive passes ahead. The dam has a very good visitor center and plenty of lawn for lounging around. At the entrance near the highway, look for rabbits. Travelers feed them lettuce; this seems to be a favorite pastime for both rabbits and people.

Ahead on US 97 Alt., Ohme Gardens sits up on a rocky bluff overlooking the Columbia. It is 3 miles north of Wenatchee. The turnoff for Ohme Gardens comes just after where U.S. Highway 2 and US 97 cross the Columbia River and become US 97 Alt. Make sure to keep to the right and follow the signs for US 2 and US 97 west toward Leavenworth and Seattle.

Just off the highway, at 2900 Euclid Avenue, is a visitor information center run by the Washington State Apple Commission. The interpretive displays are good, and you can sample an apple and a can of apple juice. A close inspection of the can's label will reveal how much of the juice is from New Zealand apples.

As you head west on US 2/US 97, snow on the Cascade mountain peaks ahead may be visible into August. The drive is in the Wenatchee River Valley, with its rich green growth and fruit orchards. The growth is more lush here than in the Columbia Valley; there is a lot more moisture here.

Wenatchee River County Park is on the left 5 miles before Cashmere. It is located right on the river, with picnic grounds and camping facilities. Wenatchee River rafters and floaters leave the river at this park. The RV grounds rarely appear full.

Cashmere was first known as Mission, after the Catholic mission built here in 1863. In 1903 it took the name of India's Vale of Kashmir, to emphasize its fertility. As if it needed emphasis. The whole Wenatchee Valley is a fruit garden.

Four miles beyond Cashmere is Peshastin Pinnacles State Park, on the right side of the highway. It is indicated by a sign with a logo of a rock climber. This is a popular spot for sport climbers because of the 200-foot sandstone spires that give rock climbers a good workout. There are also 1.6 miles of good hiking trail in this day-use park.

The highway crosses the Wenatchee River just before Dryden, at Milepost 107, and there are orchards on both sides of the drive. Dryden centers

Cherries growing near Lake Chelan.

on apple and other fruit production. Packing and storage sheds line the railroad tracks.

US 97 will shortly turn left toward Cle Elum and Ellensburg. This is the road over Blewett Pass (see Drive 16), an alternate winter route to Seattle. This description stays on US 2 west, to Leavenworth.

As you near Leavenworth, the Wenatchee Valley narrows, leaving the fruit orchards behind. Leavenworth thrives on tourism. Nearly every weekend, in downtown City Park, you will find one or more arts and crafts shows, concerts in the gazebo, storytellers, and strolling musicians.

22

Sherman Pass Loop

General description: This 193-mile loop twice crosses Roosevelt Lake (Columbia River) on small ferries, then travels through the Colville Indian Reservation range and forest lands and the highest mountain pass (5,575 feet) that is open year-round in Washington, after which it closely follows the shore of Roosevelt Lake for 70 miles.

Special attractions: Fort Spokane, Franklin D. Roosevelt Lake, Colville Indian Reservation, Sherman Pass, Eocene fossil beds, Spokane Indian Reservation.

Location: Northeastern Washington.

Highway number: Washington Highway 21, Washington Highway 20, Inchelium-Kettle Falls Road, Washington Highway 25, Miles-Creston Road, Bachelor Drive, U.S. Highway 2.

Travel season: The road is open year-round.

Camping: There are Park Service campgrounds on Roosevelt Lake and two Forest Service campgrounds.

Services: Full traveler services are available in Republic and Kettle Falls.

For more information: National Park Service Headquarters (Coulee Dam National Recreation Area), Colville National Forest, Kettle Falls Ranger District, Republic Ranger District, Stonerose Interpretive Center, Republic Visitor Information Center, Republic Area Chamber of Commerce, Fort Spokane (see Appendix A).

 The drive

The town of Wilbur is on U.S. Highway 2 between Spokane and Coulee City. It is easily reached via Washington Highway 174, 19 miles southwest of Grand Coulee Dam. Begin the drive at Wilbur and head north on Washington Highway 21 toward Roosevelt lake.

Here on the south side of Roosevelt Lake, away from the reservation, there are no trees. Everything is sagebrush range with little coulees, big coulees, and bumpy hills. This is a very dry environment, much like the Palouse southeast toward Oregon and Idaho. The drive crosses a dozen miles of rolling wheatfields and then descends steep bluffs to Roosevelt Lake.

There is a big RV park just above Keller's Ferry, where gas and groceries are available. Nearby is a Park Service campground. The Keller Ferry

Drive 22: Sherman Pass Loop

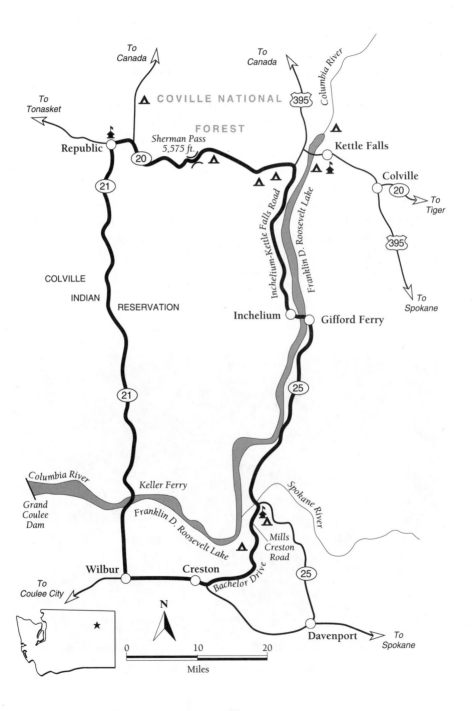

To Canada

To Canada

Columbia River

To Tonasket

COVILLE NATIONAL

FOREST

395

Republic

Sherman Pass
5,575 ft.

Kettle Falls

20

Colville

21

20

Inchelium-Kettle Falls Road

Franklin D. Roosevelt Lake

To Tiger

395

COLVILLE

INDIAN

RESERVATION

Inchelium

Gifford Ferry

To Spokane

21

25

Columbia River

Keller Ferry

Spokane River

Grand Coulee Dam

Franklin D. Roosevelt Lake

Mills Creston Road

To Coulee City

Wilbur

Creston

Bachelor Drive

25

N

Davenport

To Spokane

0   10   20

Miles

Marina here sees four thousand people a day on a busy weekend. This is the place to rent a houseboat.

The ferry crossing on Lake Roosevelt, one of the few free ones in Washington, takes about ten minutes. The vessel, the *Martha S.*, has been operating here since 1948. It is the only Washington State Department of Transportation ferry that does not operate on Puget Sound. This lake, actually a section of the Columbia River, has 630 miles of public shoreline. There are plenty of bears, deer, and cows on the sandy beaches.

From the ferry landing the drive travels 10 miles along a north-south extension of Lake Roosevelt, which is actually the Sanpoil River, and then 53 more miles of rangeland to Republic. The highway follows the course of the Sanpoil River north across the Colville Indian Reservation and passes small farmsteads, grazing cattle, and stands of ponderosa pine. Where the valley narrows it becomes thick with pine, cottonwood, and larch trees.

The landscape on this section of the Colville Indian Reservation is entirely different from the Colville road in Drive 20. This is all forested, with scrub trees and very tall pines right along the edge of the lake. The town of Keller, 10 miles from the landing, is very small. But it does have its own post office. Three miles past Keller, Brush Creek comes in from the left to join the Sanpoil.

Just above the little horse ranch at Milepost 96 on the right side of the

Free Gifford–Inchelium Ferry across Roosevelt Lake.

river, a huge rock looms. It looks just like a giant bullfrog and is about the size of a couple of houses.

A few road signs caution that you are traveling through open range-land, and the warning should be heeded. There are occasional groups of unfenced bovines munching at the side of the road. Once in a while the drive passes a crossroad, a house, or a ranch. The small amount of traffic serves to remind you just how sparsely populated some vast areas of the West are.

The drive passes between steep canyon walls with trees growing all the way up to the top. The Sanpoil River stays with the drive nearly to Republic. A terrific climbing rock thrusts up on the right at Milepost 121. This rock might well be named the Colville Chief, in honor of the Stawamus Chief on the coast of British Columbia. This one is about one-third the size, however, and there are no climbers on it; at least, not yet.

About 2 miles after crossing the West Fork of the Sanpoil River, the drive leaves the reservation and enters the Colville National Forest. This is just after the Thirteen-Mile trailhead access.

The canyon narrows and truck-size boulders of chunky columnar basalt can be seen scrambled all alongside the river. Just before Republic, the valley broadens out a little. There is now some actual farmland in addition to all the ranch land. Occasional deer nibble in the pastures. Other animals in the Colville National Forest include black bears, coyotes, squirrels, chipmunks, cougars, bobcats, lynx, and pine martens. Birds species include three-toed woodpeckers, great-horned owls, and mountain bluebirds.

At the southern end of Republic, WA 21 joins Washington Highway 20 and turns right. But proceed straight ahead on Clark Avenue into town for an interesting stop. Republic sits on the bottom of a 50-million-year-old lake bed. It is rich in Eocene fossils of fish, insects, and plants. Travelers are welcome to try their hand at a surface dig. The Stonerose Interpretive Center, in an old house at 15 North Kean Street across from Patterson Park, offers advice, samples for sale, rental tools, and tours of the site at the edge of town. One recent visitor unearthed a chip of dawn redwood metasequoia, today found only in China. She was allowed to keep the 48-million-year-old sample.

Republic began as Eureka in 1885, due to gold mining in the area. Two active gold mines remain, and the local weekly newspaper prints the prices of gold and silver at the top of the front page. One thousand bicyclists pedal through Republic every season on the cross-country BikeCentennial Trail, some in groups of fifty or a hundred. The highlight of this leg of their trek is Sherman Pass, which, at 5,575 feet, is the highest mountain pass in Washington that is open year-round.

Take WA 20/WA 21 east from Republic and pass the Eastside RV Park on the right. The 35 miles between Republic and Kettle Falls is a Forest Service scenic drive called the Sherman Pass Scenic Byway. Attractions along the way include horse and wagon trails, camping most anywhere, hiking, mountain biking, fall foliage touring in late October, and huckleberry picking. The Republic Ranger District is planning a year-round, hut-to-hut system for skiers, bikers, and hikers.

The scenic byway route over the pass was first used by the San Poil Indians who traveled to Kettle Falls to fish. By the twentieth century it was a wagon road. For more than fifty years it was heavily used by miners and, later, loggers. It was finally paved in 1954.

After nearly 3 miles, WA 20 and WA 21 split. Stay on WA 20 as it turns south on its way to Kettle Falls. Eight miles from Republic, the highway enters the Colville National Forest and climbs through ponderosa pine, Douglas-fir, and larch. Ninebark and oceanspray grow on the hotter south-facing slopes.

This is a winding road, nestled among the trees. Once in a while a deer will gracefully hop across the road and over a fence. There are occasional open pastures, which allow a view of rounded, forested peaks in the distance.

The drive is soon at 4,000 feet, where 20,000 acres of forest were burned in 1988 by lightning strikes. The damage is visible up to the right, where you can see stark 30-foot tree stumps with no branches on them. A blanket of grass grows underneath. This terrain is similar to that north of Sandpoint on the Idaho Panhandle. The Sundance fire there burned so hot (2,200 degrees!) that it burned the soil two feet deep. Grass is still the only plant that will grow there.

This burned area goes on for 7 miles. There is little variety in the landscape, just tall trees with no green about them, covering entire mountainsides. After awhile the fire damage is visible on both sides of the road.

A mile from the 1988 White Mountain burn area, the top of Sherman Pass has an entrance to the Kettle Crest National Recreation Trail. Take the dirt road on the left for about an eighth of a mile. The lot is for people using the trail, so they don't have to leave their cars parked and vulnerable on the highway. There is a car-only campground and several hitching posts for horses. The scenic trail is a short, ten-minute walk, which leads to vistas of surrounding peaks as well as a look into how fire helped shape the landscape. Sherman Pass Campground is near Sherman Overlook, just east of the pass.

As you head down the east side of the pass, WA 20 passes through even more verdant tree stands. But in the height of the summer travel season, the campgrounds and historic sights are nearly empty. The Canyon Creek Campground is also a historic site and is located on the right where

Fort Spokane.

Canyon Creek flows into Sherman Creek. There are not many services here (one big hand-operated water pump serves for all), but the creekside setting is peaceful. This is also the Log Flume Interpretive Area, known as Camp 5 in earlier days of intensive commercial logging. From this point, and running 5 miles to the Columbia River, workers built a wooden flume that used water to flush logs from the woods to a large sawmill. A delightfully informative 0.5-mile-long interpretive flume trail winds from camp through the woods to Sherman Creek.

Continuing east, the drive turns south in about 3.5 miles onto Inchelium-Kettle Falls Road. WA 20 continues past the turnoff for 7 miles to Kettle Falls, but this drive leads to Inchelium on the Colville Indian Reservation side of the Columbia. At the turnoff, the road crosses Sherman Creek and parallels it for about 1 mile. The drive is still in the Colville National Forest, and the Sherman Creek Campground is located where the creek meets the Columbia. Fewer than 2 miles ahead on Inchelium-Kettle Falls Rd., Haag Cove Campground is also beside the river.

The drive turns inland from the cove for about 3 miles of gentle curves through forest. Below Staehly Mountain it leaves the national forest and enters the Colville Indian Reservation. The setting is rural in the extreme, pristine actually, as the drive continues south along the west shore of Roosevelt Lake. Elevation here is 2,000 feet.

The town of Inchelium is a sub-Indian Agency. It has a gas station and a post office and is 3 miles from the next ferry crossing. Follow signs to the Gifford–Inchelium Ferry, leaving town on the Inchelium–Covada Road. In less than 1 mile turn left, following the sign for the ferry.

The free ferry makes a round-trip every half hour beginning at 6:30 A.M. The last run of the day to Gifford is at 10:30 P.M. There are rest rooms on both sides of the crossing. While waiting for the ferry on a hot day, stand in the water to cool off your feet and take some pictures of the incoming ferry and the beautiful vista beyond.

Upon arriving on the eastern side of the Columbia, turn south on Washington Highway 25. The road hugs the shoreline, offering a good chance to look out over the river. After several miles, the drive pulls away from the river and climbs to a plateau of golden hay fields. The plateau is actually more of a big ledge, with rocks and forests above. The river seems far away, down to the right. The drive stays high for the next 20 miles, until it crosses the Spokane River at Fort Spokane. Visible across the river are great white cliffs that appear to break straight down to the water's edge.

Near the town of Hunters, there is a campground. Just follow the sign 1 mile to the left from town.

The town of Fruitland, 3 miles ahead on WA 25, has gas, groceries, and a post office. The towns and countryside on this side of the river lend

Franklin D. Roosevelt Lake.

the impression that a lot more people used to live here than do now. The next town, Enterprise, has a nice grange, but cows are the only population left.

Just after Enterprise, the drive enters the Spokane Indian Reservation. As on the Colville Reservation, this is unfenced cattle rangeland. There is also the occasional bee farm and horse ranch, plus stands of pine. For several miles the road goes straight as an arrow. This plateau reaches 2,300 feet elevation before it descends for 4 miles to Lake Roosevelt again.

On this, the reservation side of the lake, two magnificent sculptures of Indian warriors announce the Two Rivers commercial area. Here there is an RV park, rental houseboat marina, and the Two Rivers Casino.

This is also where the Spokane River flows into Lake Roosevelt. The drive leaves the Spokane Reservation and crosses the river into Lincoln County. On the other side there is a nice park on the right and a campground on the left.

This is Fort Spokane, part of the Coulee Dam National Recreation Area. There is a visitor center, but very little is left of the fort. The army abandoned it in 1898, and then it was used by the Spokane Tribe until 1929. What was left after years of fires and vandalism was either sold or moved to the Indian Agency at Nespelem.

Just past Fort Spokane on WA 25, the drive turns right onto Miles-Creston Road. Creston is about 17 miles from this intersection. The view from above, opposite the Two Rivers Ranch, takes in the river and lake with swarms of boats going in all directions.

The drive passes houses and farms along this section above Roosevelt Lake. As you drive along the ledge about 500 feet above the water, the views seem to extend for miles. As the road twists and climbs, the lava rocks alongside appear as if they had been poured out of the side of the hill. Past the turnoff for the Seven Bays Airport and Marina, there are big basaltic upthrusts straight ahead. The beauty of the scene here, with these haystack rocks, rivals the drive through the Yakima Canyon (Drive 18).

Past the Hawk Creek Campground on the right and the sheer rock wall, there are signs posted on the wooded area to the left that say, "Feel free to hunt." Now *that's* posted!

The drive levels off in wheat country above 2,000 feet. It started as the Miles-Creston Rd., continued through Olsen Canyon, and is now Bachelor Drive, as it crosses the Bachelor Prairie and joins US 2 about 2 miles before Creston.

At US 2, turn right toward Creston, Wilbur, and Wenatchee. In Creston, find Deb's on the left, a cowboy bar and restaurant formerly owned by a 1950s rodeo star who lives down the street. The espresso sign across from Deb's can be translated to read, "Welcome Seattleites." US 2 is a favored scenic route east to Spokane for people who have the time to avoid the interstate and drive through communities where folks still hang their laundry out on the line to dry.

Unlike the Palouse, with its dry land wheat farming, the fields on this plateau are all irrigated. Between Creston and Wilbur the wheat fields seem to go on forever. Wilbur, the end of the drive, announces itself with stacks of silos and water towers ahead. Wilbur welcomes travelers with a few motels, RV park, groceries, a gas station, a department store, pizza, and yes, even espresso.

23

Kettle Falls to Crawford State Park

General description: This 73-mile drive begins on the Columbia River at Kettle Falls and goes east through the Colville National Forest before following the Pend Oreille River north to Crawford State Park (day use only, closed Tuesdays and Wednesdays) on the Canadian border. There is no border crossing here.

Special attractions: Colville National Forest, Little Pend Oreille Wildlife Area, Boundary Dam, Gardner Cave, Saint Paul's Mission.

Location: Northeast corner of Washington.

Highway number: Washington Highway 20/U.S. Highway 395, Washington Highway 31, Boundary Road.

Travel season: Year-round

Camping: Colville National Forest campgrounds along the Little Pend Oreille River.

Services: Full traveler services in Kettle Falls and Colville. Limited services on the rest of the drive.

For more information: Colville National Forest, Kettle Falls Area Chamber of Commerce, Colville Chamber of Commerce, Kettle Falls Ranger District, Little Pend Oreille Wildlife Area, Washington State Parks (see Appendix A).

 ## The drive

Begin this drive where Washington Highway 20 and U.S. Highway 395 meet and cross east over the Columbia River to Kettle Falls. There is an immediate left turn onto Portage Road to the Kettle Falls Historical Center (open summers only, Wednesday through Sunday) and Saint Paul's Mission. As an introduction to the mission and Kettle Falls on the Columbia, a self-guided tour of the Historical Center's "People of the Falls" is in order.

Proceed past the center for about 0.5 mile on the dirt road through the pine forest to Saint Paul's Mission. It was built in 1847 out of squared logs and is still in excellent shape. A short path behind the mission leads to a bluff overlooking Roosevelt Lake. Kettle Falls is directly below, submerged under 90 feet of water.

Until 1941, when Grand Coulee Dam created Roosevelt Lake, Kettle Falls was 33 feet high, rich in migrating salmon, and the annual meeting

Drive 23: Kettle Falls to Crawford State Park

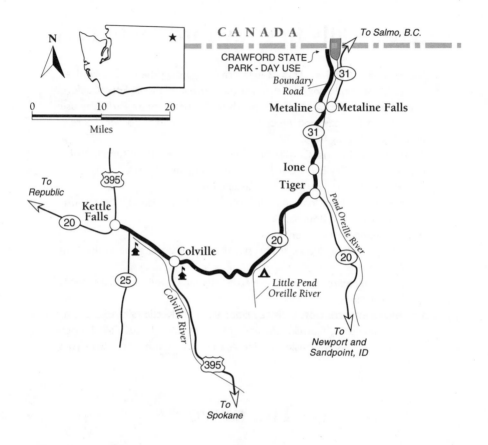

grounds of hundreds of Indians during fishing season. A huge sharpening stone for the fishing spears still sits on the bluff.

In 1974, the lake was lowered for work on the dam and the original falls were exposed. Indians from many tribes came here to celebrate, but that was the last time the falls were visible.

Returning to the highway, turn left (east) onto WA 20/US 395 and drive into the town of Kettle Falls, "home of 1,256 friendly people and one grouch." The grouch serves for a year from a popular selection process. Like most towns in this part of Washington, Kettle Falls began as a mining center and later added logging to its economic base. Both are still mainstays of the town. In 1992, a local woman won the Miss America pageant.

The drive to Colville follows the course of the Colville River. Colville is a city of wide streets, much in the manner of Spokane, and more appealing than the smaller mountain towns of Washington. The width of streets, at least those in Salt Lake City, was determined by the width of the turning circle needed by a team of oxen. Old-growth trees in the center of town are a pleasant surprise. Traffic signs warn motorists of the presence of bicyclists. Colville is on the BikeCentennial cross-country route for summer bicycle tours.

Make sure to stay on WA 20, as US 395 turns south toward Spokane. The drive takes Third Avenue, which becomes Colville-Tiger Road (also WA 20). Before WA 20 leaves town going east toward Tiger, there is a Washington State Department of Wildlife Trout Hatchery on the left. Logging trucks also use the next 36 miles of WA 20 to Tiger, so keep an eye out for them.

For a few miles, the drive passes through a valley in wheat country once again, but soon enough it gets into the Selkirk Mountains, passing through evergreen forests and next to a chain of glacial lakes.

Six miles east of Colville, the 7-mile-road to the Little Pend Oreille Wildlife Refuge offices takes off to the right. The refuge is a mountainous yellow pine forest managed for white-tailed deer. There are also plenty of bald and golden eagles, black bears, mink, grouse, songbirds, waterfowl, beavers, and muskrats. To get there, turn right onto Kitt-Narcisse Road and follow it 2.2 miles to a fork. Take the right fork on what is now a dirt road called Bear Creek Road and drive 3.3 miles to the log headquarters building.

This stretch of highway, 9 miles east of Colville, is a bit like southern Ohio with its rolling hillsides. The drive meanders and climbs through bold greenery and stands of trees, interspersed with rolling fields. The deer blend in easily with the occasional herd of cows. Not all cows are fenced in however, so be wary of those beasts who stand by the side of the road wondering where to go next.

Camping and fishing spots are many along the Little Pend Oreille. Halfway to Tiger, the drive climbs to 3,000 feet in elevation. In the winter, this is a prime recreation area for snowmobilers and cross-country skiers. A sign informs travelers that part of the highway is kept clean by the Driftriders Snowmobile Club. Summer sees trail riders, on horseback, on the many maintained trails in the forest. ORV riders also have their own trail, the Radar Dome ORV Trail, and there are campgrounds operated by the Washington Department of Natural Resources.

The thickly forested hills stretch as far as the eye can see and are cause for amazement. Forest roads wind into the countryside in many places. Then suddenly the drive runs alongside the glacially formed Lake Gillette and the even longer Lake Thomas. There are some Colville National Forest campgrounds to the right. Visitor information is available here; just watch for the sign.

Boundary Road to Crawford State Park.

WA 20 continues past lakes and meadows and through thick forest that would reclaim the highway if it could. It grows to within 5 feet of each side and the canopies meet above the road. Approaching the Pend Oreille River, the drive winds down alongside Renshaw Creek to the community of Tiger, 27 miles south of the Canadian border.

Turn left here, to go north on Washington Highway 31. Tiger is the oldest pioneer settlement in Washington. The state's first post office is here, located in the former general store that is now the Tiger Museum. The post office boxes still hold unclaimed letters from the 1940s.

Driving north along the river, keep in mind that farm vehicles always have the right of way. This is a quiet, little-traveled part of the state. A Pend Oreille County travel pamphlet misses its own irony when it states, "It is a mecca for the outdoorsman and his family." The 100-mile-long Pend Oreille is one of only two American rivers that flow north. Five hydroelectric dams stanch its flow as it heads across the Canadian border to join the Columbia River.

Slightly more than 3 miles from Tiger is the town of Ione. It has an airport, RV park, supermarket, gas station with propane, laundromat, restaurant, and motel. There is also a campground with a pool in Ione Riverfront Park.

Coming here for a vacation is a bit like going to rural Mexico; if something goes wrong you've got to walk around and talk to people to see if anybody knows anybody who knows how to fix it. From Ione, maps show a series of dirt roads through the forests to the west. In particular, Smackout Pass Road is supposed to meet Washington Highway 25 on the Columbia River. But in and around Ione, there are no signs indicating Smackout Pass Road, or any other road into the mountains for that matter. Signs are torn down in several places on this drive, and some signs are edited with notations on duct tape. Local people, including the postmistress, may be no help either. She never heard of such a road, and a couple of old guys say that they have never been out that way. So here is some advice: stay on the paved roads in northeastern Washington.

Continue north of Ione on WA 31, still following the Pend Oreille River, and after about 3 miles there is a deep gorge on the right. The steep rock cliffs are part of Box Canyon. A one-lane dirt road leads 0.1 mile to a scenic overlook revealing Box Canyon Dam, a county property built to supply local electrical power. There is one picnic table at this little park.

The drive continues north alongside the river and canyon. The altitude here is 2,300 feet. The Pend Oreille narrows through Z Canyon shortly before WA 31 comes into Metaline. The entire river used to look like this rampaging torrent before the dams were built. Metaline has less than two hundred people, but it has a motel, a gas station, and a nice city park on the river. This whole area was, and to a lesser extent still is, rich in minerals, hence the name Metaline. There are mines and gravel pits all up and down the Pend Oreille Valley.

Driving north, after about 0.5 mile, you will notice signs on the left to Crawford State Park, Gardner Cave, and Boundary Dam. You can turn here after a visit to Metaline Falls across the river.

Continue north on WA 31, and very shortly it will cross the river on that incredible-looking bridge visible ahead on the right. Metaline Falls had a "gold by the pound" reputation that caused it to boom in the 1890s. Then for a long time the town's lifeblood was the Portland Cement factory, now closed. The cement and red brick produced here helped build much of downtown Spokane. But now, behind the town, is a 40-foot high pile of cement manufacturing waste about a quarter of a mile long.

Metaline Falls has the feel of a ghost town. The Pend Oreille Apartments were built in 1929 as a hotel, but never used. Twenty years later the building was converted to apartments. But eleven years later, in 1960, it was closed and remained empty for another thirty years. Other enterprises in town have proved more viable, including what look like perpetual yard sales. Gas and food are available, and the Cutter Theater on Park Avenue is a performing arts center with live music and theater in the summer, attracting people from Montana, Idaho, and eastern Washington. The building was originally a school built of locally kilned bricks. The movie house has a

Box Canyon Dam on the Pend Oreille River.

regular Saturday matinee. The visitor center is in an antique railroad car in the city park.

Returning on WA 31 toward Metaline, 0.5 mile before town turn right on Boundary Road (also called County Road 62) toward Gardner Cave and Crawford State Park. As the road climbs up, the Salmo Priest Wilderness and Colville National Forest are visible across the valley. Watch for cattle munching by the side of the road. Fences are not yet needed for the lifestyle of this corner of Washington.

The vistas are good up here as the drive parallels Flume Creek. It presently crosses Beaver Creek, which runs below Beaver Mountain. There are beaver dams to be seen on the left. The beavers have created small lakes from the roadside creeks, and they attract more wildlife than Boundary Lake. Look for the deer, elk, raccoons, geese, and ducks that gather at sunset.

The big set of powerlines on the left comes from Boundary Dam, the next stop on this drive. The dam blends into the rugged terrain so well that road signs are necessary to let travelers know it is there. The access road to the dam is on the right, 11.5 miles from the WA 31 turnoff. It goes directly to the base of the dam, and visitors are welcome to park and walk right inside, under 400 feet of rock.

Inside it looks like the mountain interior set for *The Guns of Navarone*, with its huge tunnels and bore holes. There is even a mud wren nest in the ceiling. The cavern carved into this Precambrian granite mountain is 17 stories high and more than 0.25 mile long. It is owned by Seattle City Light and produces one-tenth of Washington's electrical power.

Once back on Boundary Road, the drive to Crawford State Park and the Gardner Cave is only 1.5 miles. The day-use park (closed Tuesdays and Wednesdays) has twelve picnic sites. It is wooded and cool in the summer heat, but the main attraction is the Gardner Cave. It is one of the two largest limestone caves in the state, eroded over the last 70 million years by groundwater seepage. The eerie pillars are still forming from the meeting of stalactites and stalagmites. This whole area was compressed ocean floor 500 million years ago, so the limestone seen today was formed from ancient compressed sea life. Pending funding, and on weekends and holidays between May 1 and September 20 only, there are ranger-led tours at 10 A.M., 2 P.M., and 4 P.M. Those are the only times you can enter the caves.

The Pend Oreille River flows from here into Canada, turns left, and flows into the south-flowing Columbia, which itself flows into the United States about 13 miles west of Crawford State Park.

24

Spokane River Loop

General description: This 72-mile loop begins in Spokane city traffic, but leaves it to run alongside the Spokane River and Long Lake before passing through rangelands of the Inland Empire.

Special attractions: Spokane River, Long Lake Pictographs, Spokane Plains Battlefield, canoeing, kayaking, horseback riding.

Location: Eastern Washington.

Highway number: U.S. Highway 2, U.S. Highway 295, Washington Highway 291, Washington Highway 231.

Travel season: The road is open year-round.

Camping: Riverside State Park, Long Lake Campground.

Services: All traveler services are available in and around Spokane. Other communities on the drive have cafes and gas stations.

For more information: Spokane Area Chamber of Commerce, Spokane Area Convention & Visitors Bureau, Spokane Area Visitor Information Center, Department of Natural Resources (see Appendix A).

 ## The drive

Begin the drive by going north on downtown Spokane's Division Street, which is also U.S. Highways 2 and 395. The route can be reached from downtown or by taking exit 281 from Interstate 90.

Once on Division Street, the drive will continue north for 4 miles from I-90. Riverside State Park is 10 miles from the start of the drive. Within a few blocks of I-90 there are easy-to-follow signs to a visitor information center to the left.

Traffic is usually thick on Division Street, so relax. You can catch a glimpse of the Spokane River Centennial Trail on the approach to the Senator Sam Guess Memorial Bridge. The trail runs along the south side of the river all the way from Riverfront Park in Spokane to Lake Coeur d'Alene in Idaho. It was built for bicyclists, joggers, and walkers.

Shortly after crossing the bridge, there is an opportunity for a side trip (a few blocks) to see the Bing Crosby Collection on the campus of Gonzaga University. To get there, turn right on Sharp Avenue. The Bing Crosby Home is in one block on the right, on the southeast corner of Addison Street at East 508 Sharp Avenue. Visitors are welcome 8 A.M. to 4:30 P.M. Monday

Drive 24: Spokane River Loop

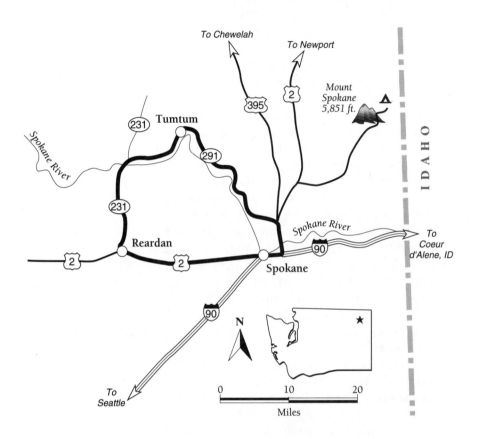

through Friday. Bing Crosby grew up here just one block from the university (from which he dropped out), and the former school library, endowed by Crosby, houses a special memorial to him. The building is now the Crosby Student Center and houses the Crosbyana Room. It contains his complete album collection, his Oscar for "Going My Way," and his "White Christmas" platinum record, which sold 200 million copies.

To reach the Crosby Student Center, continue east on Sharp Avenue for three more blocks to Cincinnati Street and turn right. The parking lot two blocks ahead is close to the center. During the school year, the Crosbyana Room is open 7:30 A.M. to midnight weekdays and 11 A.M. to midnight on Saturday and Sunday. In summer, the room is open 8:30 A.M. to 4:30 A.M. weekdays.

Back on Division Street, head north and pass the Northtown shopping mall on the right and a large city park on the left. From the park, the junction with Washington Highway 291 is three blocks ahead, so get into the left lane. Signs are minimal along here. Turn left onto WA 291/Francis Avenue toward Tumtum, Nine Mile Falls, and Riverside State Park. An Arby's restaurant will be on the southeast corner where the drive turns west.

This stretch of WA 291 is decidedly unscenic in the usual sense. While it is only a few blocks south of Fivemile Prairie, it is full of the usual businesses so essential to suburban communities that spread from downtown cores. There are fast-food restaurants, gas stations, sports bars, strip malls, and a few motels, as far as the eye can see.

But soon enough, after crossing Indian Trail Road and staying on Francis Avenue, the drive starts down into the Spokane River valley. A narrow vista ahead reveals the terrace-like bluffs across the valley. It looks about 2 miles to the forested plateau on the other side of the river.

Housing developments continue on the left side of WA 291, but as the road bends to the right, wooded countryside appears for the first time. Riverside State Park (on the left) gives an opportunity for a side trip. (Do not confuse this park with Riverfront Park in downtown Spokane.) The state park and its one hundred campsites are open all year. There are miles of pleasant trails for strolling. Most visitors stop to see the Bowl & Pitcher, a lava formation on the Spokane River. Even college photography classes make regular visits.

As you continue northwest on WA 291, the scene is mostly housing tracts on the left and woods on the right, as the drive edges closer to the Spokane River. The road straightens out, and by Milepost 6 it is apparent that this is a very flat valley floor. The drive here feels a bit like dry alpine California, with all the ponderosa pines. Although the river is nearby on the left, it only slowly becomes visible through the trees until the road starts running directly adjacent to the water.

As you near the river, it becomes clear that it is a major body of water. In this area it is maybe 100 feet wide, but ahead it becomes immensely wider. In fact, the Spokane River becomes Long Lake, held back by the Long Lake Dam about 24 miles ahead. For now, though, this part of the river is sometimes called the Nine Mile Reservoir. This is the water behind Nine Mile Falls, created by the dam with the big spillway at Milepost 9. Not to belabor the name, but a sign at the Nine Mile Store features fifty pounds of deer chow for $9.99.

The spillway makes it obvious that the drive is going the same northwesterly direction as the river's flow. A road sign warns to watch for ice, and from this point on the drive would be tricky to do in the winter with ice on the ground. It meanders through the forest for about 1 mile before coming

Pictographs at Long Lake.

upon the Spokane House Interpretive Center on the left. The center tells the story of the Pacific Northwest fur trade.

At Milepost 10 there is river access via a road on the left leading to a boating takeout site. This is a lovely little drive, sort of snaking around the edges of the valley floor. The drive passes from Spokane County to Stevens County as it comes upon another large section of Riverside State Park on the right, an interpretive preservation area. By Milepost 11, the drive is winding barely 10 feet from the water's edge. This is obviously more of a lake by now than a river.

But after Milepost 12, the drive begins to climb up out of the valley. The little town of Tumtum is 10 miles ahead, and Spokane is 13 miles behind. Within a few miles, near Suncrest, the drive courses a big flat plain, maybe 3 miles across, with scattered clumps of forest. At Milepost 16, a big dip in the road seems to come out of nowhere.

The Little Ponderosa Horse Ranch on the right marks the beginning of an area of small-time ranches. The mobile homes and small houses are part of the not-yet-suburban spread from Spokane down the valley. Old-fashioned northwest summer vacation housing appears after the road twists steeply back down to the river valley. "Under-maintained" would be a fair description of the cottages and mobile homes whose main purpose is nighttime shelter for outdoor recreationists.

The community of Tumtum, from the onomatopoetic Chinook word for "heart," is just ahead. Before Long Lake Dam was built, this was a noisy, pulsing bend in the river, hence the name. The drive continues along the water toward Ford and Springdale, still on WA 291.

At Milepost 23, the road leaves the water's edge and climbs up and away through a striking stand of ponderosa. It continues through upland woods for a few miles. Basalt outcroppings on the right are reminders of the volcanic origins of this region. The ridge of basalt edges slowly toward the road until, at Milepost 18, a giant boulder on the right calls for attention. This is the site of the Long Lake Pictographs and a very short archeological interpretive trail.

The site is maintained and protected by the Washington Department of Natural Resources (DNR). A chain link fence keeps visitors from getting too close to the boulder and its Indian paintings. The delicate sacred paintings are on two of the rock's surfaces; the clearer ones are on the back side. An interpretive sign explains that the " . . . origin, purpose and meaning of these paintings are a mystery to modern man." One theory suggests that young men spending their required time alone in the wilderness made the paintings as proof that they were there. Another theory relates to the desire for hunting success.

Less than 1 mile ahead is the DNR Long Lake Camp and Picnic Area. It has nine campsites and eight picnic sites, plus fishing and boating. WA

291 continues for a few miles on the flats above the lake. Two Sisters Cafe is located at Milepost 31.

At Long Lake Dam, about 1 mile before the junction with Washington Highway 231, there is a pullout with a nice view of the rocks around the dam and the dam itself. Look for a huge osprey nest on top of one of the telephone poles. When the birds are flying, they make a stark contrast to the rocks.

After the dam, the drive starts descending again. At the stop sign turn left toward Reardan on WA 231. This may appear to be in the middle of nowhere, but FedEx trucks make regular pickups and deliveries on these roads. The western boundary of the Spokane Indian Reservation is less than 1 mile up the first road on the right.

Going south on WA 231 the road crosses the Spokane River, known locally as the Little Falls Reservoir. There is a dam and power plant about 4 miles downriver.

The drive enters Lincoln County on the south side of the river, and at about Milepost 44 it begins a 2-mile climb to the plateau. Trees are quite a bit shorter here, at least by half. Up on the flats the drive courses through farming country. Toward Devil's Gap on the left is a wildlife viewing area.

This is irrigated farming country, as evidenced by the rolling watering systems. The road is straight as an arrow as it passes under the transmission lines from Long Lake Dam. Most of the fences are torn and rent, a sign that the days of livestock are past. Some of the farms are for sale.

The drive passes through an old fire zone and heads for a few miles up a narrow canyon, a coulee, with a lot of tangled growth and trees falling over the creek. Up on the next plateau are signs of greater prosperity. Just before Reardan you will see an ostrich farm on your right. The penned birds look like gigantic turkeys.

At Reardan find the junction with US 2, which the drive takes east and back to Spokane. Reardan has a couple of gas stations and cafes. Turn left onto US 2, which for several miles passes through flat range areas. US 2 was the main east-west route between Seattle and Spokane until I-90 was built. But it is still the scenic choice for those travelers who find I-90 uninspiring and boring. The towns and communities on US 2 lend a layer of reality to traveling that families may be seeking.

From Milepost 265, Spokane lies 22 miles ahead. Within about 4 miles, gently rolling land begins, and farmsteads appear well away from the highway. The road is straight, and in the distance ahead planes from the Spokane Airport and Fairchild Air Force Base can be seen taking off and landing. The Air Force picked this location because of the weather and the great distance from the Cascade Mountains, which were seen as a barrier to airborne invasion during World War II.

At about Milepost 270, the highway goes over a little crest, giving a view of a broad expanse of farmland followed by forested areas that continue way to the right and left. This vantage gives some idea of the scope of the Channeled Scablands created by the Spokane Flood of nearly twenty thousand years ago. Some geologists think there may have been more than one flood caused by the same type of event: melting glaciers at the end of the last ice age. An ancient Montana lake covering more than 3,000 square miles called Glacial Lake Missoula crashed through, weakening ice dams. In just a few days, the rushing waters flattened the eastern Washington landscape and carved coulees all the way to the Columbia River.

The woods start at the community of Deep Creek, but extend mostly north and south. Across the highway from the Air Force base lies a great spread of flat, treeless land dotted by new houses on 5- and 10-acre plots. It is quite an arresting sight. At the eastern end of the base on the right is the U.S. Air Force Survival Training School. It can be reached by turning right on Rambo Road. The obstacle course visible from the highway looks just like the ones in the movies, full of impediments to climb over, crawl under, and run around.

The next town, Airway Heights, got its name for obvious reasons. In between the Air Force base and the airport, Boeing Spokane is not far ahead. Nearby, to the left, is the Spokane Plains Battlefield. It is the site of the last major Indian battle of the Inland Northwest. The Coeur d'Alene, Palouse, and Spokane tribes were defeated here in September of 1858.

After the turnoff to the airport, the drive descends a bit from the plateau.

25

Palouse Country

General description: This 98-mile drive goes south, near Washington's border with Idaho, through gently rolling farmlands and rural towns.
Special attractions: Uniontown fence, Washington State University, Steptoe Butte State Park.
Location: Southeastern Washington.
Highway number: Washington Highway 27, U.S. Highway 195.
Travel season: The road is open year-round.
Camping: Chief Timothy State Park (8 miles beyond Clarkston, the end of the drive).
Services: Full traveler services are available at both ends of the drive and in Pullman. Smaller towns along the way offer some services.
For more information: Clarkston Chamber of Commerce, Pullman Chamber of Commerce, City of Palouse, Oakesdale Chamber of Commerce, Tekoa Chamber of Commerce, Washington State Parks (see Appendix A).

 The drive

This drive through Palouse Country winds over and around gently rolling farmlands and rural towns. Wheat is the main crop, but lentils and peas are also grown in abundance. Palouse hills were formed by one million years of accumulated glacial and wind-blown silt from the Columbia River during the last ice age. The drive is most beautiful in the spring when the wheatfields are a luxuriant green. Late summer is another excellent time to visit, when the golden fields bow in the winds and the wheat's hues change with the day's light.

Begin the drive by taking exit 289 from Interstate 90, just east of Spokane, and turning south on Washington Highway 27 through the town of Opportunity. WA 27 is also Pines Road. Opportunity, with all of its business and heavy traffic, looks like everybody else got here first to stake their claim. The area was a real estate developer's dream in 1905, when it was developed by the Modern Irrigation and Land Company. Promoters held a contest to pick a name for this town in the Spokane Valley, and a Miss Laura Kelsey won $10 for her suggestion of Opportunity. Just continue straight south through town on WA 27, passing several major intersections with traffic lights.

Drive 25: Palouse Country

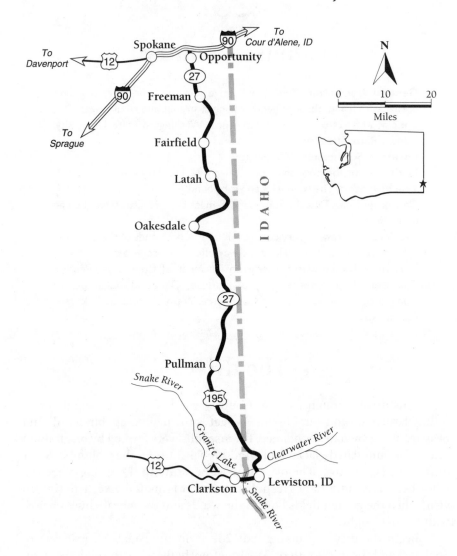

There are not many signs for WA 27, but just keep driving straight on Pines Road. The drive passes an immense hospital-green water tower on the left, seen from some distance before. Another tower, identical to the first, is ahead just out of sight on the horizon.

Presently, WA 27 angles to the left to a traffic light about 50 yards beyond the split with Pines Road, which goes straight. After that intersection, the drive is almost in the country, finally. There is still plenty of 1970s housing on both sides of the highway. Many of the trees blown down by the storms of the winter of 1996 lie where they fell.

The drive leaves the Spokane Valley now as it climbs left, over, and through the hills ahead. It takes a long gradual ascent, a three to four percent grade that winds a bit. The landscape is much more forested along here. There are ravines heading up to the right and a short ridgeline on the left. The extent of the gorgeous skyline ahead is revealed at Milepost 80 as the drive reaches the top of this low elevation range. In another mile, Hidden Hollow Drive takes off to the left.

Just before the town of Mica, named for its mineral deposits, mountains of red brick appear to encroach on the highway. Mica has maybe forty or fifty houses on the left side of the road and a gravel quarry on the right. Now the drive starts to enter more farmland as it passes the Palouse Highway to Valleyford, which takes off to the west.

Just ahead is the first of many big, red barns on the drive. The adjacent elevator system that distributes wheat to the silos is almost a diagram for how wheat storage is handled. This system is one of the biggest of those visible from the drive.

Coming into the community of Freeman, just past Milepost 76, about all there is to see is the Freeman Store, with gas and movie rentals, right next to a high school whose sports teams are known as the Freeman Scotties. An actual railroad station was located here in 1889, and the town was named for its telegrapher, Truman W. Freeman.

After Freeman, the drive enters the first of the Palouse-type contoured hills on the right, interspersed with forested ravines and valleys as far as the eye can see.

This road is so sparsely used by cars that bicycle racers use it for training. Some of the towns even identify local routes especially for bicyclists. WA 27 is quite a meandering road, with no sharp turns. It takes the course of least resistance through, over, and around the contoured hills. The hills grow larger as the drive continues south.

Before the turnoff into the town of Rockford, a narrow highway underpass requires cars to stop if trucks or school buses are coming the other way. Continuing straight on WA 27, the drive will come to Fairfield in 6 miles and Oakesdale in 32.

Beyond Milepost 68, the contoured fields rise on both sides of the road. Summer wheat gives an eerie beauty to this stretch. It seems sometimes that these hills are in rows, going off into the distance as a ridge whose height does not vary.

Drive slowly through Fairfield for a good look at all kinds of farm machinery. The town is almost a museum, with farm implements piled up all over the place. There is a nice little park too, smack in the center of town in the shadow of the silos. It has a basketball court, RV dump, and a playground. Even this far from Seattle, espresso is available at the gas station.

From Fairfield, the drive follows Union Creek for about 4 miles, then picks up Hangman Creek for about 10 miles through Latah clear to Tekoa (pronounced TEE-koh). The creek flows north to Spokane.

At Milepost 62, the road sweeps around to the left a little, revealing terraced farm hills as far as the eye can see. This is an excellent view of the expanse of the Palouse. *Palouse* was the name of an Indian tribe who lived in the region, and it also resembles a French word for "ground covered with short, thick grass." French-Canadian fur traders were among the first whites here.

After Latah, an 1892 Western-looking town with some abandoned gas stations, Latah Motors, and a post office, WA 27 takes a turn to the right toward Tekoa. The town is the end of the John Wayne Trail, a gravel trail that replaces tracks laid by the Milwaukee Railroad in 1908. It runs 213 miles between Tekoa and Easton, near Snoqualmie Pass on I-90.

At Milepost 53, the drive leaves Spokane County and enters Whitman County. There is no shoulder on this road, and a safe maximum speed is about 50 mph. The John Wayne Trail runs alongside on the right.

Still only 50 miles from Spokane, Tekoa announces itself with the huge trestle over Slippery Gulch ahead. WA 27 goes through the center of town where "Phantom of the Gulch" may be playing at the Empire Theater. WA 27 turns right toward Oakesdale at the stop sign. Then the drive turns left around an empty brick building that looks like an old Masonic temple, then past a huge silo.

US 195 near Colton.

At Milepost 48, the drive crosses over the gulch. WA 27 follows a creek to the southwest from Tekoa for 1.5 miles, then the road turns west and picks up another creek for a bit over 4 miles. Then it picks up a third creek for 1.5 miles, and yet another for the last few miles into Oakesdale. The pattern continues after Oakesdale with Spring Creek and Kelly Creek to Garfield.

The first road sign warning drivers to be on the lookout for farm machinery is ahead, by Milepost 46. There is a gorgeous vista of rolling wheatfields to the southwest. In a few miles, what looks from a distance like weird sculptural art is actually farm machinery alongside the road.

Approaching Oakesdale, there is a stop sign just beyond the hillside cemetery on the right. At the stop sign, continue on WA 27 to the left toward Oakesdale, which the drive enters in about fifty yards. High school sports are community events, as shown by the sign on the right boasting of all the championships that the local high school teams have won.

At the next stop sign in downtown Oakesdale, turn left to continue on WA 27. A side trip is possible here, to Steptoe Butte State Park. In less than 1 mile on WA 27, turn right onto Hume Road following the sign for Colfax. The park is on the right in about 8 miles. It has the best view of the country-side around, and for this reason it was used as a reconnaissance point in the battles of the 1850s. There is a nearby 25-foot granite memorial that marks the Steptoe Battlefield, site of the last local Indian victory over the U.S. Army, in May of 1858. Besides the view, the park is good for bird watching, hang-gliding, hiking, and picnicking.

Continuing south from Oakesdale on WA 27, the town of Palouse is 36 miles ahead. The number of silos in and around Oakesdale is impressive.

"Lentils $1," says a sign in the window of Oakesdale Grain Growers. Colfax, to the west of Oakesdale thinks of itself as Lentil Central, and Pullman, south on this drive, holds an annual National Lentil Festival held in late August. Ninety-five percent of the nation's lentil crop comes from the Palouse.

Unlike in the Midwest, the barns in the Palouse do not have old signs or murals painted on them. Here, the barns are just plain barns, and at least three-quarters of them are painted red. The tint does not seem to alter from one to the next.

Between the collections of farmhouses and barns, there are great stretches of contoured fields on the hilly lands. Aside from the railroad tracks and electric lines on the right, the rest is just knobby fields as far as the eye can see, which is not very far when the road is down in the gullies.

Just before Milepost 28, the drive enters the Palouse Conservation District. On the left is the ubiquitous stand of silos, but ahead on the right are six rusty ones laying on their sides. Upon entering Garfield, observe the 25 mph speed limit. These Palouse communities are serious about their speed limits.

Garfield enjoys tall ponderosas, 70 or so feet high, on the right. Houses line both sides of the street through town, but there are no sidewalks. WA 27 turns left ahead and goes through the center of town. Several of the buildings are brick, one of them three stories high.

Leaving Garfield, WA 27 crosses the railroad tracks and continues south to Palouse, 9 miles ahead, and Pullman, 24 miles. Coming over the rise after Milepost 19, you get a great vista of the narrow canyon, hills, and bumps ahead. The view continues as the drive descends past a lot of farm equipment and sheds on the right, red of course. The Palouse River on the right is the most substantial waterway on the drive.

Palouse is yet another residential farming community, but it has a lot more trees than most. Big, tall ponderosas line both sides of the street through town. Palouse is a very pleasant community, refreshingly acknowledging the strengths of farming as a way of life.

At the blinking yellow light, continue straight on WA 27. There is a city park on the right, and shortly after, the drive crosses the Palouse River. It leaves town up the other side of the valley. Some of the town is on the little hillsides, but most of it is low in the valley.

By Milepost 10 the drive is climbing a bit to a level where the hills are smaller. Within a few miles the drive is flat and straight.

Pullman, a large city by this drive's standards, is bisected by the South Fork of the Palouse River. It is the home of Washington State University,

John Wayne Trail and Hangman Creek.

which occupies a 600-acre hilltop. At the stoplight just after Milepost 1, WSU is to the left on Stadium Way. WA 27 continues straight.

Pullman is just before the end of WA 27, but the drive continues south on U.S. Highway 195 toward Lewiston. Lewiston is in Idaho actually, and this is the only scenic drive in this book that enters another state to reach its destination. The drive will end in Clarkston, Washington, just across the Snake River from Lewiston.

The drive joins US 195 South in progress south of Pullman, and continues through rolling farmlands for mile after mile. Near the community of Chambers, the WSU Livestock Center is on the right.

In Uniontown, after Milepost 6, some of the residents apparently have some time at the end of the day to work on their art. The first and only artistically painted barn is here. It is fairly splashed with bright blues, yellows, and greens. Also, there is a great long fence made entirely of wagon wheels, gears, and myriad other round shapes from old farm machinery. The fence is composed of more than one thousand pieces and was twenty-five years in the making. It surrounds a farmhouse and 3 acres of pasture.

The drive enters Idaho and joins US 95 going south toward Lewiston. This is still US 195. At the crest of Lewiston Hill, 2,756 feet in elevation, there is a frontage road to the right that gives an outstanding view below of the Clearwater and Snake rivers and the port cities of Lewiston and Clarkston. Seagoing freighters still dock in Lewiston to load grain and other cargoes for distant lands.

Back on the drive, the downgrade is 7 percent for 6 miles. This is an impressive descent, especially with the views ahead and to the right.

After crossing the Clearwater River on the Lewis and Clark Trail, the drive will turn right onto US 12 West at an intersection with a traffic light. The route follows alongside the Lewiston Levee around the business district, which is struggling for economic survival if the number of closed stores are any indication. On the levee is a hiking and wheelchair trail that is an extension of the Lewiston Wildlife Preserve on the Clearwater River. That would explain all the ducks.

Stay on US 12 over the Snake River, crossing via a large drawbridge. There is a visitor information center one block past the Motel 6. Washington Highway 129 to the left leads 3 miles to the Hells Canyon National Recreation Area Office. For camping, Chief Timothy State Park is on US 12, 8 miles west of Clarkston on the Snake River. The park is closed November through February.

Appendix A
Addresses and Phone Numbers

Drive 1

Mount Baker Ski Area
1017 Iowa Street
Bellingham, WA 98226
(360) 734-6771

Mount Baker-Snoqualmie National
    Forest
1022 First Avenue
Seattle, WA 98104
(206) 442-5400

Mount Baker-Snoqualmie National
    Forest
21905 64th Avenue West
Mountlake Terrace, WA 98043
(206) 775-9702

Outdoor Recreation Information
    Center
915 Second Avenue, Suite 442
Seattle, WA 98174
(206) 220-7454

Mount Baker Ranger District
2105 Highway 20
Sedro Woolley, WA 98284
(360) 856-5700

Glacier Public Service Center (open
    mid May through October)
P.O. Box C
Glacier, WA 98244
(360) 599-2714

Bellingham-Whatcom County
    Convention & Visitors Bureau
904 Potter Street
Bellingham, WA 98226
(800) 487-2032
www.bellingham.org/pnm.html

Whatcom County Parks
3373 Mount Baker Highway
Bellingham, WA 98226
(360) 733-2900 or from county
phones 592-5161

Drive 2

DNR Northwest Region
919 North Township Street
Sedro-Woolley, WA 98284-9395
(360) 856-3500.
(800) 527-3305 (statewide general
    information)

Drive 3

San Juan County Parks
(360) 378-2992

San Juan Island Chamber of
    Commerce
P.O. Box 98
Friday Harbor, WA 98250
(360) 378-5240

San Juan Islands Visitor Information
    Service
P.O. Box 65
Lopez Island, WA 98261
(360) 468-3663

Moran State Park
Star Route, Box 22
Eastsound, WA 98245
(360) 376-2326
(800) 233-0321
TDD(360) 664-3133

Washington State Ferries
801 Alaskan Way
Seattle, WA 98104-1487
(800) 84-FERRY (Washington only)
  or (206) 464-6400

Doe Bay Village Resort
Star Route 86
Olga, WA 98279
(360) 376-2291

West Beach Resort
Eastsound, WA 98245
(360) 376-2240

Obstruction Pass
Department of Natural Resources
Olympia, WA 98504-7000
(360) 856-3500 or (800) 527-3305

Drive 4

Larrabee State Park
245 Chuckanut Drive
Bellingham, WA 98226
(360) 676-2093

Bellingham-Whatcom County
  Convention & Visitors Bureau
904 Potter Street
Bellingham, WA 98226
(800) 487-2032
www.bellingham.org/pnw.html

Bellingham Parks and Recreation
3424 Meridian Street
Bellingham, WA 98225
(360) 676-6985

Taylor United (oyster farm)
188 Chuckanut Drive
Bow, WA 98232
(360) 766-6002

Drive 5

Monte Cristo Enterprises, Inc.
Box 737
Granite Falls, WA 98252
Message phone (360) 691-6448

Darrington Ranger District
1405 Emmens Street
Darrington, WA 98241
(360) 436-1155

Verlot Public Service Center
33515 Mountain Loop Highway
Granite Falls, WA 98252
(360) 691-7791

Mount Baker-Snoqualmie National
  Forest
21905 64th Avenue West
Mountlake Terrace, WA 98043
(360) 775-9702

Granite Falls Chamber of Commerce
P.O. Box 28
Granite Falls, WA 98252
(no phone)

Arlington Chamber of Commerce
P.O. Box 102
Arlington, WA 98223
(360) 435-3708

Darrington Chamber of Commerce
Box 351
Darrington, WA 98241
(360) 436-1260

Snohomish County Parks &
  Recreation
2828 Rockefeller
Everett, WA 98201
(206) 339-1208.

Washington State Parks and
  Recreation Commission
7150 Cleanwater Lane
P.O. Box 46250
Olympia, WA 98504-2650
(360) 902-8563

Washington State Department of
  Natural Resources
P.O. 47016
Olympia, WA 98504-7046
(360) 902-1650

Drive 6

Ebey's Landing National Historical
  Reserve Trust Board
P.O. Box 774
Coupeville, WA 98239
(360) 678-6084

Cascade Loop Association
P.O. Box 3245
Wenatchee, WA 98807
(509) 662-3888

Hatzoff Productions
2326 Sixth Avenue
Seattle, WA 98121
(800-458-5335)

Greenbank Farm
Whidbeys
One Stimson Lane
Woodinville, WA 98072

Oak Harbor Chamber of Commerce
P.O. Box 883
Oak Harbor, WA 98227
(360) 675-3535

Oak Harbor City Hall (City Beach RV
  Park)
Oak Harbor, WA 98277
(360) 679-5551

Island County Fairgrounds
819 Camano Avenue
Langley, WA 98236
(360) 221-4677

Drive 7

Gifford Pinchot National Forest
6926 East Fourth Plain Boulevard
P.O. Box 8944
Vancouver, WA 98668-8944
(206) 750-5045

Goldendale Observatory State Park
1602 Observatory Drive
Goldendale, WA 98620
(509) 773-3141
(800) 562-0990

Mount Adams Ranger District
2455 Highway 141
Trout Lake, WA 98650
(509) 395-2501

Drive 8

Columbia Gorge Interpretive Center
P.O. Box 396
Stevenson, WA 98648
(509) 427-8211

Columbia River Gorge National
  Scenic Area
Forest Service Information Center
1131 SW Skamania Lodge Drive
Stevenson, WA 98648
(509) 427-2528

Skamania County Chamber of
   Commerce
167 NW 2nd Street
PO Box 1037
Stevenson, WA 98648
(509) 427-8911

Drive 9

Forks Chamber of Commerce
P.O. Box 1249
Forks, WA 98331
(800) 44-FORKS

Forks Timber Museum & Visitor
   Center
P.O. Box 873
Forks, WA 98331
(360) 374-9663

Hoh Rain Forest Visitor Center
HC 80, Box 650
Forks, WA 98331
(360) 374-6925

Hoh Valley Adventures River Rafting
HC80, Box 671
Forks, WA 98331
(360) 374-4288

Hurricane Ridge Visitor Information
   Center
(360) 452-4501

Kalaloch Visitor/Ranger Station
Milepost 157
Kalaloch, WA 98331
(360) 962-2283

Lake Crescent Lodge
416 Lake Crescent Road
Port Angeles, WA 98363
(360) 928-3211

National Park Service Information
   Center
915 Second Avenue, Room 442
Seattle, WA 98174
(206) 220-7450

North Olympic Peninsula Visitor &
   Convention Bureau
338 West First Street, Suite 104
P.O. Box 670
Port Angeles, WA 98360
(360) 452-8552
(800) 942-4042

Olympic Game Farm
1423 Ward Road
Sequim, WA 98382
(360) 683-4295
(800) 778-4295

Olympic National Forest
1835 Black Lake Blvd. SW
Olympia, WA 98502-5623
(360) 956-2300

Olympic National Park Headquarters
600 East Park Avenue
Port Angeles, WA 98362
(360) 452-4501 (headquarters)
(360) 452-9235 (recorded
   information)

Port Angeles Chamber of Commerce
12 East Railroad
Port Angeles, WA 98362
(360) 452-2363

Port Townsend Chamber of
   Commerce
2437 East Sims Way
Port Townsend, WA 98368
(360) 385-2722

Quinault Rain Forest Visitor
  Information Center
Route 1, Box 40
Quinault, WA 98575
(360) 288-2644

Sequim-Dungeness Valley Chamber
  of Commerce
P.O. Box 907
Sequim, WA 98382
(360) 683-6197
(800) 737-8462

Drive 10

Makah Cultural and Research Center
P.O. Box 95
Neah Bay, WA 98357
(360) 645-2711

Makah Tribal Museum
P.O. Box 160
Neah Bay, WA 98357
(360) 645-2711

Neah Bay/Makah Tribal Council
P.O. Box 115
Neah Bay, WA 98357
(360) 645-2201

Neah Bay/Ozette Chapter
Clallam Bay-Sekiu Chamber
P.O. Box 355
Clallam Bay, WA 98326
(360) 963-2339

Drive 11

Bowerman Basin
National Audubon Society
Washington State Office
P.O. Box 462
Olympia, WA 98507
(360) 786-8020

Grays Harbor Chamber of Commerce
506 Duffy Street
Aberdeen, WA 98520
(360) 532-1924

Grays Harbor National Wildlife
  Refuge
(360) 532-6237

Grays Harbor Tourism Council
2109 Sumner Ave., Suite 202
Aberdeen, WA 98520
(360) 459-0877

Ocean Shores Chamber of Commerce
P.O. Box 1447
Ocean Shores, WA 98569
(360) 289-4411
(800) 874-6737

Drive 12

Willapa National Wildlife Refuge
Julia Butler Hansen National Wildlife
  Refuge for the Columbian White-
  tailed Deer
P.O. Box 566
Cathlamet, WA 98612
(360) 795-3915

Grays Harbor National Wildlife
  Refuge
c/o Nisqually National Wildlife
  Refuge
100 Brown Farm Road
Olympia, WA 98516
(360) 532-6237

Long Beach Peninsula Visitors
  Bureau
P.O. Box 562
Long Beach, WA 98631
(360) 642-2400
(800) 451-2542

Skamokawa/Lower Columbia
  Economic Development Council
P.O. Box 98
Skamokawa, WA 98647
(360) 795-3996

Drive 13

National Park Service
Pacific Northwest Regional Office
83 South King Street, Suite 212
Seattle, WA 98104
(206) 220-4000

Mount St. Helens National Volcanic
  Monument
Route 1, Box 369
Amboy, WA 98601
(360) 247-5473

Cowlitz County Department of
  Tourism
207 Fourth Avenue North
Kelso, WA 98626
(360) 577-3137

Weyerhauser Forest Learning Center
P.O. Box 188
Longview, WA 98632
(360) 414-3439

Mount St. Helens Visitor Center
3029 Spirit Lake highway
Castle Rock, WA 98611
(360) 274-2100

Coldwater Ridge Visitor Center
3029 Spirit Lake Highway
Castle Rock, WA 98611
(360) 274-2131

Gifford Pinchot National Forest
  Headquarters
6926 East Fourth Plain Boulevard
P.O. Box 8944
Vancouver, WA 98668-8944
(360) 750-5001

Packwood Ranger District
Packwood, WA 98361
(360) 494-5515

Randle Ranger District
P.O. Box 670
Randle, WA 98377
(360) 497-7565

Drive 14

Mount Baker-Snoqualmie National
  Forest
21905 64th Avenue West
Mountlake Terrace, WA 98043
(206) 775-9702

National Park Foundation
1101 17th Street NW, Suite 1102
Washington, DC 20036

North Cascades National Park
  Superintendent
2105 Highway 20
Sedro Woolley, WA 98284
(360) 856-5700

North Cascades Visitor Center
502 Newhalem Street
Newhalem, WA 98283
(206) 386-4495

Okanogan National Forest
1240 Second Avenue S
P.O. Box 950
Okanogan, WA 98840
(509) 422-2704

Rendezvous Outfitters, Inc.
P.O. Box 728
Winthrop, WA 98862
(509) 996-3299

Ross Lake National Recreation Area
Forest Service/North Cascades
  National Park
2105 Highway 20
Sedro Woolley, WA 98284
(360) 856-5700

Seattle City Light Skagit Tours
1015 Third Avenue
Seattle, WA 98104-1198
(206) 684-3030
(206) 233-2709

North Cascades National Park
Skagit and Wilderness District Office
728 Ranger Station Road
Marblemount, WA 98267
(360) 873-4500

Drive 15

Monroe Chamber of Commerce
211 East Main Street
Monroe, WA 98272
(360) 794-5488

Leavenworth Chamber of Commerce
P.O. Box 327
894 Highway 2
Leavenworth, WA 98826
(509) 548-5807

Leavenworth Ranger District
600 Sherbourne
Leavenworth, WA 98826
(509) 782-1413

Sultan Chamber of Commerce
P.O. Box 46
Sultan, WA 98294
(360) 793-2211

Wenatchee National Forest
215 Melody Lane
Wenatchee, WA 98801-5933
(509) 662-4335

Drive 16

Leavenworth Ranger District
600 Sherbourne
Leavenworth, WA 98826
(509) 782-1413

Cle Elum Ranger District
803 West Second Street
Cle Elum, WA 98922
(509) 674-4411

Wenatchee National Forest
215 Melody Lane
Wenatchee, WA 98801-5933
(509) 662-4335

Drive 17

Wenatchee National Forest
215 Melody Lane
Wenatchee, WA 98801-5933
(509) 662-4335

Mount Baker-Snoqualmie National
  Forest
21905 64th Avenue West
Mountlake Terrace, WA 98043
(206) 775-9702

Drive 18

American Hop Museum
22 South B Street
P.O. Box 230
Toppenish, WA 98948
(509) 865-HOPS(4677)

Central Washington Agricultural
  Museum
4508 Main Street
Union Gap, WA 98903
(509) 457-8735 or (509) 248-0432

Greater Wapato Chamber of
Commerce
P.O. Box 157
Wapato, WA 98951
(509) 877-3322

Hispanic Chamber of Commerce of
Greater Yakima
P.O. Box 2712
Yakima, WA 98907
(509) 952-6771)

Toppenish Chamber of Commerce
11A South Toppenish Avenue
P.O. Box 28
Toppenish, WA 98948
(509) 865-3262

Toppenish Mural Society
P.O. Box 212
Toppenish, WA 98948
(509) 865-4345

Bureau of Land Management
Wenatchee Resource Area Office
1133 North Western Avenue
Wenatchee, WA 98801
(509) 662-4223
(800) 47-SUNNY (camping planner
pamphlet)

Von Hellstrum Inn (Sears kit house)
51 Braden Road
Sunnyside, WA 98944
(509) 839-2505

Yakima Nation RV Park
280 Buster Road
Toppenish, WA 98948
(800) 874-3087

Yakima Valley Visitors & Convention
Bureau
10 North Eighth Street
Yakima, WA 98901-2515
(509) 575-1300
(800) 221-0751

Drive 19

Gifford Pinchot National Forest
6926 East Fourth Plain Boulevard
P.O. Box 8944
Vancouver, WA 98668-8944
(360) 750-5000

Mount Rainier Guest Service
Star Route
Ashford, WA 98304
(360) 569-2275

Mount Rainier National Park
Superintendent
Tahoma Woods, Star Route
Ashford, WA 98304
(360) 569-2211 (recorded updates
on road conditions and park
information)

Naches Ranger District
10061 Highway 12
Naches, WA 98937
(509) 653-2205

Packwood Ranger District
13068 U.S. Highway 12
Packwood, WA 98361
(360) 494-5515

Randle Ranger District
10024 U.S. Highway 12
Randle, WA 98377
(360) 497-7565

Rainier Mountaineering, Inc.
(conducted climbs)
201 St. Helens
Tacoma, WA 98042
(206) 627-6242, or
Paradise, WA 98398
(360) 569-2227 (June to September)

Drive 20

Brewster Chamber of Commerce
P.O. Box 1087
Brewster, WA 98812
(509) 689-3589

Bridgeport Visitor Information
Center
1015 Columbia Avenue
Bridgeport, WA 98813
(509) 686-4101

Chief Joseph Dam Visitor Center
P.O. Box 1120
Bridgeport, WA 98813
(509) 686-5501

Colville Confederated Tribes
P.O. Box 150
Nespelem, WA 99155
(509) 634-4711

Colville Confederated Tribes
Museum
516 Birch Street
Coulee Dam, WA 99116
(509) 633-0751

Fort Okanogan State Park
c/o Alta Lake State Park
Star Route, Box 40
Pateros, WA 98846
(509) 689-2798

Four Winds Guest House B&B
301 Lincoln Street
Coulee Dam, WA 99116
(800) 786-3146, (509) 633-3146

Grand Coulee Dam Area Chamber of
Commerce
306 Midway, Hwy. 155
P.O. Box 760
Grand Coulee, WA 99133
(509) 633-3074

Grand Coulee Dam Visitor Arrival
Center
WA 155 between Coulee Dam and
Grand Coulee
P.O. Box 620, Code 141
Grand Coulee, WA 99133
(509) 633-9265

Roosevelt Recreational Enterprises
Reservations Office
P.O. Box 587
Grand Coulee, WA 99133-0587
(509) 633-0201
(800) 648-LAKE (within Washington
only)

National Park Service Headquarters
1008 Crest Drive
Coulee Dam, WA 99166
(509) 633-9441

Omak Visitor Information Center
401 Omak in East Omak
Route 2, Box 5200
Omak, WA 98841
(509) 826-4218

Chelan Ranger District
428 West Woodin Avenue
Route 2, P.O. Box 680
Chelan, WA 98816
(509) 682-2576
(509) 682-4584

Entiat Ranger District
P.O. Box 476
Entiat, WA 98822
(509) 784-1511

Entiat Valley Chamber of Commerce
(509) 784-1500
(800) 7-ENTIAT

Lake Chelan Visitor Information
    Center
102 East Johnson Street
P.O. Box 216
Chelan, WA 98816-0216
(509) 682-3503
(800) 4CHELAN

Lakeshore RV Park (Chelan)
P.O. Box 1669
Chelan, WA 98816
(509) 682-5031

Washington State Apple Commission
    Visitor Center
2900 Euclid Avenue
P.O. Box 18
Wenatchee, WA 98807
(509) 663-9600

Washington State Parks
(800) 233-0321

Colville National Forest
Federal Building
765 S. Main Street
Colville, WA 98114
(509) 684-3711

National Park Service Headquarters
1008 Crest Drive
Coulee Dam, WA 99166
(509) 633-9441

Fort Spokane
c/o National Park Service
    Headquarters
1008 Crest Drive
Coulee Dam, WA 99166
(509) 633-9441

Kettle Falls Ranger District
255 West 11th
Kettle Falls, WA 99141
(509) 738-6111

Republic Area Chamber of
    Commerce
P.O. Box 502
Republic, WA 99166-0502
(509) 775-3222

Republic Ranger District
P.O. Box 468
Republic, WA 99166
(509) 775-3305

Republic Visitor Information Center
61 North Kean Street
P.O. Box 1024
Republic, WA 99166-1024
(509) 775-3387
(509) 775-3216 (Town Hall)

Stonerose Interpretive Center
15 North Kean Street
P.O. Box 987
Republic, WA 99166
(509) 775-2295

Drive 23

Colville Chamber of Commerce
309 South Main
P.O. Box 267
Colville, WA 99114-0267
(509) 684-5973

Colville National Forest
Federal Building
765 S. Main Street
Colville, WA 98114
(509) 684-3711

Kettle Falls Area Chamber of
  Commerce
265 West Third Street
Kettle Falls, WA 99141
(509) 684-5973
(509) 738-6514

Kettle Falls Ranger District
255 West 11th
Kettle Falls, WA 99141
(509) 738-6111

Little Pend Oreille Wildlife Area
(509) 684-8384

Washington State Parks
(800) 452-5687 (reservations)
(800) 233-0321 (information)

Drive 24

Washington State Department of
  Natural Resources
Northeast Region
P.O. Box 190
225 South Silke Road
Colville, WA 99114-0190
(509) 684-7474

Spokane Area Chamber of Commerce
West 1020 Riverside Drive
P.O. Box 2147
Spokane, WA 99210
(509) 624-1393

Spokane Area Convention & Visitors
  Bureau
926 West Sprague, Suite 180
Spokane, WA 99204
(509) 624-1341
www.spokane-areacvb.org

Spokane Area Visitor Information
  Center
201 West Main Avenue
Spokane, WA 99201
(509) 747-3230
(800) 248-3230

Drive 25

Clarkston Chamber of Commerce
731 Fifth Street
Clarkston, WA 99403
(800) 993-2128
(509) 397-3712

Pullman Chamber of Commerce
North 415 Grand Avenue
Pullman, WA 99163
(800) 365-6948
(509) 334-3565

City of Palouse
PO Box 248
Palouse, WA, 99161
(509) 878-1811

Oakesdale Chamber of Commerce
PO Box 184
Oakesdale, WA, 99158
(509) 285-4200

Tekoa Chamber of Commerce
PO Box 682
Tekoa, WA, 99033
(509) 284-3271

GENERAL
Washington State Tourism Division
P.O. Box 42500
Olympia, WA 98504-2500
(800) 544-1800, ext. 2

Appendix B
Further Reading

Best Places Editors. *Olympic Peninsula Best Places*. Sasquatch Books: Seattle 1996.

Brewster. David and Stephanie Irving. *Northwest Best Places*. Sasquatch Books: Seattle 1993.

Douglas, William O.. *Of Men and Mountains*. Chronicle Books: San Francisco 1990.

Easterbrook, Don. *Geology and Geomorphology of Western Whatcom County*. Western Washington State College Geology Department: Bellingham, Wash. 1977.

Halliday, Jan and Gail Chehak. *Native Peoples of the Northwest*. Sasquatch Books: Seattle 1996.

Hunn, Eugene S.. *Nch'i-Wána "The Big River" Mid-Columbia Indians and Their Land*. University of Washington Press: Seattle 1995.

La Tourrette, Joe. *Washington Wildlife Viewing Guide*. Falcon Press: Helena, Mont. 1992.

McLuhan, T.C.. photographs by Edward S. Curtis. *Touch the Earth, a Self-Portrait of Indian Existence*. Simon & Schuster: New York 1971.

Miles, John. *Impressions of the North Cascades: Essays About a Northwest Landscape*. The Mountaineers: Seattle 1997.

Phillips, James W.. *Washington State Place Names*. University of Washington Press: Seattle 1990.

Prater, Yvonne. *Snoqualmie Pass, From Indian Trail to Interstate*. The Mountaineers: Seattle 1981.

Roe, JoAnn. *North Cascadians*. Madrona Publishers: Seattle 1980.

Satterfield, Archie and Dianne J. Boulerice Lyons. *Washington Handbook*. Moon Publications, Inc. Chico: Calif. 1994.

Index

About the Author

Back in high school Steve Giordano thought he'd like to be a writer some day. After twenty-five years, he realized it would never happen unless he made it happen. So he wrote some stuff and took it to a writer/editor buddy at a local newspaper for his advice. He said, "Steve, I've been looking for a monthly columnist—would you like to start with this piece?" It took the next ten years to become an overnight success. Most of Giordano's friends think he's retired and having a good time on the road.

Giordano's books include *Now Hiring: Ski Resort Jobs* and *The Seattle Dog Lover's Companion*. He contributes chapters annually to the guidebooks *Skiing America* and *Ski Europe* and is currently second vice-president of the North American Ski Journalists Association. He has written materials for two CD-ROMs: *Mount Everest, Quest for the Summit of Dreams*, for Peak Media, and *Leonardo*, for Corbis Corporation.

Steve has lived in Bellingham, Washington since 1970.

The author and friends.

FALCON GUIDES are available for where-to-go hiking, mountain biking, rock climbing, walking, scenic driving, fishing, rockhounding, paddling, birding, wildlife viewing, and camping. We also have FalconGuides on essential outdoor skills and subjects and field identification. The following titles are currently available, but this list grows every year. For a free catalog with a complete list of titles, call FALCON toll-free at 1-800-582-2665.

SCENIC DRIVING GUIDES

Scenic Driving Alaska and the Yukon
Scenic Driving Arizona
Scenic Driving the Beartooth Highway
Scenic Driving California
Scenic Driving Colorado
Scenic Driving Florida
Scenic Driving Georgia
Scenic Driving Hawaii
Scenic Driving Idaho
Scenic Driving Michigan
Scenic Driving Minnesota
Scenic Driving Montana
Scenic Driving New England
Scenic Driving New Mexico
Scenic Driving North Carolina
Scenic Driving Oregon
Scenic Driving the Ozarks including the
    Ouchita Mountains
Scenic Driving Texas
Scenic Driving Utah
Scenic Driving Washington
Scenic Driving Wisconsin
Scenic Driving Wyoming
Back Country Byways
National Forest Scenic Byways
National Forest Scenic Byways II

HISTORIC TRAIL GUIDES

Traveling California's Gold Rush Country
Traveler's Guide to the Lewis & Clark Trail
Traveling the Oregon Trail
Traveler's Guide to the Pony Express Trail

WILDLIFE VIEWING GUIDES

Alaska Wildlife Viewing Guide
Arizona Wildlife Viewing Guide
California Wildlife Viewing Guide
Colorado Wildlife Viewing Guide
Florida Wildlife Viewing Guide
Idaho Wildlife Viewing Guide
Indiana Wildlife Vewing Guide
Iowa Wildlife Viewing Guide
Kentucky Wildlife Viewing Guide
Massachusetts Wildlife Viewing Guide
Montana Wildlife Viewing Guide
Nebraska Wildlife Viewing Guide
Nevada Wildlife Viewing Guide
New Hampshire Wildlife Viewing Guide
New Jersey Wildlife Viewing Guide
New Mexico Wildlife Viewing Guide
New York Wildlife Viewing Guide
North Carolina Wildlife Viewing Guide
North Dakota Wildlife Viewing Guide
Ohio Wildlife Viewing Guide
Oregon Wildlife Viewing Guide
Tennessee Wildlife Viewing Guide
Texas Wildlife Viewing Guide
Utah Wildlife Viewing Guide
Vermont Wildlife Viewing Guide
Virginia Wildlife Viewing Guide
Washington Wildlife Viewing Guide
Wisconsin Wildlife Viewing Guide

■ *To order any of these books, check with your local bookseller
or call FALCON ® at **1-800-582-2665**.*

Visit us on the world wide web at:
www.falconguide.com